ANGER IN THE AIR

This book is dedicated in loving memory of my father, Richard Hunter, who gave me the hope and determination to be the woman I am today. His unconditional love and commitment to my mother, my sisters, and me will always be remembered.

Anger in the Air
Combating the Air Rage Phenomenon

DR JOYCE A. HUNTER
Associate Professor
Saint Xavier University, Chicago, Illinois, USA

ASHGATE

© Joyce A. Hunter 2009

All rights reserved. No part of this publication may be reproduced, stored in a retrieval system or transmitted in any form or by any means, electronic, mechanical, photocopying, recording or otherwise without the prior permission of the publisher.

Joyce A. Hunter has asserted her moral right under the Copyright, Designs and Patents Act, 1988, to be identified as the author of this work.

Published by
Ashgate Publishing Limited
Wey Court East
Union Road
Farnham
Surrey, GU9 7PT
England

Ashgate Publishing Company
Suite 420
101 Cherry Street
Burlington
VT 05401-4405
USA

www.ashgate.com

British Library Cataloguing in Publication Data
Hunter, Joyce A.
  Anger in the air : combating the air rage phenomenon
  1. Air rage 2. Aeronautics, Commercial - Passenger traffic
  3. Aeronautics, Commercial - Security measures
  I. Title
  363.1'24

  ISBN: 978-0-7546-7193-0

Library of Congress Cataloging-in-Publication Data
Hunter, Joyce A.
  Anger in the air : combating the air rage phenomenon / by Joyce A. Hunter.
    p. cm.
  Includes bibliographical references and index.
  ISBN 978-0-7546-7193-0 -- ISBN 978-0-7546-8022-2   1. Air rage. 2. Anger. 3.
  Aggressiveness. I. Title.
  HE9787.3.A4H86 2009
  363.12'4--dc22

                                                                    2008053600

Mixed Sources
Product group from well-managed forests and other controlled sources
www.fsc.org Cert no. SGS-COC-2482
© 1996 Forest Stewardship Council
FSC

Printed and bound in Great Britain by
TJ International Ltd, Padstow, Cornwall

Contents

Acknowledgements

Commit to the Lord Whatever You Do and Your Plans Will Succeed.

—Proverbs 16:3

I would not have been able to write this book without the personal hands-on experience I acquired while working as a representative for a major airline for over three decades. It was my front line experience as a reservation sales agent, ticket sales agent, executive account agent, and, finally, an account manager that afforded me the opportunity to understand and learn how to deal with a raging travelling public.

Not too many years ago, airlines were judged on the service they gave passengers; to be highly rated, an airline had to deliver impeccable customer service. As I finished this examination of air rage, I realized that it was the gruelling customer service training, ingrained in my spirit, that had taught me the true essence of what customer service entails and how it should be implemented. My training in the airline industry taught me years ago that many explosive situations could be resolved amicably if the airline representative was willing to listen, show compassion, be informative, and generally give "smiling customer service" when dealing with irate customers.

I wish to acknowledge the following people for their incredible contribution to this book. To my mother, Elizabeth Hunter, the greatest woman I have ever known, everlasting thanks. She gave me hope, support, encouragement and unconditional love, and she stood by me throughout the completion of this manuscript.

To my sisters, Joan, Brenda, and Gloria, for planting the seed, watering it, and watching it grow to maturity. You all gave me the hope, support, and guidance needed to complete this journey.

Special thanks go to Penny Kramer, without whose valuable editorial help this book could not have been written. Penny, you were the Rock of Gibraltar and the guiding light for this project.

To all the experts who have written and researched this phenomenon before me and have been kind enough to allow me to share their ideas, opinions, and suggestions for curing this phenomenon, namely Dr Andrew Thomas, Dr Leon James, Dr Diane Nahl, Michael Boyd, Angela Dahlberg, Elliott Neal Hester, and retired Captain Steven Luckey, I would like to express my thanks and appreciation.

Chapter 1
Anger in the Air

8/11

On August 11, 2000 (which I refer to as 8/11), on a routine flight from Las Vegas to Salt Lake City, a muscular young man stood up out of his seat and a turning point was reached in passengers' attitude towards flying.

At the gate earlier, 19-year-old Jonathan Burton, tall, blonde, and square jawed, with an open smile and a football player's build, had just said a cheerful goodbye to his mother. An hour later, eyes dilated, he was pacing up and down the aisle, telling a flight attendant, "I'm fine. It's just the drugs." Suddenly he charged from the back to the front of the plane, screaming, "I can fly this plane!" before leaping up and kicking through the cockpit door.[1]

Reports vary on what happened in the pandemonium that followed, but all agree that a few male passengers jumped up and blockaded the cockpit while a female flight attendant and several other male passengers eased Jonathan, who had recently watched a TV special on plane crashes,[2] towards a seat on the exit row. As they did so, he suddenly lunged for the emergency exit, screaming that he had to get out of the plane. Passengers again restrained and soothed him, asking questions to distract him from his fear. They seemed to have calmed Burton down, when a passenger said, he "went ballistic" on hearing that an off-duty policeman had come to help. Powered by panic and adrenaline, he seemed unstoppable as he kicked, bit, and punched as many as eight men, hitting the policeman hard enough to spray blood around the cabin.[3]

At that point it was as if an emotional switch had been thrown. The passengers, presumably bursting with their own adrenaline, began pounding and kicking Burton all over his body, pinning him to the floor long after he'd gone limp. Within hours, Burton died of strangulation.[4] According to the autopsy report, when police

---

1   Timothy Roche, "Homicide in the Sky," *Time,* October 2, 2000, found at http://www.time.com/time/magazine/article/0,9171,998079,00.html.

2   "Air Rage Death Clarified," *Las Vegas Review-Journal,* September 17, 2000, found at http://www.reviewjournal.com/lvrj_home/2000/Sep-17-Sun-2000/news/14407481.html.

3   Roche, 2000.

4   "A Death on Descent," *CBS News,* September 21, 2000, found at http://www.cbsnews.com/stories/2000/09/21/national/main235154.shtml.

walked on the plane they found him lying face down, "with at least one individual standing on his neck."[5]

Known as a gentle soul who'd won an award for his work with the elderly, Burton had no history of mental illness.[6] The autopsy showed just barely detectable trace amounts of cocaine and THC (the active ingredient in marijuana) in his system—probably not from recent use and not enough to account for his outburst.[7] The death was ruled a non-criminal homicide, and no charges were filed.[8]

What turned Jonathan Burton from a harmless passenger into a threat to the safety of Flight 1763? And what turned his fellow passengers from supportive helpers into a death-dealing mob? This book will examine the potential answers to those questions and look at what can be done to minimize future such "air rage" episodes.

The media frenzy over the 8/11 incident first brought the phenomenon of air rage (so named because of its similarity to drivers' irrational bursts of road rage) to widespread public attention both because it was shocking and grisly and because it was the first incident in which an American had died. But Jonathan Burton's death was just the culmination of an explosion of air rage incidents in the years leading up to 8/11. Between 1994 and 1997, the number of air rage incidents reported around the world had more than quadrupled from 1,132 to 5,416[9]—and as many as 30 times that number had been swept under the rug by image-conscious airlines. The International Air Transport Association that represents the airline industry worldwide said there were 10,000 incidents of air rage in the United States in the year 2000.[10]

It's significant that during the same period, from 1995 to 2000, airlines were experiencing a considerable decline in service.[11,12] Overbooked flights, persistent delays, and shabby aisle treatment at the hands of surly flight attendants contributed to declining service rankings for even top airlines, including American, Delta,

---

5   Michael Janofsky, "US Declines to Prosecute in Case of Man Beaten to Death on Jet," *New York Times,* September 21, 2000, found at http://query.nytimes.com/gst/fullpage. html?res=9406E5DE103BF932A1575AC0A9669C8B63.

6   Roche, "Air Rage Death Clarified."

7   Roche, "A Death on Descent."

8   Janofsky, "US Declines to Prosecute."

9   E.W. Fine, Air Rage Behavior: Implications For Forensic Psychiatry, paper presented at the 2001 symposium conducted at the meeting of The American College of Forensic Psychiatry, April 2001, p. 3, found at http://www.forensic psychonline.com/psychiatry2001.html.

10   Anonymous and Andrew R. Thomas, *Air Rage: Crisis in the Skies* (Amherst, NY: Prometheus Books, 2001), p. 23.

11   Angela Dahlberg, *Air Rage: The Underestimated Safety Risk* (Aldershot, UK: Ashgate, 2001), pp. 60–61.

12   U.S. Dept. of Transportation. *Air Travel Consumer Report* (Washington, DC: Office of Aviation Enforcement and Proceedings, 2001), found at http://www.dot.gov/airconsumer.ost.gov/report.htm.

USAir, and United.[13] For passengers, the results were infuriating, and the question arose: Did this epidemic of poor service spawn the metastasizing rage?

It's hard to remember now, but throughout their first 60 years of existence, the airlines were known for providing champagne service. Because theirs was the gold standard for customer care, other industries looked to them as models of how to keep customers happy. However, when the airline industry was deregulated in 1978, airline service and the quality of the flying experience began to deteriorate in the United States.[14] And when bargain airlines arrived on the scene in 1992, offering fares as much as 70 percent lower than the rest of the industry, airlines across the board were forced to cut fares to compete. To keep profits up, they switched from selling relatively few high-priced tickets to a smaller group of pampered customers, to selling low-cost tickets in bulk. The result of lower prices, a lower profit margin, and more riders was a drastic cut in services.

For passengers, says Andrew Thomas, co-author of *Air Rage: Crisis in the Skies*, it was like going from shopping at an elite emporium like Harrods or Nordstrom, to standing in line at WalMart.[15] As a result, since low-cost fares came in, airlines have been barraged with complaints about poor service, and the Airline Quality Rating, an annual analysis of Department of Transportation Statistics, says no airline is immune.[16] Even Delta, Southwest, and Northwest Airlines, all previously known for some of the best service within the industry, have seen their customer service ratings fall sharply.

By 1995, providing good customer service had apparently ceased to be a driving force in the industry. Companies that used to live by the motto, "The customer is always right—even when he's wrong" seem to have replaced that with, "The airline is always right—no matter what." They strive to achieve maximum profits at any cost, with a blatant lack of accountability for customer satisfaction. This refusal to recognize the importance of customer service has created a dangerous and detrimental environment for the flying public. Airline personnel's lack of courtesy, respect, civility, and sensitivity to customers' needs has helped fuel the growing epidemic of air rage.

The consequences are more than unpleasant. Air rage is the single greatest threat to the flying public. On August 11, 2000, it was the raging passenger who was killed; but had Jonathan Burton gotten into the cockpit, the death toll could have included everyone on the plane. Air rage has already left airline attendants with stab wounds, bruises, internal bleeding, torn kneecaps, and a broken back

---

13   M. Drummond, "Customer Service Woes: At a Time When Companies Should be Doing Everything in Their Power to Keep Customers and Keep Them Happy, Many Aren't." *Business 2.0.*, June 4, 2001, found at http://www.business2.com/articles/web/0,1653,15896,FF.html.

14   Anonymous and Thomas, p. 83.

15   Ibid.

16   T. Harrison and J. Kleinsasser, *Airline Quality Rating, Press Release*, 1999, found at http://www.unomaha.edu/~unoai/aqr/aqr99press.html.

and neck. But when a passenger gets totally out of control at 30,000 feet, it can take the airplane down, as passengers on All Nippon Airways learned on July 23, 1999. Shortly after their jumbo jet took off from Tokyo's Haneda Airport, a crazed passenger pulled a knife on a flight attendant and forced his way into the cockpit. He told the co-pilot to leave, stabbed the captain to death, and took over the controls. Luckily, the co-pilot and two airline employees were able to storm the cockpit, and a non-uniformed pilot was able to land the plane, but not before the plane had come within seconds (and 300 meters) of crashing into the ground.[17]

And that was before 9/11.

9/11

At 8:46 a.m. on September 11, 2001, American Airlines Flight 11 flew into the World Trade Center and time stood still. Frozen in fear, Americans watched as planes flew into buildings, people jumped out of hundred-story windows, and screams could be heard for blocks. Then the Twin Towers crumbled into dark clouds of dust that swallowed chunks of downtown New York.

The 9/11 tragedy that altered every aspect of American life permanently changed the course of air travel. Now our images of flying include an airplane piercing a building against a sunny blue sky, blocks-long lines of passengers herded through security checkpoints, and the ever-present threat of more humiliating body searches, not to mention hijacking—all of which add to passengers' anger and anxiety as they walk into an airport or onto a plane.

The 9/11 terrorists succeeded in "grafting a virulently toxic psychology into the very DNA of air travel," said pilot and columnist Patrick Smith. "Not entirely surprising…in a society that increasingly encourages fear, front and center over rationality or common sense."[18]

As a result, 9/11 has compounded the growing epidemic of passenger rage, while making it more urgent than ever that airlines around the world find ways to prevent it. Airlines used to brag of "something special in the air." On September 11, that "something" turned into a toxic mix of fear and anger that would slowly seep into the hearts and minds of airline travelers and personnel alike, further eroding the civility of travel that was once an integral part of the industry's culture.

For a short time after 9/11, the number of air rage incidents in America seemed to decrease because fewer passengers were flying, and those who did were on their good behavior. But the heightened tension these attacks added to the flying experience just increased the chances of air rage in years to come. Studies showed

---

17   Elliott Neal Hester, "Flying in the Age of Air Rage," Travel and Food section, *Salon.com*, September 7, 1999, found at http://www.salon.com/travel/diary/hest/1999/09/07/rage/index.html.

18   Patrick Smith, "Ask the Pilot," *Salon.com*, May 28, 2004, found at http://dir.salon.com/story/tech/col/smith/2004/05/28/askthepilot88/.

that airline passengers, filled with post-World Trade Center attack anxiety, were more likely than ever to lash out at fellow travelers and airline staff, warned psychiatrist Dr Graham Lucas.[19]

"Despite a drop in passenger numbers of as much as 30 percent in the past four months, air rage incidents [in England] have not reduced," Dr Lucas, a British adviser to the Civil Aviation Authority (CAA), told a Royal Society of Medicine conference on the risks of international travel in January 2002. Although no published figures existed at that time, according to the United Kingdom Department of Transport, early indications from the CAA showed that air rage incidents after September 11, were at a similar level, despite fewer passengers.[20]

By September 2007, air rage had again become such a problem that United Airlines created an internal committee to review air rage incidents.[21] That month, author Andrew Thomas said, "Abnormal, aberrant or abusive behavior in the context of the air travel experience is back with a vengeance."[22]

9/11 Blowback: Vigilante Injustice

The 9/11 attacks made it especially urgent to deal with air rage. In the future, when pandemonium begins to break out in an airline cabin, personnel won't be sure whether they're dealing with an enraged passenger or a terrorist until after the incident is over, at which point it may be too late. In addition, pilots, locked in their cockpits since 9/11, won't be there to help. Onlookers, panicked at the thought of terrorism, may overreact as they race to subdue a troublemaker—or, thinking it's "just a blowhard," fail to restrain a terrorist. That fact alone makes it doubly important in a post-9/11 world to recognize, understand, and contain air rage much more effectively than we have to date.

At the 2002 Royal Society of Medicine conference, Dr Lucas predicted that "twitchy" passengers could be expected to overreact to anything that struck them as unusual. Paradoxically, their pre-emptive efforts to prevent terrorism could actually put the plane in greater danger. Islamic groups confirmed Dr Lucas' fears. A report by Robert Mendick in *The Independent* newspaper said that four months

---

19   Robert Mendick, "Drink Does it. Sex Does it. But the Real Reason Air Rage is Rising is 11 Sept," *The Independent,* January 13, 2002, found at http://www.independent.co.uk.

20   Ibid., para. 3.

21   Kelly Yamanouchi, "United's New Committee Targets 'Air Rage,'" *Denver Post,* September 17, 2007, found at http://www.denverpost.com/business/ci_6913089.

22   Marilyn Miller, "Air Rage Taking Off, Expert Says," *Akron Beacon Journal,* September 28, 2007, quoting Andrew Thomas, found at: http://www.ohio.com/business/10099131.html.

after 9/11, Muslim passengers even hesitated before walking to the restroom on planes for fear of being "surrounded" by fellow passengers.[23]

"If there is a kerfuffle on the plane", said Dr Lucas, who is also a consultant specializing in aviation psychiatry at the Priory Clinic in West London, "passengers may well now suspect it's a terrorist incident rather than just some drunken person." That natural mistake could turn a small incident into a major fracas, endangering a planeload of people.[24]

In addition, post 9/11 passengers could be expected to drink more to drown their fears, further increasing the chance of air rage, said Professor Cary Cooper, a behavioral psychologist at University of Manchester Institute of Science and Technology. In almost half the officially recorded air rage cases, alcohol was "a contributory cause."[25]

But the bigger risk comes from "sensitive" passengers, suspicious of other passengers' behavior, Professor Cooper said. "My real fear is anybody who behaves in a strange way on a plane is now at risk of attack." Nervous passengers may target even the most innocuous of their fellow flyers, especially if they are Arab or Asian, Mednick reported. In one case, Murtaza Walji, a father of two from Birmingham, England, was flying from New York to Seattle shortly after 9/11 when a passenger behind him became extremely loud and abusive.

"She was shouting at me. Maybe she was scared but she was blaming me for what had happened in New York," said Mr Walji, 44. "There were a lot of people on the plane but I was the only Asian." At the end of the flight, the woman even called security and police, who stopped Mr Walji as he got off the plane.[26] *Muslim News*, which began compiling a list of Islamophobic attacks after September 11, had already documented six verbal or physical assaults in the first four months after the disaster. Editor Ahmed Versi estimated that many more had gone unreported.[27]

What is Air Rage?

In the decade before 9/11, the experience of flying was already more than stressful. Faced with long ticket lines, overbooked planes, sardine seating, bad cabin air, delayed flights, missed connections, lost luggage, and rude personnel, some overwrought passengers had already begun bursting into uncontrolled eruptions of anger. They screamed at, harassed, beat, or stabbed flight attendants. They also attacked pilots, took over plane controls, and tried to open exit doors at 30,000 feet—and in one creative case, a well-dressed but overly lubricated executive in First Class expressed his feelings by climbing up on the food cart and relieving

---

23   Mendick, 2002.
24   Ibid.
25   Ibid.
26   Ibid.
27   Ibid.

himself. Noting the similarities to drivers' irrational explosions of road rage, observers dubbed these outbursts "air rage."

But because they were in the air, these explosions of anger were far more dangerous than even a shootout on the highway. Since airline personnel can't just toss the troublemaker off the airplane (unless they're like one airline pilot we'll hear about later who landed on a desert island and left the rager there), they're forced to handle erupting craziness at 30,000 feet, which can be deadly. On December 29, 2000, a hysterical male passenger stormed the cockpit and tried to grab the controls of a British Airways jet flying from London to Nairobi, sending the Boeing 747 into a terrifying two-mile dive. Many screaming passengers in the planeload of 398 people, which included British rock singer Bryan Ferry, first hit the ceiling and then slammed against the front of the plane as it plummeted thousands of feet. The jumbo jet came within four or five seconds of flipping on its back, after which the co-pilot would not have been able to regain control.[28]

When Did Air Rage Start?

In the early 1990s, the term "air rage" was completely foreign to the average traveler, partly because the phenomenon itself was less common, and partly because the industry was not anxious to publicize the problem. Not having a specific term for the phenomenon made it easier to ignore, so airlines used euphemisms, reporting only that "an irate passenger" had "caused a disturbance." By not naming the problem, the industry could treat each incident as if it were an isolated case, unrelated to business as usual.[29]

But it was more than a disturbance in January 1999 when a drunken passenger allegedly harassed the woman beside him, ripping off her headphones and biting them in half before punching the door window of a British Airways jet, smashing the window's inner layer and threatening to cause decompression at 35,000 feet. Passengers feared that "disturbance" could take their plane down. It took four flight attendants and four passengers to subdue this "irate passenger" before the "disturbance" was over.[30]

It's thought the term air rage was first coined in the 1990s by the news media to refer to unruly passengers as a variation on the term "road rage," a term coined, appropriately enough, in Los Angeles in 1984 by a *Los Angeles Times* reporter when he was covering the story of a truck driver who shot at another driver who cut him off on the freeway.[31]

---

28 "BA Jet Plunges in Cockpit Struggle," *BBC News,* December 29, 2000, found at http://news.bbc.co.uk/2/hi/uk_news/1092164.stm.

29 Dahlberg, p. 1.

30 Hester, "Flying in the Age of Air Rage."

31 Gary Martin, Road Rage. *The Phrase Finder,* found at http://www.phrases.org.uk/meanings/303700.html.

Only as the media began to report air rage incidents did the term begin to creep into public use. Now there are as many definitions of air rage as there are researchers, but they all agree that air rage includes "any behavior that threatens the safety of a customer or crew member."[32] The term includes everyone from a passenger who refuses to turn off his cell phone to one who stabs a crew member or tries to open an exit door mid-flight. According to Angela Dahlberg, author of *Air Rage: The Underestimated Safety Risk,* "The term 'air rage' is a label now used by the media not only for high profile cases but [to encompass] all forms of passenger behavior causing a disturbance."[33] The phrase may describe anyone from an entitled first-class passenger throwing a fit when he can't get his preferred dinner to a schizophrenic suffering a complete psychotic break.

For years, to avoid publicity, airlines allowed passengers to get away with blatantly violent or dangerous behavior that would have resulted in arrest at sea level. Even when wildly abusive passengers were arrested, the companies rarely filed criminal charges. This book will examine the conditions and attitudes in the airline industry that could allow even dangerous passenger behavior to be shrugged off or ignored.

However it's defined, says author Andrew Thomas, air rage is by far the greatest threat to the safety and security of the 1.5 billion passengers who travel by air each year, because even one small incident that disables airline safety systems or distracts the pilot at a crucial moment could bring down an entire airliner.[34]

Before 9/11

Before 9/11, according to a study reported in 2000 by the Aviation Safety Reporting System at the National Aeronautics and Space Administration (NASA), unruly passengers could cause a pilot to make serious flying errors, partly because, in 40 percent of the 152 cases NASA analysts studied, pilots either left the cockpit to help flight attendants deal with a dangerous situation or were otherwise distracted by the crisis to the point that, in half the incidents, it adversely affected the pilot's performance.[35] Addressing the United States House of Representatives Sub-Committee on Aviation on June 11, 1998, Captain Stephen Luckey, Chairman of the National Security Committee of the Air Line Pilots Association (ALPA) called

---

32   K. Tyler, "Afraid to Fly and it Shows. Air Rage is an Escalating Problem. So, Why Don't Airlines Adequately Train Their Employees for This?" *HR Magazine,* 2001, 46(9), found at http://www.shrm.org/hrmagazine/articles/0901.

33   Dahlberg, p. 1.

34   Anonymous and Thomas, p. 25.

35   National Aeronautic and Space Administration (NASA), Aviation Safety Reporting System (ASRS), "Passenger Misconduct: Effects on Flight Crews," *Callback,* April 2000, 250, 1–2, found at http://asrs.arc.nasa.gov/callback_issues/cb_250.htm.

passenger interference "the singularly most pervasive security problem facing the airline industry, not only in the U.S., but around the globe."[36]

Because airlines had in many cases switched from three-pilot to two-pilot airplanes, Captain Luckey said, "sending a pilot into the passenger cabin to help resolve a dispute seriously diminishes the safety of the flight. This is particularly so in the event of an altercation, which could result in an incapacitated pilot and a resulting one-pilot aircraft."[37]

FAA's Three Levels of Trouble

Flight crews need to recognize quickly when behavior that is simply irritating is about to escalate into verbal threats or even physical assaults. To help them identify problems, airline employees have been given diagnostic yardsticks to help them assess the level of threat each behavior represents so they can decide how to respond. These disruptive behaviors include: assault; sexual harassment (which includes sexual advances, gestures, and innuendoes as well as touching or groping); verbal abuse and threats, and violence.

Before 9/11, the Federal Aviation Administration (FAA) divided passenger misconduct into three categories:

- Category One: A flight attendant reminds a passenger to carry out an instruction—say to turn off a cell phone or put up a tray table—and the customer does so. No further action is required and the incident isn't reported.
- Category Two: A passenger ignores flight attendants' requests that he comply with federal regulations like fastening a seat belt or stopping verbal abuse or other disruptive behavior that interferes with cabin safety. The attendant has to take further action, like asking the pilot to come enforce the request. The passenger may become verbally abusive and take a while to comply, but eventually does.
- Category Three: This is what the FAA means when it refers to air rage. A category three incident is one that endangers someone on the plane. During a category three event, one of the following problems occurs: a passenger's continuing interference disrupts a crew members work; the passenger's behavior either injures or threatens to injure a passenger or crew member; the pilot finds it necessary to make an unscheduled landing, and/or crew

36   Statement of Captain Stephen Luckey, Chairman, National Security Committee, Air Line Pilots Association, Before the Subcommittee on Aviation, Committee on Transportation and Infrastructure, U.S. House of Representatives, Passenger Interference with Flight Crews and the Carry-on Baggage Reduction Act of 1997, June 11, 1998, found at http://cf.alpa.org/Internet/TM/tm061198.htm.
37   Ibid., para. 2.

members find it necessary to put the passenger in restraints such as flex cuffs.[38]

In his *Salon.com* column, veteran flight attendant Elliott Neal Hester described a striking example of a category three event:

> On March 16, 2000, aboard Alaska Airlines flight 259 from Puerto Vallarta, Mexico, to San Francisco, a man…broke through the cockpit door and attacked the pilots. Provoked (or so his attorney claims) by a bad reaction to blood-pressure medicine, Peter Bradley, 39, shouted, "I'm going to kill you," and lunged for the controls.

> Having been alerted of the impending attack, the co-pilot was armed with an ax. He fought with Bradley, suffering a cut to his hand that would require eight stitches. Struggling to fly the plane during this tight-quartered assault, the pilot made an urgent plea for help over the intercom. At least seven passengers responded. The 6-foot-2, 250-pound assailant was snatched from the cockpit, wrestled to the ground, bound hand and foot with plastic restraints and taken into custody by federal authorities upon landing in San Francisco.[39]

The goal of the FAA in creating these categories is to minimize the possibility that passengers' behavior will cross over into category three, which is considered the danger zone, and bring some type of civility back to air travel.

After 9/11

September 11 was a cold, calculated political act of terrorism, not a spontaneous outburst of air rage. However, said author Andrew Thomas, airlines' head-in-the-sand approach to air rage played into the terrorists' hands because they had relied on the fact that pilots routinely left the cockpit to calm angry passengers.[40] That's one reason that, since 9/11, pilots have stopped helping attendants deal with passengers.

In a post-911 world, Thomas says, the situation has changed. To combat terrorist attacks in which an attacker could invade the cockpit and incapacitate pilots, airlines have massively reinforced cockpit doors. Unfortunately, this has

---

38   Robert Bor, Morris Russell, Justin Parker, and Linda Papadopoulos, Managing Disruptive Passengers: A Survey of the World's Airlines, 1999, found as a 2000 reprint at http://www.skyrage.org/pdf/academic/ rbor.pdf.

39   Elliott Neal Hester, "Cockpit Assault," *Salon.com*, April 8, 2000, found at http://archive.salon.com/travel/diary/hest/2000/04/08/cockpits/index.html.

40   Michael McConnell, "Air Rage Takes Back Seat in Our Post-9-11 World," *Detroit Metro Connections*, September 19–October 2, 2002, found at http://metro.heritage.com/dtw100202/story3.htm

given rise to another problem, pilots' isolation from the rest of the plane, which leaves the flight attendants to deal with problems on their own.

"Pilots are locked in the cockpit because of potential terrorist attacks," says Andrew Thomas. "There is no authority figure today to offer any calming effect. The people on the front line today are underarmed and undertrained." As a result, he said, he's seeing more passengers trying to jump in and help the flight crew calm problem passengers.[41]

To address this problem, some airlines are installing video monitors that allow the pilots to see what's happening in the cabin without opening cockpit doors. A British company called AD Aerospace has sold the FlightVu system of closed circuit television systems to companies including British Airways, Britannia, AirAsia, Corsair, Germania, and Jet Blue.

According to AD Aerospace documents, the FlightVu CDMS consists of:

...two or three CCTV cameras linked to a LCD monitor or monitors strategically mounted forward of the pilots' positions. The system provides the flight crew with clear, forward viewing, real-time video of the area outside the cockpit door.

The CCTV cameras are flush mounted, in low-profile housings colour coordinated to the aircraft interior, outside the secure cabin door and in the galley area.[42]

In addition, infrared illuminators make it possible to see what's happening even when the cabin lights are out.[43] However, the presence of monitors leaves open the question of what the pilots can do when they see a problem in the cabin, if they can't safely open the cockpit door and go help.

Fifty Ways to Say "Bad Actor": Definitions and Descriptions of Air Rage

Experts on workplace violence around the world have arrived at their own definitions of air rage. Andrew Thomas defines air rage as "a type of behavior that is abnormal, aberrant, or abusive within the context of generally accepted social norms and values. In other words, when someone acts crazy or menacing."[44] He also says this "abnormal, aberrant and abusive behavior" is displayed by thousands of airline passengers each year, calling it, "by far today's greatest threat to the safety and security of the flying public."[45]

---

41   "Air Rage Increasing, Expert Says," *Akron Beacon Journal*, September 28, 2007, found in Securityinfowatch.com, at http://www.securityinfowatch.com/article/printer.jsp?id=12650.

42   "Corsair Selects FlightVu CDMS for Aircraft," August 24, 2004, found at http://www.ad-aero.com/news_nr_details.php?news_id=33.

43   Ibid.

44   Anonymous and Thomas, p. 21.

45   Ibid., p. 11.

Veteran flight attendant and Salon.com columnist Elliot Neal Hester says air rage incidents can run "the gamut of behavioral maladies from severely rude and obnoxious behavior (for example, when a passenger verbally threatens to punch a flight attendant) to outright physical assault,"[46] while AirSafe.com calls air rage "extreme misbehavior by unruly passengers."[47]

The International Transport Workers Federation, which represents five million transportation workers in 693 labor unions around the world, defined air rage as "disruptive passenger behavior ranging from non-compliance with safety instructions through to actions amounting to verbal harassment or physical assault directed at staff, passengers or the aircraft."[48]

Considering all the definitions used today, it seems that air rage behavior runs the gamut from A to Z: aggressive, boisterous, contemptuous, drunk, egotistical, facetious, grandiose, hallucinogenic, insulting, judgmental, kooky, lewd, malicious, nasty, obnoxious, pushy, quarrelsome, rude, sarcastic, troubled, uninhibited, violent, wicked, xenophobic, yammering, and, finally, just plain zonked.

Road Rage Versus Air Rage: Similarities and Differences

Air rage episodes are less frequent than road rage incidents, partly because driving is part of daily life for more people. Even so, researchers say air rage has much in common with road rage. According to authors Leon James and Diane Nahl, both air rage and road rage are triggered by the inability to cope with the challenges of congested traffic.[49] And, just like aggressive driving and road rage, air rage is so common that most travelers are unaware that they have it. It is just part of the background feeling that goes along with the stress of travel and transportation.

Of course, because road rage happens in a car on the ground, the aggressors act it out differently. David A. Gershaw, emeritus professor of psychology at Arizona Western College, says road rage is "aggressive driving—attempting to injure or kill another driver because of a traffic dispute," that "involves unusually aggressive responses to a variety of traffic incidents." As with air rage, he says that relatively small perceived slights can set off the driver:

> "Road ragers" may be upset by rather minor driving errors, like not using a turn signal. They may become enraged by a bigger infraction, like tailgating. They may retaliate with their car by forcing someone off the road, or they may follow the driver until he stops. Then they get out of their car and attack the driver in

---

46   Hester, "Flying in the Age of Air Rage."

47   AirSafe.com, 2002, para 1.

48   University of Nebraska at Omaha, "Organization Theory and Behavior" (PA 8090), *Air Rage,* 2002, p. 2, found at http://www.unomaha.edu/~wwwpa/pa8090/ryberg/airrage.htm.

49   Annette Santiago, "Air Rage," *AviationNow.com*, August 10, 2001, found at http://www.drdriving.org/rages/.

person. Such attacks may include the use of a gun or any handy weapon, like a tire iron or a purse.

"Road rage" is thought to be a factor in two thirds of all automobile accident fatalities. According to the US Department of Transportation, approximately 250,000 people have been killed and 20 million injured in traffic crashes between 1990–96. They estimate that two thirds of deaths are at least partially caused by aggressive driving.[50]

Road ragers may be male or female, of any age, race or income level, and Gershaw says that they may not be angry in daily life—until they get behind the wheel of a car. "However, persons who are typically cynical, rude, angry or aggressive get angry more often," Gershaw says.[51] They "rage" at home, at work, and on the road, which suggests that intermittent rage may often be a lifestyle for some people, where one sort of rage segues into another.

It would be an interesting psychological study to cross-reference the backgrounds of those convicted to air rage incidents to see if road rage was also part of their background. Many investigators have observed the importance of escalation in road rage incidents. In his Congressional Testimony on Aggressive Driving in 1997, Dr. Leon James describes the cycle of arousal or rage, focusing on how it can be extinguished, only to flare up again:

The natural cycle of verbal road rage begins with an explosion of invectives and accusations, silent or out loud, reaching a rapid peak that lasts a few seconds, then lessens with a temporary feeling of relief from the pent-up pressure of frustration or fear. What happens next depends on conditions. In some minor but annoying events, conflicting exchanges die down after a few moments when the physiological symptoms of anger dissipate, receding into the subconscious, put to sleep, but ready to awaken at the next opportunity, maybe only a minute or two later. The cycle of anger can be rekindled just by seeing the other car, or it can die down if the target driver avoids eye contact, verbal replies, and other forms of provocation.[52]

Air rage is similar to road rage in that it is aggressive, anonymous, and often related to situations where a person is lashing out due to feeling trapped or crowded.

---

50   David A. Gershaw, "A Line on Life: Road Rage," February 21, 1999, found at http://www.members.cox.net/dagershaw/index.html.

51   Ibid.

52   Testimony by Dr. Leon James, Professor of Traffic Psychology, University of Hawaii, Honolulu, Before the Subcommittee on Surface Transportation and Infrastructure, U.S. House of Representatives, July 17, 1997, found at http://www.drdriving.org/articles/testimony.htm.

But the air rage victim doesn't seem to experience the temporary relief observable in the angry driver after the initial explosion of road rage.

Even worse, angry outbursts on planes often draw just the kind of attention designed to *increase* the rage by making the offender feel even more trapped, crowded, or controlled. Unlike raging drivers, airline passengers don't have the option of removing themselves from the irritant by getting off at the nearest freeway exit. Crowded conditions, cramped seating, and no freedom to get away from the annoying stimulus can operate as a constant re-irritant similar to raging drivers' continuing contact with the drivers who enraged them.

The most common tip in anger management is to walk away from a possible fight, go somewhere else, and cool off. On an airplane there are no "other places" to go.

As with air rage, there is no absolute definition of what constitutes road rage, but the parallels between road rage and air rage are easy to see in the following table.[53]

How Often Does Air Rage Occur—and Why Don't We Know?

No one knows for sure how often air rage occurs. That's because airlines aren't required to report these in-flight brawls unless they want to—and given a choice, they'd really rather not.

Avoiding Bad Publicity

"It doesn't make airlines look good if they report violent incidents on their aircrafts," says Dawn Deeks, a spokeswoman for the Association of Flight Attendants, which represents 50,000 flight attendants from 26 airlines. Until the FAA requires airlines to report every air rage incident, she says, the problem will be swept under the rug. "The numbers are meaningless unless there's a reporting mechanism in place that says every incident needs to be reported."[54]

That's why the first thing that strikes one when investigating air rage is how little reliable data there is on how many attacks occur. The number of cases of air rage has been estimated at anywhere from 250 to 10,000 or more each year. As long as the airlines can decide whether or not to report a given incident, the statistics will be questionable. "The number and severity of incidents appears to be on a steady rise, but there is a wide disparity among the diverse sources of reporting,"

---

53   K. Michelle Scott, "The Phenomenon of Road Rage: Complexities, Discrepancies and Opportunities for CR Analysis," *The Online Journal of Peace and Conflict Resolution,* Fall 2000, found at http://www.trinstitute.org/ojpcr/3_3scott.htm.

54   Jessica Wehrman, "'Air Rage' is Back," Scripps Howard News Service, January 14, 2002, found at http://www.knoxstudio.com/shns/story.cfm?pk=AIRRAGE-01-14-02&cat=AN.

Table 1.1   Similarities between air rage and road rage

Causes of Air Rage	Causes of Road Rage
Increased congestion at the airport and aircraft	Increased congestion on roadways
The need to "save face" and overcome feelings of being disrespected by airline staff	The need to "save face" and overcome feelings of being disrespected by another driver
An innate human drive to aggression	An innate human drive to aggression
An overriding human need for "space," which causes some passengers to become territorial and guard against another passenger's infringement on their space	An overriding human need for "space," which causes some drivers to become territorial and guard against another driver's infringement on their space
An ignorance about the rules of the airline industry	An ignorance about the rules of the road
Dehumanization of the other	Dehumanization of the other
A cultural propensity to promote and reward behavior that is competitive, tenacious, and aggressive	A cultural propensity to promote and reward behavior that is competitive, tenacious, and aggressive
An attempt to attain power in an otherwise powerless existence	An attempt to attain power in an otherwise powerless existence
Increased commuting distance and durations	Increased commuting distance and durations
The need to assert one's identify and maintain control in a situation where one fears losing control	The need to assert one's identity and maintain control in a situation where one fears losing control
An overriding focus on individualism that produces a "me first" mentality	An overriding focus on individualism that produces a "me first" mentality
Oppressive social conditions that produce feelings of alienation in individuals	Oppressive social conditions that produce feelings of alienation in individuals

Source: Independently compiled from K. Michelle Scott, "The Phenomenon of Road Rage: Complexities, Discrepancies and Opportunities for CR Analysis," *The Online Journal of Peace and Conflict Resolution,* Fall 2000, found at http://www.trinstitute.org/ojpcr/3_3scott.htm.

says Dahlberg. "Figures cited by flight and cabin crew labor associations differ from figures cited by industry, IATA, ICAO, and NASA."[55]

These reports capture only a fraction of what's really happening on flights, a flight attendant union reported in 2000, because only the most serious incidents are reported.[56] The Airline Pilot's Union (ALPA) agrees, saying, "Official statistics do not always tell the whole story. In fact, cockpit crews and flight attendants are still often discouraged by airlines from reporting cases of air rage in an effort to keep an aircraft as close to schedule as possible."[57]

In an August 2007 article, Dr Andrew Thomas, founder and editor-in-chief of the *Journal of Transportation Security* [JOTS], suggests that this situation of inadequate reporting had not changed in the intervening six or seven years:

> In the U.S. there have been 1,750 documented air-rage incidents since 2000, according to the Federal Aviation Administration. Thousands of more incidents have gone unreported. Data from the FAA, which only tracks the handful of incidents that are reported by the airline crews, show the average number of rage incidents was about 248 a year from 2000 through 2006. From 1995 through 1999, there were 198 incidents a year on average. The reporting mechanism is woefully inadequate for the problem. There could be as many as 10,000 actual air-rage incidents a year in the U.S. alone.[58]

That said, existing data does give some sense of the problem. In an Australian Services Union survey, 97 percent of customer service employees at the budget airline Jetstar said passengers had subjected them to air rage, and 59 percent said it happened every day. Eighty-one per cent suffered verbal threats, while 29 percent said they were attacked physically. Airline personnel reported being choked, kicked, spat upon, strangled, punched, slapped, pushed, shoved, and struck with a bottle.[59]

In a year when the FAA reported 283 episodes of air rage among all 83 United States airlines, United Airlines alone reported more than 600.[60] If one airline experienced 600 episodes, it's likely that 83 taken together experienced—well,

---

55   Dahlberg, p. 7.

56   "Airlines Tolerate Air Rage," *USA Today*, March 21, 2001, found at http://archives. californiaaviation.org/airport/msg13957.html.

57   Anonymous and Thomas, p. 103.

58   Andrew Thomas, "The Continuing Scourge of Air Rage," *Jagua Forbes Group and Security Technologies International,* August 2007, found at http://www.jagwaforbes. com.au/continuing-scourge-air-rage.

59   "Jetstar: Low Cost but at What Cost?" Australian Services Union Zero Air Rage survey, on *ASU net, the ASU Website*, February 21, 2005, found at http://www.asu.asn. au/media/airlines_general/20050221_airrage.html.

60   Hester, "Flying in the Age of Air Rage."

more than 200. Many observers accept Thomas's estimate of 10,000 or more incidents a year.[61]

Avoiding Lawsuits

There are many reasons airlines drag their feet about reporting air rage. For one thing, reports can open them up to lawsuits. Some raging passengers have even had the nerve to sue the airlines themselves. In a 1999 Salon.com article, flight attendant Elliott Neal Hester describes an incident precipitated by "the passenger from hell," a hostile, drunken man named Adam Ratliff who appeared to be sniffing drugs. Early in the flight, Hester said:

> ... a loud, somewhat primordial scream ripped through the cabin.
>
> "ARRRRGGGH .. ARRRRGGGH!!"
>
> It sounded as if a large, carnivorous animal had escaped from the cargo hold and was terrorizing passengers at the rear of the airplane. When I swung around, I realized I was only half right. A wild-eyed male passenger was terrorizing passengers at the rear of the plane. His arms flailed, his head jerked spasmodically—he looked like the deranged criminal in a low-budget biker flick.[62]

Throughout the flight, Ratliff continued screaming obscene insults and threatening anyone who tried to quiet him down. Two flight attendants and a flight engineer kept the feral passenger at bay while terrified passengers moved out of his area of the plane. Warned by the pilot that he would be arrested when the plane landed, Ratliff made a beeline for the rest room, where he presumably flushed his illegal drugs. He was arrested upon his arrival.

Not long afterward, a private investigator visited Hester at his home, saying that he was working for Ratliff's lawyer and he wanted to hear details of the flight. Hester described the ordeal and then asked when Ratliff would be going to trial:

> "Trial?"
>
> "Yeah," Hester said. "He's being prosecuted for his actions on the airplane, right?"

---

61   Anonymous and Thomas, pp. 22–23.
62   Elliott Neal Hester, "The Passenger from Hell," *Salon.com*, August 17, 1999, found at http://dir.salon.com/story/travel/diary/hest/1999/08/17/passenger/.

"Oh, hell, no," the investigator said. "Mr. Ratliff is suing your airline. We believe he was intoxicated before boarding and should never have been allowed on that airplane. Your airline is at fault."[63]

Avoiding Being Branded a Troublemaker

Another cold reality stifles the impulse to report air rage. As long as the FAA doesn't require incidents to be reported, any employees who do talk about an incident may be treated by the airlines and their coworkers as troublemakers. Knowing this, employees hesitate to speak out, especially if it might mean losing their jobs. As a result, a cloud of silence descends over most air rage incidents.

Airlines' drive to preserve the sunny façade of endlessly happy flights is a remnant of the old airline culture of service that assumed "the customer is always right." Even when passengers are violent, any crew members who shine a light on their boorish behavior are seen as painting an unhappy picture of the onboard experience and inviting unseemly publicity.

The High Cost of Responsibility

The major airlines have expressed reluctance to discuss or report air rage incidents because of the fear that bad publicity will tarnish the industry's image. One has to wonder which unblemished area they think could be further tarnished at a time when airlines rank in the bottom three industries in service provided. Rather than so energetically protecting a sadly fallen image, the airlines might be better occupied in cleaning and polishing the service provided, so that it can stand up to scrutiny.

Another reason airlines are reluctant to admit fault is the all-too-real threat of legal liability. Sadly, in the current lawsuit-saturated business world, stepping up and saying "we're responsible" can be admissible evidence in a court of law that can cost a company millions. Initially less expensive but also highly damaging is the bad publicity of major press coverage of airline mistakes. These are real issues that industry executives have to deal with in order to stay in business.

One problem with the "no comment" approach, however, is that when airline officials keep silent on problem issues, it makes life even more difficult for those airline employees who are out there facing demanding passengers on the air travel front lines every day. They have limited options when it comes to saying nothing, and stonewalling irate passengers only results in employees and their airlines' being branded as poor service providers. Air rage incidents continue to cause a great deal of apprehension and frustration for airline personnel who must have a continuous working relationship with the traveling public.

---

63   Ibid.

Why Aren't Offenders Prosecuted?

From the time the first recorded air rage incident was reported in 1947, perpetrators have walked away from incidents scot-free. As is so frequently the case in air rage reports, details of that first incident are sketchy. All we know is that an unruly intoxicated male passenger on a flight from Havana, Cuba, to Miami, Florida, physically assaulted and injured another passenger with a bottle of alcohol. While being subdued, the passenger assaulted and injured three crew members. When the flight reached Miami, the passenger was removed and arrested by the authorities. No charges were brought, because no one knew who had jurisdiction to prosecute him.[64]

Half a century later, methods of dealing with incidents of air rage haven't changed much. A 1999 survey of flight attendants at 17 airlines by the Association of Flight Attendants (AFA) revealed that they often receive little training in defusing unruly passengers. Most said their carriers had no policy on air rage. Only 3 of the 17 airlines gave workers what they considered adequate training to deal with the problem. "No surprise then," the report concluded, "that some disruptive passengers simply walk away when a flight lands, though interfering with a crew member is a federal offense."[65]

Jurisdiction Unknown: Welcome to Bangor

One more unique feature of air travel that allowed the first air rage perpetrator to walk free in 1947 still allows offenders to avoid prosecution today. Air rage incidents happen in the air as the plane crosses from one local jurisdiction to another, making it hard to determine which law enforcement agency has jurisdiction to prosecute the raging passenger. Usually if a flight is diverted because of a serious incident, the local authorities will be involved, but other law enforcement agencies may be involved as well.

One city, Bangor, Maine, population 32,000, seems to have sorted out this problem. Bangor has become the destination of choice for flights that are diverted because they run into trouble over the Atlantic. Larger airports have too much traffic to accommodate surprise landings, but Bangor has welcomed diverted flights with open arms, turning the processing of unruly passengers into a thriving business. In a 2004 *Washington Post* article, Sara Kehaulani Goo explained why Bangor was the perfect spot for an unexpected stop:

> Nestled in the northeastern corner of the country, Bangor International has ... a runway more than two miles long, a U.S. attorney's office and FBI agents who

---

64 Michael P. Sheffer, "The Problem Passenger: A History of Airline Disruption; 1947 to Present," 2000, found at http://www.skyrage.org/PDF/SKYRAGE/scsi.pdf.
65 "Airlines Tolerate Air Rage."

live within minutes of the terminal. For airline pilots, the combination makes Bangor a favorite unscheduled landing spot.

The incidents are so common that local nurses say they often treat patients from the diverted flights: an assaulted flight attendant, a heart attack victim, a woman in labor.

"It's not a major thing" to get a patient from a diverted flight, said Karla Adams, a local nurse at St. Joseph Hospital in Bangor.[66]

Long before the terrorist attacks, Goo said, Bangor became the favorite spot for airlines to dump and run, quickly dropping unruly passengers and getting back in the air:

From his small office tucked into a corner near the Delta Air Lines ticket counter, Bangor police sergeant Donald "Ward" Gagner serves as the resident expert when it comes to diverted flights—he once handled two in one day back in 2001. A tall, imposing figure, Gagner said he and his law enforcement colleagues have earned the respect of transatlantic pilots who know Bangor can swiftly take care of any trouble on board and send the plane back into the sky.

"Yeah, try to land an unscheduled flight in Boston or New York," said Gagner, who said it would take hours to get a plane on its way again at those busy airports. "Someone called [diverted flights] our cottage industry." Then lowering his voice, he jokes, "We take out your garbage."[67]

Gagner told the reporter he'd developed a technique to calm down booted passengers, many of whom initially put up a fight or made a scene on the plane. Once they're in handcuffs in the squad car, he said, the obstreperous former passengers tend to calm down. "We give them a reality check," he said. "We handcuff them, sit them in the car and then pull out just a bit, and let them watch the aircraft" leave them behind. "Soon, they are very cooperative."[68]

Air Rage Eclipsed by 9/11

Even though the September 11, 2001, attacks caused Americans to beef up airline security, Thomas suggests that the result wasn't greater protection from air rage. On the contrary, he said in the August 2007 article cited previously, the tremendous

66   Sara Kehaulani Goo, "Bangor is Used to Surprise Landings," *Washington Post,* October 17, 2004, p. A-3, found at: http://www.washingtonpost.com/wp-dyn/articles/A38685-2004Oct16.html.
67   Ibid.
68   Ibid.

investment of resources in stopping deliberate, politically motivated terror attacks may have distracted airport and airline personnel from dealing with nonpolitical attackers who are simply out of control.

"The severity of an attack by a drug courier or an upset passenger who didn't get an upgrade is not nearly as strong as a determined terrorist who is on a mission to sacrifice his life in order to bring down an airliner," Thomas said.[69] But, while the threat of terrorism is horrifying, he said, it distracts from the more prevalent problem of air rage:

> The actions of disruptive passengers are often the most overlooked element when trying to recognize the role violence plays within the aviation system. Although terrorist and criminal acts against aviation receive much more attention from both policy planners and the media, disruptive passengers pose a much more pervasive, ongoing threat. The sheer number of cases that take place every year evidences this.[70]

Given these four factors—the FAA's failure to require reporting of air rage, the airlines' reluctance to publicize anything as bad for business as violence on planes, the crew members' lack of training in handling incidents, and law enforcement's uncertainty about who should prosecute the offenders—it's not surprising that even the FBI has trouble getting comprehensive information on air rage. As Harry A. Kern points out in an FBI Law Enforcement Bulletin:

> Gathering and assessing information concerning air rage incidents can prove difficult. Not only do reporting practices vary between governmental agencies and airline companies, but the reporting mechanisms used often contain only some essential information, omitting many details concerning the factors surrounding these incidents. This may result in incomplete (as pertinent details surrounding these incidents may be omitted), as well as inconsistent and conflicting reporting (as many of these incidents may be mislabeled as air rage). Additionally, the records of many governmental agencies and airline companies prove difficult to obtain.

> Airline company policies differ as to when air rage incidents are reported, or not, and when to leave the decision to employee discretion. Inadequate communications, worker shortages, time pressures, employee fear, and staff-performance measurement systems that may encourage conflict avoidance versus resolution, all may contribute to potential offenders' boarding of airplanes. Differing policies of, and representation by, unions, such as those representing pilots, flight attendants, and other industry personnel, add to the overall mix of

---

69 Thomas, "The Continuing Scourge of Air Rage."
70 Ibid.

describing, reporting, and subsequent actions taken, or not taken, in response to the problem of air rage.[71]

When even the top law enforcement agency in the United States cannot obtain complete information, it is hardly surprising that no one has a clear picture of the problem. As Agent Kerns puts it, "Until more fully defined, air rage only can function as a popular term, not a legal one. Greater comprehensive research and more complete data can help in the recognition, assessment, and control of air rage incidents."[72]

The Genesis of Anger: What Causes Air Rage?

To understand the causes of air rage we first need to understand rage itself. Knowing how and why anger gets triggered in the body and mind is the best way to understand why it gets out of hand. We'll explore the genesis of anger briefly in the following paragraphs, and at greater length in Chapter Two.

Brain Chemistry: The Fight-or-Flight Reflex

While most of us in a civilized society control our angry impulses, we've all known those brief moments when we "weren't ourselves," when something took hold of us for just a second and we lashed out, or cut someone off in traffic, or laid on the car horn angrily. Where does that sudden unexpected flash of anger come from?

It grows out of a primitive physical coping mechanism, the "fight-or-flight" reflex that enabled human beings to survive in prehistoric times—and that can kill us now. Unknown to us, the minute we start to panic or become enraged about anything from a traffic jam to a fight with a ticket agent, this primitive fight-or-flight reflex kicks in, flooding our bodies with stress hormones, including adrenalin and cortisol, that enable us to fight or run for our lives, just as if we were a prehistoric man escaping from a saber-toothed tiger. The minute our mind screams "Code Blue!" these powerful hormones surge through our bodies, revving up our heartbeats, blood pressure, and blood sugar so we can run faster and fight harder than we ever could in everyday life. Meanwhile, non-emergency services like digestion and thinking shut down, as oxygen-carrying blood races to the arms and legs, where the body thinks it's needed for a fight. To repeat—once the adrenalin and cortisol are flooding the system, the ability to think clearly and make good judgments evaporates.

In the modern world, where we're not in danger of becoming a tiger's lunch, this cascade of hormones leaves us all charged up with no place to go. The resulting

---

71   Harry A. Kern, "The Faces of Air Rage," The FBI Law Enforcement Bulletin, August 1, 2003, found at http://www.encyclopedia.com/doc/1G1-107930060.html.
72   Ibid.

energy surge implodes in our body—and sometimes explodes on a plane. The jolt of hormones can change passengers or crew members' disposition in the blink of an eye, causing them to act without thinking, overwhelmed by the internal physical drive to lash out.

By one estimate, Americans average 50 brief fight-or-flight episodes a day. (That's why an estimated 60 to 90 percent of all doctor visits are for stress-related illness.) One implication of that fact is that on a bad plane trip we may be more capable of succumbing to a spike in stress hormones than we know—though most of us may limit our reaction to a quickly regretted curse or hand gesture.

Psychologist and anger management specialist Robert McCrary cites two sources for anger: (a) Frustration: Not getting what one wants, especially if one was expecting to get it, and (b) Feeling that others do not respect one or care how one feels.[73]

Luckily, stress is in the eye of the beholder. One person's catastrophic flight delay is another's chance to finish a novel before the plane reaches the gate. But at this point, air travel is overly stressful for almost everyone. And new research shows that in some people who have suffered childhood trauma, the brain's wiring has been physically changed to make them see any event, from a boss's failure to smile in the hall to a five-minute wait on the runway, as more stressful than it really is.

It helps to keep this fight-or-flight reflex in mind when considering causes of air rage. In this book, we'll look at the impact of each stressor—helpless waits in long security lines, the implied threat of terrorism at every turn, claustrophobic seating, under-oxygenated cabin air, lost luggage, fear of flying, and rude airline personnel, to name just a few—on our fight-or-flight reflexes and stress hormones. We'll also consider what kind of dance those hormones do in our bodies and brains when low cabin pressure, chemicals in cabin air, missed meals, fatigue, dehydration, and alcohol are thrown into the mix.

Then we'll consider three questions: How can airline officials reduce sources of aggravation to keep their passengers' stress from spiking? How can airline personnel help overwrought passengers who are well on their way to "fight-or-flight" recover their peace of mind? And finally, when all else fails, how can airline personnel cope with people destined to lose control, or prevent them from boarding a plane in the first place? The answers to these three questions can help make flying the pleasant, civilized and exciting experience it used to be.

In investigating these questions for this book, passengers and airline personnel were surveyed to see whether premier service and the expectation of premier service really do make passengers less prone to air rage.

---

73 Robert John McCrary, "Anger Management: A 'How-To' Guide," G. Werber Bryan Psychiatric Hospital, Columbia, SC, 1998, found at http://www.state.sc.us/dmh/bryan/webanger.htm.

The Glory Days: Champagne Service

Today, as travelers all over the world make their way to airports and brace themselves for the drudgery and humiliation of security checks, it is no wonder that the traveling public is fueled with anger, thinking it shouldn't be this hard. They remember that as recently as the 1990s, there were no security lines extending for city blocks. No one had to contemplate being subjected to an invasive personal search or walking through a metal detector.

Back then, passengers' biggest concerns were to arrive at the airport on time, stroll onto the aircraft, claim their reserved seats, select their favorite meals, and gather their carry-on luggage when they arrived safely at their destination.

The traveling public might wonder whatever happened to the "good old days" of airline travel before 1992. Then the airline industry culture was built on a foundation of politeness and impeccable customer service. Travelers selected air carriers based on the level of service they offered, and as the date of a trip approached, they felt excitement and anticipation. Next to safety, service was the industry's highest goal. Arguing with customers was unheard of.

Civility was the order of the day. There was no room for a rude airline employee, and it was inconceivable that a passenger would behave inappropriately in an airport or on a plane. The airline culture was built on a belief in treating the traveling public with respect, compassion, human dignity, and understanding. Airlines that exhibited sincerity, concern, compassion and understanding were held in high esteem.

From Heroic to Hip to "Cattle Class": A Brief History

The first commercial flights in the late 1920s and early 1930s were seen as heroic experiences. The very first flight attendants were teenage boys and young men, but in the 1930s they were soon replaced by female registered nurses, because those few members of the general public who did fly were concerned about rampant air sickness in tiny planes that couldn't climb above turbulence, as well as more serious risks to life and limb. Most of the people flying in the early 1930s were wealthy executives flying on business, plus a few favored socialites. The best-known woman in the air was First Lady Eleanor Roosevelt, who crisscrossed the country by plane to make various political and goodwill trips.

When Bette Davis said, "Fasten your seatbelts, it's going to be a bumpy night" before entering a turbulent party in the 1950 movie "*All About Eve,*" most Americans had never been on an airplane, but everyone knew what she was talking about. Even though ordinary people could only imagine such a high-flying life, they had all seen movies about airplanes, and Davis' words captured how airplane travel was seen at that moment in time: glamorous, dangerous, and wickedly fast in every sense of the word. In the next couple of decades, more and more people began to add airplane travel to their lives, but it was still a luxury experience. Ticket prices were so tightly controlled by government regulation that the airlines had to compete by offering more and better services, a more enjoyable flying experience, and an atmosphere that would lure customers away from the competition.

As planes got larger and more comfortable, air travel soon entered an era of glamour, culminating in the 1960s and '70s, when flying was an elite, prestigious form of transportation and "flying high" was a term that denoted exuberant high living. In the 1940s and '50s and well into the '60s, passengers set off for the airport dressed in their Sunday best. Men wore suits and ties and women wore white gloves and hats. And as they entered the airport, they sported company manners to match their clothes.

In the hedonistic 1960s, Braniff Airlines painted their airplanes in bright pastels and signed up designer Emilio Pucci to design their new stewardess uniform in fluorescent colors. In 1966, their mildly provocative slogan was "Does your wife know you're flying with us?" Pucci's fluorescent colors reflected the contemporary association between "modern," "hip," and "psychedelic." This carefully crafted association between fun, hipness, and flying seemed to work. "In the first quarter of 1966, Braniff carried nearly 40 percent more passengers than in the same 1965 period," *Fortune* magazine reported, "almost twice the increase for the industry as a whole."[74] Other airlines followed suit, trying to capture the modernistic mood of the decade.

Simply put, people wanted to fly. Flying itself was a high-speed, high-class experience that was within the grasp of anyone with the money for a ticket. The term "the jet set" arose to describe "wealthy people who lead a life of fast travel and expensive enjoyment."[75]

From their formal, semi-military role as nurses, stewardesses had evolved into sex symbols by the 1960s and '70s. In his article, "Where Did All the Stewardesses Go?" Joshua Zeitz reported that in 1971, National Airlines, determined not to be outdone by Braniff:

> ... ran a now-famous campaign featuring Cheryl Fioravente, a real-life flight attendant, with the slogan "Hi, I'm Cheryl—Fly Me." To which Continental responded, "We Really Move Our Tails for You," prompting National to change its slogan to "We'll Fly You Like You've Never Been Flown Before." And on and on. (Air France: "Have You Ever Done It the French Way?" Air Jamaica: "We Make You Feel Good All Over.")

---

74 "The Girls who Painted the Planes: Introducing the Air Strip," *Fortune Magazine,* August 1966, page 146, found at http://www.ciadvertising.org/studies/student/96_fall/lawrence/braniff.html.

75 "Jet set" definition, found at http://www.allwords.com, 2003.

With such goings on, and Southwest Airlines requiring its flight attendants to slip into hot pants before performing safety checks on the cabin doors, something had to give.[76]

The airlines were selling a sophisticated, colorful, fun experience. Even in 1980s and '90s airline employees flocked to be part of the industry. According to 16-year veteran flight attendant, now syndicated columnist Elliott Neal Hester, "The ability to fly for next to nothing is the reason I took this job."[77]

United Airlines' more family-oriented, but equally legendary 1965 slogan, "Fly the Friendly Skies" became so popular that it has entered the vernacular. (In the aftermath of the 9/11 attacks, the phrase often seems bitterly ironic, as friendliness becomes ever harder to find in the air or in the terminal.)

The downward slide in service started with airline deregulation in 1978, but it didn't really accelerate until low-cost, no-frills carriers like Southwest, Midway, and ValuJet became wildly successful in 1992. Then everything changed as airlines' luxury image and sterling service went into a tailspin, and the era of budget airlines and zero-frills flying blossomed. To compete, airlines had to sell cheaper tickets to more people. The focus of the airline industry turned to the quantity of customers they could cram into a plane, rather than quality of service once they got there. As a result, says air rage expert Andrew Thomas, most customers found themselves flying "Cattle Class."[78]

To save money while adding more flights and passengers, airlines also cut staff levels. In the summer of 2006, there were 70,000 fewer airline workers handling 100 million more passengers than in 2002. Planes were fuller than they had been since they were used to fly troops in World War II, meaning that more ticket holders were getting delayed or bumped from flights.[79] On-time performance in the first seven months of 2007 was its worst since records have been kept, and more than a million pieces of luggage were lost, damaged, delayed, or pilfered by U.S. airlines from May to July, 2007.[80] And the frontline airline workers forced to cope with the

---

76   Joshua Zeitz, "Where Did All the Stewardesses Go?" *AmericanHeritage.com,* March 22, 2007, review of Femininity in Flight: A History of Flight Attendants, found at   http://www.americanheritage.com/articles/web/20070322-airlines-stewardness-flight-attendant-pullman-porters-unions-austin-powers_print.shtml.

77   Elliott Neal Hester, "The Sky's the Limit," *Salon.com*, 2002, found at http://archive.salon.com/travel/diary/hest/2000/03/21/flyfree/index1.html.

78   Anonymous and Thomas, p. 88.

79   Jeff Bailey, "Rough Summer is on the Way for Air Travel," *New York Times,* May 21, 2006, found at http://www.nytimes.com/2006/05/21/business/21AIRTRAVEL.htm.

80   "2007: The Year of Mishandled Luggage," *CBS 4* online service, October 1, 2007, found at http://www.topix.com/content/cbs/2007/10/2007-the-year-of-mishandled-luggage-6 and also found at the *CBS News* site, http://cbs11tv.com/consumer/airports.airlines.travel.2.507448.html.

fallout from angry passengers had taken pay cut after pay cut for their trouble.[81] One result may have been the deterioration of their attitudes.

Whatever the cause, a willingness to help, an attitude of gratitude, common courtesy, and knowledge are hard to find in many airline employees today. When overworked, overwhelmed, or rude employees make customers feel they're getting bad service, they become frustrated and angry. Not surprisingly, a survey from the National Quality Research Center at the University of Michigan confirmed what many already know: the three industries that are seen as providing the worst service are phone companies, utilities—and airlines.[82]

As of 2007, airlines have continued cutting every possible frill to keep costs down. Today, in order to save fuel and squeeze in more passengers, even seat padding has been minimized—and, as we all know, the rows of seats have been placed closer together.[83]

Today Southwest Airlines marketers would probably blush to remember their politically incorrect "stewardess in hot pants" days. As a budget carrier, Southwest has become one of the most profitable airlines in the world. In a complete departure from their hot pants presentation, a 2006 Southwest advertising slogan gently satirizes the in-flight announcement, "You are now free to move about the cabin" by proclaiming, "you are now free to move about the country." Anyone who has traveled in recent years knows that while the plane itself may be "free to move about," the passenger has little such freedom while the plane is in the air.

Airline travel, once a joyfully anticipated event, has been reduced for most fliers to deeply dreaded drudgery. Service is minimal, stress is ever-present, and security is tight. Passengers have learned to expect delays, to tolerate having their shoes removed and searched for explosives, and to surrender any small belongings that might conceivably be used as a weapon or to hide a weapon. Still, people who can afford it will continue fly because flying is still the fastest available form of transportation, even when it tortures the traveler with delays, indignities, and sometimes fear. By the beginning of the twenty-first century, Gallup polls said, "While most Americans have flown commercially at least once during their lives, the percentage of those who fly in an average year amounts to about half of the adult population."[84] Luxury and glamour were long gone. Flying was still fast, in the sense that it's the quickest way to reach a destination, and there can be danger, although commercial air travel is not the kind of risk that acts as a magnet for daredevils.

---

81   Bailey, "Rough Summer."

82   Drummond, ibid.

83   George Hobica, "How to Upgrade Your Seat Cheaply," posted April 17, 2008, on *Airfarewatchdog.com*, found at http://www.aviation.com/travel/080418-upgrade-your-seat-cheaply.html.

84   Mark Gillespie, "Public Confident in Security of Airline Travel," February 15, 2002, found at http://www.gallup.com/poll/5335/Public-Confident-Security-Airline-Travel.aspx.

The decline in airline customer service is particularly frustrating to those who remember what a beacon of excellence airline service once was. It has slipped far from that high historical standard, and customers pay the price in irritation, even as they reap the savings of low fares. As pilot, Patrick Smith puts it:

> I am known to wax on about the salad days of flying, but don't get me wrong: I neither believe, nor have written, that luxurious pretensions deserve a place in modern-day aviation. People sitting in coach aren't covetous of a velvet-clothed cheese cart or a serving of grilled salmon with braised fennel and leeks. What they yearn for is a halfway comfortable seat, something to do, and for God's sake an occasional bottle of water.[85]

Even those who don't mourn the days of high quality service have reasons to fear the increase in disruptive passenger behavior that has been the source of serious injuries and deaths. The failure on the part of the airline industry to curtail this behavior jeopardizes virtually every individual who boards an aircraft.

Some observers feel the perception of shabby customer service can be reversed with changes in customer orientation of service providers.[86] In his online newsletter, Michael Boyd, president of a company called Airline Services Training, Inc., said the problem of customer alienation:

> ... cannot be solved unless it is honesty and clearly identified. When it comes to why consumers dislike airlines, we'll be blunt: too many airlines have not bothered to try to identify what makes air passengers go bonkers. The industry has babbled about it for the past two years, yet the angry mobs are still forming like a re-run of Bastille Day.

> The choice is clear. Airline front offices can either move now to really put the customer first. Or they can let Congress try it.[87]

In researching this book, I examined whether improved customer service and the expectation of better service would in fact reduce air rage. Chapters 2 and 3 examine how airline policies are helping to trigger air rage. Chapters 4 and 5 look at the passenger's problems, from substance abuse and mental illness to rage addiction, that cause air rage. Chapter 6 examines the genesis of rage itself, and

---

85   Patrick Smith, "Ask the Pilot," *Salon.com,* December 6, 2002, found at http:// archive.salon.com/tech/col/smith/2002/12/06/askthepilot21/index.html.

86   M.K. Brady and J. Cronin, Jr., "Customer Orientation: Effects on Customer Service Perceptions and Outcome Behaviors," *Journal of Service Research,* 3(3), 241–251.

87   Michael Boyd, "The Airline CEO Challenge: Experience What You Put Your Passengers Through," *Hot Flash,* July 23, 2001, found at http://www.aviationplanning. com/airline1.htm#Abuse.

Chapter 7 discusses ways to solve the air rage problem, including the results of my studies on how a customer's perception of the service they're offered affects their approval of other passengers' enraged behavior, and their willingness to take part in such behavior themselves.

Chapter 2
The Perfect Storm: Airline Policies that Cause Air Rage

On July 29, 2007, a Continental flight was making the long flight from Caracas, Venezuela, to Newark, New Jersey, when their plane was diverted to Baltimore, Maryland, where it sat on the tarmac for five hours. The 120 passengers were locked in the plane as they ran out of food, water, and toilet paper, the toilets became filthy, and people became ill. After five hours with no information, the beleaguered passengers, including a diabetic, a pregnant woman, and a number of children and old people, staged a gentle protest, clapping in rhythm and drumming on overhead bins. Now there was action. Officers and customs officials boarded the aircraft and escorted passengers off the plane to the airport—where they were made to feel like criminals as a policewoman with a dog yelled at them to "Stay against the wall!" and they had a hard time getting wheelchairs for the sick people.

When they finally reached Newark, the exhausted travelers were desperate to rebook missed connections, but "the service just got worse," one told the *New York Times*. Agents shouted at them, telling passenger Caroline Murray to "shut up about her connecting flight." When another passenger vehemently insisted on being put on a flight that night, "They made him say he was sorry before he could continue speaking to someone," Murray said. When she finally reached the front of the line and complained about the service, an agent called her a bad name.

The Baltimore plane was just one of hundreds of planes trapped on airport tarmacs in the first half of 2007, but the others were trapped longer—for six, eight, or even twelve hours.[1]

****

Eight minutes before departure time, a father, mother and their two children raced to the gate at a dead run, having been delayed by a major snowstorm. When they presented their tickets to the agent, she sneered, "You failed to meet our ten-minute rule," and flipped the tickets back at the bewildered father, said airline consultant Michael Boyd. "We're already processing our stand-bys, and your reservation is canceled. You can standby for a later flight, but they're all full." Not understanding

---

1   Joe Sharkey, "On The Road: Right There on the Tarmac, the Inmates Revolt," *New York Times*, August 14, 2007, found at www.nytimes.com/2007/08/14/business/14road. html; and "29ᵗʰ July 2007—Baltimore, USA" incident cited in AD Aerospace, "Is FlightVu the Answer?" found at http://www.ad-aero.com/products_witness_news.php.

what she was talking about, the father protested, Boyd said. "A supervisor arrives, who haughtily re-affirms the sentence handed down by the gate agent. There is no appeal: the family is guilty of violating the airline's sacred ten-minute rule." Meanwhile the agent standing next to the family kept calling out the names of stand-by passengers to give them the family's seats. Facing the prospect of having his family stranded, Boyd said, "Papa's tone goes up a decibel or two, 'But you have seats and you're giving them to other people! We have reservations!' Again, the gotcha-sneer from the supervisor. 'Not any more you don't. And if you raise your voice at me again, I'll have you arrested.'"[2]

****

As we've seen, rage is often triggered by our "fight-or-flight" reflex, which kicks in when we feel threatened. Air travel today presents the harried traveler with a perfect storm of "fight-or-flight" triggers. By 2007, almost one in three planes arrived late,[3] 100,000 flights were cancelled in one month,[4] and 56,000 passengers were involuntarily bumped from their flights.[5] That year, one out of every 138 checked bags was lost or damaged,[6] and hundreds of planeloads of passengers sat locked in planes on airport tarmacs for six to twelve hours at a time.[7] In other words, said expert Andrew Thomas, "the system was broken."[8]

On top of that, said Boston University psychologist Tom Cottle, "air travel is a breeding ground for anxiety caused by fear of death, discomfort in crowds, separation from home and family and fouled-up sleep cycles. Passengers are subjected to rules about where to stand or park their cars; creepy language that's used nowhere else ('your final destination') and class tensions at the baggage counter: 'This line, which is very short, is for the first class, and this line is for the rest of you slobs.'"[9]

---

2   Michael Boyd, "'Abusive' Passengers. Ever Wonder How Some Get That Way?" *Hot Flash*, 2001, found at http://www.aviationplanning.com/airline1.htm#Abuse.

3   "Travel: Lose Your Cares, Luggage, Sanity," *CBS News online*, October 1, 2007, found at http://www.cbsnews.com/stories/2007/10/01/travel/main3314904.shtml.

4   Chris Isidore, "Your Vacation at Risk," *CNNMoney.com*, July 12, 2007, found at http://money.cnn.com/2007/07/12/news/companies/canceled_flights/index.htm?postversio n=2007071211.

5   Jeff Bailey, "Bumped Fliers and No Plan B," *New York Times*, May 30, 2007, found at www.nytimes.com/2007/05/30/business/30bump.html?pagewanted=print.

6   Susan Glaser, "Be Sure to Pack Some Patience for Your Journey," *Cleveland Plain Dealer*, November 16, 2007, p. A1, found and available for sale at http://pqasb.pqarchiver. com/plaindealer/search.html.

7   Sharkey, ibid.

8   Anonymous and Andrew R. Thomas, *Air Rage: Crisis in the Skies* (Amherst, NY: Prometheus Books, 2001), p. 35.

9   Joanna Weiss, Associated Press (unnamed) article of August 17, 1999, cited in Elliott Neal Hester, "Flying in the Age of Air Rage," *Salon.com*, September 7, 1999, found

The minute we walk into an airport, we surrender control over our lives. As a result, even if we're not conscious of it, everything from fear of flying or panic about missing a flight to anger at being wedged into a suffocating seat can set off alarm bells in our brains, sending a cascade of stress hormones into our bloodstreams. Add to that the unhealthy chemical brew in cabin air mixed with a pre-flight jolt of liquor or drugs and the policy of pushing liquor sales on flights, and you've created a toxic stew of brain chemistry that sets up some passengers to explode. And that's before we've been insulted by a rude ticket clerk or bumped from a flight.

"Anyone who steps onto a plane has a certain potential for violence," said Terry Riley, a psychologist who trains airline staff. "Usually we're able to keep ourselves under control, but if too much stress builds up, it can break down our inhibitions, and the fewer the inhibitions we have, the more powerfully the violence can break through."[10]

Who's to Blame: Airlines or Passengers?

Air rage observers fall into two camps: those who think it's largely caused by arrogant airline policies that treat customers like cattle, and those who think it's caused by an increasing tolerance of rage in a spoiled society—in other words, those who blame the airlines and those who blame the passengers. As we'll see, both factors play a role.

Andrew Thomas makes a case that air rage increased when airlines switched from selling fewer tickets to buttoned-down wealthy and middle-class passengers, to mass marketing tickets to a larger, less sophisticated population that cared less about manners than standing up for themselves. Coming at a time when society at large seemed to value self-assertion and self-esteem more than politeness, this new group of passengers felt free to make a ruckus when life onboard the plane didn't go their way.

The bad behavior of this growing population was more than matched by that of rich entitled executives, snobs, and celebrities who thought the world revolved around them and weren't afraid to say so.[11] These included the woman who delayed a plane's departure for a full hour, arguing that she shouldn't have to stow her Gucci bag for takeoff. (The rest of the passengers applauded when she was marched off the plane.)[12]

And the problem was aggravated, says retired pilot Steven Luckey, because obnoxious flyers' behavior was rarely punished, often ignored, and sometimes even rewarded with a free drink or an upgrade to first class to shut the loudmouths

---

at http://www.salon.com/travel/diary/hest/1999/09/07/rage/index1.html.

10   Terry Riley, interview by email with the author, September 24, 2008.

11   Anonymous and Thomas, pp. 83–85.

12   "1ˢᵗ August 2006—Hong Kong" incident cited in AD Aerospace.

up.[13] Fuel these two populations with drugs and alcohol, take away their cigarettes, throw in a few passengers with uncontrolled mental illness and "rage disorder," and, some folks say, you've pretty much explained air rage.

Others say no. They say intolerable and dehumanizing airline policies are also pushing normally civil people over the edge. This chapter and the next will examine the airlines' role in triggering air rage. Chapters 4 and 5 will then examine passengers' role in the problem.

How Did It Start?

The problem is not one specific incident, said a longtime airline professional, but an attitude that runs through the whole industry. Most travelers can cope with a cancelled flight or lost bag "if there's a helpful, even sympathetic, and knowledgeable professional on the other side of the counter who sincerely tries to help and seems to care," he said, but the airlines' stance is more like comedian Lily Tomlin's old "Ma Bell" routine: "We don't care; we don't have to."[14]

That cynical attitude, the unnamed professional wrote in an ABC News.com article in 2006, is due partly to wretched employee morale caused by plummeting salaries and pensions and the rush of layoffs that leaves fewer tired, overworked, disgruntled workers to serve more passengers under worse conditions than ever before.[15]

In 1978, while still maintaining the air traffic control system, the federal government deregulated the airlines, starting the deterioration of airline customer service as we knew it.

The problems with deregulation continued to escalate in the 1980s, when Congress refused to set a mandatory floor of minimum ticket prices. As airlines competed to offer the lowest priced tickets in a highly competitive market, they found themselves actually having to charge less for a ticket than it cost to fly the passenger to avoid losing their customers in those markets—even if they went bankrupt in the process.[16]

To keep that up, airlines tried to save money in every possible area, ABC's reporter said, until they were "facing the unexpected truth that when your prices are too low and costs have to be cut, the only place to turn is to the workers themselves, the very people who are still giving reasonably good service (or were at that time)."[17] Which is where we are today: With costs cut to the bone, fliers get

---

13   Steven Lucky (Capt., Northwest, Ret.), "Air Rage," *Air Line Pilot,* September 2000, p. 18.
14   "Why Airline Service Suffers," *ABC News online,* April 4, 2006, found at http://abcnews.go.com/print?id=1800726.
15   Ibid.
16   Ibid.
17   Ibid.

fewer of the amenities—little touches like pillows, friendly smiles, food, water, people to take your ticket, pilots to fly your plane—not to mention enough planes to fly in.

The High Cost of Disposable Customers and Employees

It seems the airline industry's main goal is to save money by filling every plane to capacity. This need to pack each flight to the walls is a major contributor to air rage.

Quoting a 2005 airline quality survey conducted by Wichita State University in Kansas, ABC.com said, "The degree to which U.S.-based airlines and their people are dedicated to giving their customers good and attentive service is at an all-time low, and sinking fast. ... Complaints about airline performance overall increased 17 percent in 2005 over the previous year, and the rate of 'mishandled' bags jumped significantly as well."[18]

Unfortunately, the attitude of airline personnel today is, "You, the public, need us ... we don't need you." Airline customer satisfaction has deteriorated to its lowest level in three years, according to a June 2008 J.D. Power and Associates survey about North American carriers.[19]

Worst of all, the airline executive said, when money is the standard by which success is measured, safety suffers. As a result of the deregulation act of 1978, "both service and safety became cost-accountable items," the author said. "Since a new breed of airline accountants could see no difference between the cost of a sandwich and the cost of safety, everything was subjected to massive and often dangerous cuts."[20]

Cruising for a Bruising: Air Rage 2000

By 2000, the broken air travel system was already producing rage. Even though the majority of airline passengers in a 1999 Gallop Poll reported they were "generally satisfied" with their travel experience, reported Andrew Thomas in his book, *Air Rage,* one out of every three passengers was already saying they sometimes became enraged at airlines or airline employees. For passengers who flew five or more times a year, that number rose to almost one in two. Since then, air travel conditions have only gotten worse.[21]

---

18   Ibid.
19   J.D. Power. "Airline Customers Dissatisfied," June 17, 2008, found at http://www.btnmag.com/businesstravelnews/headlines/article_display.jsp?vnu_content_id=1003817456&imw=Y.
20   Ibid.
21   Anonymous and Thomas, ibid., p. 15.

At an international aviation conference in 1999, Thomas said, United Airlines head James Goodwin said so many planes were flying that the airline industry was facing a crisis. "The skies are crowded and getting more so every day," he said, adding that, unless something was done soon, severe delays would become routine, creating backlogs with serious or even catastrophic implications.[22] By 2007, his predictions had come true.

In 2000, Thomas reported, Federal Express head Frederick Smith was also warning that flight delays and cancellations would only get worse if airlines kept scheduling too many flights for too few airports and runways. While the number of flights was exploding, Thomas said, only one new major airport (in Denver) had been built in the 1990s, few had been expanded, and the patchwork air traffic control system created in the 1940s was showing signs of age. "The overloaded air traffic control system, an antiquated hub-and-spoke (routing) system, insufficient airport capacity, more passengers flying every year, and the growth of the airline industry are making the skies above us as crowded as the highways on the ground."

American Airlines head David Carty agreed, saying that in 2000, the number of planes arriving on time in New York's busy LaGuardia Airport was 30 percent "and falling." That was down from 70 percent the previous year.

"Something's got to give," he said.[23]

In the years that followed, airlines responded to calls for fewer flights by increasing the number of flights and jamming more passengers onto each plane, trying to boost profits by running more customers through the system faster. To make that possible, they needed passengers to act like well oiled cogs in a machine, rather than fallible human beings.

More than a Nuisance: Danger Aboard

If rage resulted, it could endanger a planeload of people. On an Eva Air flight from Los Angeles to Taipei, a pop star from Hong Kong named Ronald Cheng had been drinking whiskey and champagne since takeoff. After smoking and setting off the fire alarm in the bathroom, Thomas said, Cheng emerged "completely intoxicated, very altered, and yelling for more whiskey." Eventually he started singing and shouting obscenities. When a flight attendant refused to give him more whiskey, he grabbed her in a headlock.

Hearing her screams, Captain John Erving sent his co-pilot out of the cockpit to help, at which point Cheng grabbed the officer by the throat. With no one else to fly the plane, the captain quickly woke up the reserve crew and left them "flying the aircraft in their underwear" while he raced back to rescue his copilot by knocking the singer unconscious with a flashlight. Cheng was treated by a doctor on board and the plane was diverted to Anchorage, Alaska, where he was taken off.

---

22   Ibid., p. 29.
23   Anonymous and Thomas, ibid., pp. 29–30.

Even though captains are no longer supposed to leave the cockpit to deal with a fracas in the cabin, the commotion is still on their minds. "That means the pilot is probably paying a little less attention to that line of thunderstorms ahead or to surrounding air traffic in the congested, overcrowded skies," Thomas said. "Under such circumstances, air rage can end up in a catastrophic disaster."[24]

Author Angela Dahlberg agrees, saying confidential reports to NASA's Aviation Safety Reporting System (ASRS) show that many pilot errors resulted from pilots' distraction by unruly passengers.[25] In 40 percent of the 152 cases in the NASA study, pilots either left the cockpit or were interrupted from their routine by flight attendants seeking help. In a quarter of those cases, the pilots said they committed errors such as flying too fast, going to the wrong altitude, or taxiing across runways reserved for other aircraft.[26]

Thomas took that concern a step further. "There have been dozens of unsolved accidents worldwide over the last ten years that may have been contributed to in some way by air rage," he said. "The reality remains that air rage is a real threat and it must be dealt with head-on."[27]

Impact of "Smiling Customer Service"

The contributing causes of air rage are many and intertwined. This chapter and the next will examine those that are under the airlines' control. In an extensive research project in 2004, I surveyed passengers to discover how the quality of the service they got or expected from their airlines would affect their attitudes towards air rage. I was especially interested in the way customers reacted to my request for them to complete the surveys I passed out to them. I found that when I made a point of smiling before asking them to complete a survey, customers agreed to do the survey in almost every case.

Intrigued, I tried this same technique when traveling myself, smiling when requesting information about my lost luggage, a delayed flight, or a flight misconnection, and I was always given information in a warm and friendly manner by the airline staff. The smiling technique was not new. For years, as an airline employee, I used the technique I call "smiling customer service" when approached by an irate passenger. I found that a simple smile would normally help dissipate some of their anger and rage. Smiling customer service will be discussed at greater length in Chapter 4.

The findings on some of the surveys I administered are outlined in Chapter 7. But in general, at least while filling out a customer survey, few people would concede

---

24 Anonymous and Thomas, ibid., p. 25.

25 Angela Dahlberg, *Air Rage: The Underestimated Safety Risk* (Aldershot, UK: Ashgate, 2001), p. 19.

26 Ibid., p. 5.

27 Anonymous and Thomas, ibid., p. 25.

that either expecting or getting bad service would make them more likely to have an emotional meltdown or become violent on a plane—the presumption being that they couldn't imagine engaging in air rage, no matter how bad things got. At least not in the cool light of reason.

But, in a slightly contradictory finding, the majority did say that the better the service they felt they were getting, the less likely they were to become enraged themselves—and the worse the service they expected, the more likely they were to approve of another passenger pitching a fit. Which raises the question—would it be a short hop from approving rage in other passengers when they felt calm and collected, to raging themselves when their stress hormones boiled over? In this chapter, we'll walk through the flying experience to see what stressors might push conditional "approvers" of rage into the "they're gonna blow!" category. We'll experience a typical day at the airport to see what could tip these potential rage approvers into behavior which, if not full-on air rage, would be much closer to it than anything they'd normally be capable of. Then in Chapter 3, we'll look at the airlines' personnel policies that promote rage.

Chapters 4 and 5 will examine the emotional baggage that sets some passengers up for rage, no matter how well they're treated, and consider what can be done to keep them from becoming a danger to themselves and others.

Causes of Rage: Airline Policies

Airline consultant Michael Boyd, president of Airline Services Training, Inc., says air rage isn't just a sign of an angry society. "Air rage is real and it could get worse," he says. "What airlines must understand is that this is not some external societal problem that has now spilled onto the departure concourse. It is essentially a situation that is partially—indeed, predominantly—within the airlines' control."

Airlines can either address the causes of air rage, he says, "or institute Green Beret training for employees. Unless some mega-carriers change the way they view passengers and service procedures, things are going to get worse."

Boyd, who admittedly has a dog in this fight since he runs a company that shows airlines how to improve customer service, says he thinks airlines need to clean up their acts. There's a fine line, he says in his newsletter, between air rage and "what is becoming a legitimate near-revolution of passengers." Current airline policies he says, are "abusive to not only customers, but to the front-line employees that are trying to serve them. We have a consumer base that feels trapped, airline employees that get hassled as a result, and management at some airlines that don't have a clue about what's causing it. And maybe just don't care."[28]

Both customers and employees are the victims, Boyd says. "The real cause of 'Air Rage' is fear," he says. Passengers fear they'll be mistreated by the airlines,

---

28   Michael Boyd, "Air Rage: Battle Lines are Drawn," *Hot Flash,* August 2, 1999, found at http://www.aviationplanning.com/airline1.htm#Abuse.

and employees fear the resulting customer anger will make their jobs harder. The two groups collide "at the battle lines—ticket counters, gates, airplane cabins— often ready and primed to put the other guy in his place. The result is a nasty downward spiral of service and of customer satisfaction."[29]

While there's no excuse for assaulting airline workers, Boyd says, "Many airline passengers feel as if they have been folded, spindled, mutilated, and generally treated like pests by some major carriers. The perception is that fares are higher, seats are smaller, amenities are fewer, and airlines don't really care. … It appears that some airlines have declared war on their passengers, who have fewer and fewer alternative airline options. But remember, cornered critters come out fighting."[30]

Customers agree. "We get better service in Kenya and South Africa than we do here," Chad Owens told the *New York Times*. He and his wife Wendy, who often fly to Africa, had arrived an hour and a half before flight time to get Wendy and their one-year-old daughter Brielle on a flight to Cleveland. After waiting an hour in a line of just eight people to check their bags, they were told they were too late to get on the flight. Although the plane hadn't left the gate, "They basically wrote us off," Owens said. "Nobody will even try to make an effort, say, 'Let's see if we can (get you on the flight).' … It's 'No, this can't be done.'"[31]

When passengers do speak out against mistreatment, they can be unfairly branded as troublemakers. Boyd suggests that airlines focus less on controlling abusers, and more on eliminating one cause of rage—bad treatment. "There will always be some small portion of the passenger base that will act like Neanderthals," he says. But many air rage triggers are under the airlines' control. This, he says, is because abusive passengers are "usually a subset of angry passengers" who got angry because they felt mistreated. If airlines focused on reducing dissatisfaction, Boyd says, they could reduce the number of angry and abusive passengers.[32]

MSNBC.com travel writer Ed Hewitt agrees. "The airlines hold all the power," he says. "While a power imbalance by nature is asking for trouble, it gets even worse when agents indulge in normal but unattractive human traits like spite, revenge and even skullduggery."

"Passengers have little or no recourse in the transaction—and when they are given no information, and stripped of control and perhaps even dignity ... well, we know why the caged bird sings."

"There are undoubtedly a lot of nice people in the airline business," Hewitt adds, "but their goodwill will always eventually be trumped—or even stubbed out—by the institutional indifference (some would say arrogance) of the airline

---

29   Ibid.

30   Boyd, "'*Abusive' Passengers*."

31   Laura Mansnerus, "Turbulent Manners Unsettle Fliers," *New York Times*, February 15, 2004, found at http://query.nytimes.com/gst/fullpage.html?res=9805E2D9173AF936A 25751C0A9629C8B63.

32   See also Boyd, "'*Abusive' Passengers*."

industry." For some time now, he says, "it has been the airlines' world up there, and we just live in it." But, he added, airline managers should remember that, "the airspace over our country, and the FAA that governs it, are owned and paid for by we the people."[33]

Customers as Cattle: Breaking the Passenger

"We make our passengers do business our way..." Boyd said he'd heard this statement from a top executive at a meeting at one of the nation's biggest airlines. Calling this airlines' "taproot" philosophy, Boyd said it was producing customer anger and, in isolated cases, air rage. He said the company's orders to its personnel amounted to: "Passengers will heel to our procedures, or else. ... We have flights to get out, and messing around with silly petty customer problems will not be allowed to get in the way."

He then described airline videos showing employees how to "psychologically bludgeon the passenger into submission." Each video described a case in which the airline made a real mistake. Then they showed a model employee sincerely admitting the failure, presenting the customer with a workable solution—and then telling them, "but we are unwilling to do that."

"The idea," he said, "was to let the passenger know who's in charge. Admit to the problem, outline a solution, and then openly tell the passenger that you refuse to do it. 'Slam that customer to the mat, babe. We've got an airline to run.'"[34]

Of course passenger violence can't be tolerated, he said, but that is the least of airlines' problems. "What we don't see in the evening news ... are the complaint letters, the phone calls, and the lost revenue from passengers that express themselves in more socially acceptable ways," he said. "That's the real cost of air rage. And airlines can control it."[35]

His comments have serious implications. If airline managers think the only cheap way move huge numbers of passengers fast is to make them feel powerless so they'll follow orders quickly without asking questions like unthinking cattle, that strategy could backfire. The fear of losing control is one major trigger of a fight-or-flight response that quickly spirals up to rage. Instead of treating customers as automatons that have to be controlled and feel controlled, airlines could turn personnel and passengers into willing participants in a group endeavor where everyone's working for the good of the group.

---

33   Ed Hewitt, "Air Rage: Why the Caged Bird Sings," *MSNBC.com*, October 30, 2007, found at http://www.msnbc.msn.com/id/21384567/.

34   Boyd, "Air Rage: Battle Lines Are Drawn."

35   Ibid.

Cogs in a Well-Oiled Machine

To make any money at all, the current system depends on the airport, airplanes, and people in them running smoothly, with no hitches, like an assembly line. According to Angela Dahlberg, author of *Air Rage: The Underestimated Safety Risk,* airlines need passengers to follow a large number of implicit rules. "The passenger becomes, for a limited time, an integral part of the system," she says. For the system to work, airlines assume people can operate as cogs in a complex, mechanized process that kicks in the minute they go online to order their tickets.[36]

Among other things, Dahlberg says, passengers are expected to:

* understand and be able to cope with automation and computers, and be able to get through their flight without human help;
* know all the procedures for processing passengers;
* cooperate and comply with all rules and be deferential to the staff;
* be unaffected by fear of flying or nicotine or drug withdrawal;
* stay cool in the face of stress, fatigue, lack of information and physical discomfort;
* not need a comfortable or large-enough seat, a quiet cabin, food, or drink;
* remain buckled up and seated in a cramped seat throughout the flight, but be ready to move out fast on landing.[37]

The only problem with the airlines' well-oiled machine is that human nature— in fact, nature of any kind—is the opposite of predictable or smooth-running. Unpredictable, spontaneous nature, whether in the form of weather or human emotions, will always get in the way of the planes' running on time.

Bait and Switch: Unrealistic Expectations

Airline passengers are doomed to disappointment before we start for the airport, says Captain Steven Luckey, chair of the Air Line Pilots Association. Not only is air travel less luxurious than it used to be, it's less luxurious than airlines claim it is now. Sophisticated elegant ads usually feature smiling, satisfied customers, "normally in a semi-reclined position, maybe enjoying a glass of French champagne," Luckey said in *Air Line Pilot* magazine. "The passenger is pictured gazing over an epicurean delight of some type, nestled on fine china plate presented on a linen table cover."[38] The reality is a lot less tasteful for the average

---

36   Dahlberg, p. 19.
37   Ibid., pp. 19–20.
38   Luckey, p. 18.

airline passenger.[39] "Today's air traveler is frequently crammed into a narrow, high-density seat, surrounded by carry-on luggage, grasping a tiny bag of pretzels while trying to quench a powerful thirst from a 3-ounce glass that also contains two ice cubes."[40] Welcome aboard.

Critics say airline ads create a bait-and-switch situation, setting passengers up to feel angry about their traveling experience before they even get on the plane. The gap between the service promised in advertisements and that experienced in the airport and on the plane keeps widening, especially in coach class.[41] This gap can come as a slap in the face to passengers when they walk into the crowded noisy airport to be herded onto their flight.

Captain Luckey described the average flier's day, starting with a struggle to get to the airport. "Traffic is terrible," he says, "especially around airports, which always seem to have access roads under construction. The parking lot is full, and no skycap is in sight to help with the bags. The first-class line has only three people in it, but the passenger's line (coach) is a hundred yards long and winds through a roped-off rat-maze line made up of other poor slobs who don't have the luxury of the expedited service either."

When the passenger finally gets to screening, he says, the screener wants the laptop computer booted up and the cell phone screen changed, and then the screener dumps the passenger's underwear on the table. The carry-on bag is then randomly selected for an explosive detection swipe test. Next the passenger has to stand in another long line at the gate check-in podium. Finally, just after answering "those two ridiculous questions regarding 'who slept with your luggage last night,' they're told their already oversold flight is being delayed for maintenance."[42] At this point, Luckey said:

> A bedraggled agent is trying to bribe several passengers into taking a later flight while rebooking some poor souls who were bumped off the previous flight because of an equipment substitution to an airplane with fewer seats. The agent has been on duty for an extra couple of hours because someone didn't show up for work and a supervisor forced the agent to work overtime. The air conditioning in the airport is on the fritz, and a young mother is trying to calm her red-faced infant who has been screaming at the top of his lungs for the last 20 minutes. You guessed it! The passenger has seat 26A, and the mother and baby have seat 26B."

---

39   University of Nebraska at Omaha, Organization Theory and Behavior (PA 8090), *Air Rage,* 2002, p. 2, found May 16, 2003, at http://www.unomaha.edu/~wwwpa/pa8090/ryberg/airrage.htm.

40   Luckey, p. 18.

41   Y. Wang. Annotated Bibliography on the Age of Rage: Rage Topics on Air Rage, Media Rage, Message Rage, and Office Rage, February 7, 2001, found at http://www.soc.hawaii.edu/leonj/409bs2001/wang/report_1.html.

42   Luckey, ibid.

... this situation, or a similar one, is fairly common. The airlines lost more money in a 3-year period 8 or 10 years ago than they had made in the entire previous history of the industry. The carriers had to either maximize the profit potential or go broke. They crammed passengers in, minimized the costs, and here we are."[43]

Airlines deserve some of the blame for the growing number of disgruntled and often violent passengers, says Patricia Friend, president of the Association of Flight Attendants, the country's largest flight attendant union, with 43,000 members. "Airlines' advertising unrealistically raises expectation," she says. "Passengers expect a fun, comfortable experience—and much of the time it's not."[44]

The cramped seats and indignities of coach, also dubbed "Cattle Class" by Andrew Thomas, are not featured in advertisements. When unrealistic expectations, fostered by airline marketing efforts, collide with the discomfort of low-fare travel, the result can be frustration. Low-fare charter bookings, advertised and promoted as fun events, can also set up potential customers for false expectations.

Airline industry advertisements present the flying experience as peaceful, enjoyable, and exciting, said psychologist Robert Bor in his 1999 study of air rage. "It does not require a degree in psychology to recognize that the reality of air travel is far removed from the expectations and images that the increasing number of air travelers have of the experience." Faced with a grueling ordeal rather than a pleasant flying experience, he said, passengers get frustrated, and the overly stressed cabin crew has to bottle up any anger they might feel or face losing their jobs. Frustration leads to aggression in thousands of small and large ways, and sometimes the aggression escalates to rage.[45]

The commercial air travel industry has succeeded perhaps too well at making air travel seem routine and easy, allowing passengers to forget that they're isolated in a small vessel that is quite literally up in the air. Aircraft designers, pilots, cabin crews, and other staff have created a padded, shielded environment that enables passengers to exist in a kind of cocoon. This illusion of normalcy lets them forget how isolated they are from the rest of the world for the duration of the flight and how important it is to get along with their flight crew and fellow passengers.

The public has already begun to adjust to the inconveniences of added security measures since 9/11. This experience of adjustment is closely related to passengers' reactions to the inconveniences of air travel. If their expectations are low, as encouraged by the low-fare "just peanuts" carriers, it's as if they're already mentally adjusted to the lower level of service before they reach the airport, and

---

43   Ibid.

44   Elliott Neal Hester, "Flying in the Age of Air Rage, September 7, 1999, *Salon.com*, about para. 24, found at www.salon.com/travel/diary/hest/1999/09/07/rage/print.html.

45   Bor, Robert, Proceedings of the 10th International Symposium on Aviation Psychology, Columbus, OH; May 3–6, 1999, pp. 1161–1166.

their reaction to adversity is different from that of a pampered traveler who expects the highest level of service.

Delays, Cancellations, and Bumped Passengers: "Dude, Where's My Plane?"

When we walk (or dash) through the airport, the only thing worse than realizing we left glamour behind in the ads is being told our plane left us behind in the airport. In the last ten years, there's been a steady rise in the number of cancelled and late flights. During peak times on some airlines at major airports, said Andrew Thomas, there is a one in ten chance that your flight will be canceled. In addition, more and more passengers are being involuntarily bumped off the planes that do take off.

In June 2007, airlines canceled nearly 100,000 flights—nearly twice the number of the previous June—leaving millions of travelers scrambling to find seats in a summer when 90 percent of all airline seats were filled. As a result, some passengers' trips were delayed by a day or more.[46]

According to the Air Line Pilots Association, this was partly due to the airlines' clever cost-saving measure of laying off pilots. Unfortunately, at least one airline, Northwest, fired so many pilots that there weren't enough left to fly the planes.[47] Another poorly kept secret is that some airlines canceled flights where bookings were "miserably low."[48]

In addition, more planes were late in 2007 than at any time since 2000.[49] More than one in every four planes (28.4 percent of all flights) pulled up to the gate late that year, with almost one in nine arriving more than 45 minutes late.[50] For American Airlines, that number was almost one in three (31 percent of all flights),[51] and in one amazing achievement, various airlines had eight flights that were late 100 percent of the time.[52] (One observer asked, "why not just change the scheduled arrival time?" Surprise, they already had. If they hadn't, the on-time stats would have been much worse.)

---

46   Isidore, 2007.

47   Ibid.

48   Tahir Siddiqui, "Schedule of Many Flights Disrupted" October 18, 2007, found at http://www.dawn.com/2007/10/18/local2.htm.

49   *The News Hour,* PBS, November 15, 2007.

50   FlightStat News, 2007 Performance Reports, January 12, 2008, found at http://www.flightstats.com/go/Home/spotlight.do?newsItemId=41.

51   Ibid.

52   U.S. Dept. of Transportation, Research and Innovative Technology Administration (RITA), Bureau of Transportation Statistics, "Airline On-Time Performance Slips, Cancellations, Mishandled Bags Up in June," August 6, 2007, found at www.bts.gov/press_releases/2007/dot077_07/html/dot077_07.html.

Meanwhile, in the summer of 2007, airlines bumped more passengers—a record 56,000—off oversold flights against their will than at any time in the previous ten years.[53] (The previous year, a total of 676,408 passengers, most of whom had agreed to be reimbursed for taking a later flight, were bumped.)[54] Since flights were fuller than ever, these ticket-holding refugees' odds of finding another seat were slim—which is why fewer people were giving up seats voluntarily.

"Airlines are running closer to capacity than at any point during the jet age—an expected 85 percent or so full this summer," said *New York Times* reporter Jeff Bailey, "which means all the seats on popular routes will be taken."[55] With fewer, more crowded planes, bumped passengers have precious few options and can find themselves spending days camped out gate-side. As a result, in November, 2007, President George Bush proposed doubling the refunds given to involuntarily bumped American passengers (from $400 to $800) and allowing commercial jets to use more military air space during the 12-day Thanksgiving holiday period, when a record 27 million passengers in the United States were expected to fill 90 percent of all available airline seats.[56]

Overselling flights is the way airlines avoid losing money when passengers with refundable fares don't show up for their flights. To figure out how many seats to sell twice, math whizzes up at corporate try to estimate which ticket holders are likely to lose their cab fare in Las Vegas or be too hung over after a convention in New York to make their flights, but they often guess wrong. That's why one flight from Phoenix, Arizona, to Cabo San Lucas, Mexico, took off in April of 2007 leaving 37 bumped passengers behind. Airline personnel dread the wrath of these stranded passengers so much that they'll try to fool company number crunchers and keep extra seats open on planes by making up phantom passengers, with the result that Mickey Mouse has become a frequent flier on many flight manifests.[57]

To Guarantee Delays: Schedule More Flights than the Airport Can Handle

In the United States, the seven busiest airports accounted for 72 percent of the nation's flight delays in 2007.[58] By October of that year, the situation had become so bad that U.S. Secretary of Transportation Mary Peters, under direct orders from President Bush, told airlines that if they didn't improve scheduling at New York's busy John F. Kennedy International Airport, they would face a scheduling reduction order. But the new acting FAA administrator said that would be a last resort.[59]

---

53   Bailey, "Bumped Fliers."
54   Ibid.
55   Ibid.
56   *The News Hour*.
57   Bailey, "Bumped Fliers."
58   "Travel: Lose Your Cares, Luggage, Sanity."
59   Ibid.

It's easy to see why planes leave late—airports schedule more departures than they can handle: JFK International normally has the capacity for 44 planes to take off between 8 a.m. and 9 a.m. in the morning. They routinely schedule 57 departures for that time. "The airport's making its money off of landing fees and take off fees and gate fees," said aviation industry expert Peter Goelz.[60]

"We're scheduling more planes to take off and land than can physically take off and land," said Rep. Peter DeFazio, D-Ore. "We're allowing this to go forward; we're saying the market will control it. The market doesn't control it."[61]

By the end of 2007, the United States government seemed to be giving the airlines a chance to limit flights voluntarily. However, airlines were still intending to add flights, not take them away.[62]

Why So Crowded?

Since low-cost fares flooded the American market in the 1990s, airlines have steadily been cramming more and more passengers into fewer and smaller planes. Between June 2001 and June 2006, six major airlines cut their fleets by 700 planes, or 20 percent, according to the Air Transport Association. On top of that, airlines shifted their larger planes to higher-priced, higher profit international routes.

As a result, each day in July of 2006, Delta had 81,692 fewer domestic seats to sell than they had in 2005, a drop of about 18 percent, at a time when two million more customers were flying than the previous summer. That and online booking with bargain fares meant that planes were flying full—so that one thunderstorm, one delay, could leave thousands more customers stranded. That situation was expected to get nothing but worse over time, especially since low-fare airlines' "hub and spoke" routing of all planes through one or two massive hub airports meant that bad weather in Chicago or Atlanta sent not ripples but a tidal wave of delays and cancellations throughout the whole system.[63]

"None of these airline systems ... were ever designed with these kinds of load factors in mind," said Kevin Mitchell, chairman of the Business Travel Coalition, an advocacy group based in Radnor, Pennsylvania.[64]

Delays and cancellations left parents with babies, old people, students flying on a shoestring, and unaccompanied minors stranded at airports with a limited amount of money, patience, time, and for some people, medications. Spending precious vacation days trapped in an airport lobby, sleeping curled up on a duffle bag, wasting limited funds on airport food, and then drinking to ease the pain

---

60   "The Politics of Airline Travel," *CBSNews.com*, September 27, 2007, found at www.cbsnews.com/stories/2007/09/27/travel/printable3303567.shtml.

61   Ibid.

62   Ibid.

63   Jeff Bailey, "Rough Summer is on the way for Air Travel," *New York Times*, May 21, 2006, found at www.nytimes.com/2006/05/21/business/21AIRTRAVEL.htm.

64   Mansnerus, 2004.

could certainly be read by the primitive brain as a threat to survival, sending stress hormones into overdrive and setting up passengers for rage.

Steady Decline in Service Since 1992

Customer service on the airlines is not what it used to be, primarily due to the explosion in the flying population after 1992. In 2001, the Association of Flight Attendants union was already saying that frequent flight delays, cancellations, and easy access to alcohol were among the main causes of air rage.[65] And it's a nice closed circle, because when a plane is late or cancelled, passengers tend to head for the bar to drown their sorrows. Of course, observers who thought it was bad in 2000 hadn't seen anything yet.

According to the U.S. Department of Transportation, in 2000, when fewer people were flying and only one of every four flights was delayed, cancelled or diverted, the cancellations already had an impact on 163 million passengers. Then the events of 9/11 gave airlines the excuse to reduce service and amenities further, saying they needed to cut costs in the wake of the tragedy.[66]

As a result, "We have seen an increase in these [air rage] incidents throughout the industry," said Sara Nelson, a spokeswoman for the Association of Flight Attendants at United. "The biggest frustration is delays and cancellations, and that has the added problem of people sitting at airports and going to a bar and drinking alcohol. Alcohol is a leading cause of air-rage incidents."

More passengers with fewer employees to help them, the frustrations of traveling, fewer amenities and packed planes increase "the opportunity for passengers to show their unreasonable side," Nelson said.[67]

Andrew Thomas agreed, saying, "as the broken system negatively affects greater numbers of passengers, it plays a larger and larger role in creating a stressful environment that can potentially lead to air rage."[68]

The steep slide in service in response to the flood of new low-fare passengers during the 1990s can be seen in changing numbers:

- *Delays:* In 2000, the average flight delay was 52 minutes. In the first 11 months of 2000, the FAA reported, 83 percent of these delays occurred on the ground: 49 percent during gate departure, 26 percent while the plane

---

65 BNET Business Network, "Airlines Reject AFA Attacks on Air Rage, Alcohol Policies," *World Airline News,* July 31, 2001, may be found through *Google.com* or at http://findarticles.com/p/articles/mi_m0ZCK/is_28_11/ai_76547444.

66 B. Shoenfeld, "We're Fed Up!" *Cigar Aficionado,* July/August 2002, found at http://www.cigaraficionado.com/Cigar/Aficionado/Archies/200208/fa802.html.

67 Kelly Yamanouchi, "United's New Committee Targets 'Air Rage,'" *Denver Post. com*, September 17, 2007, found at http://www.denverpost.com/business/ci_6913089.

68 Anonymous and Thomas, p. 39.

was taxiing out, and eight percent while the plane was taxiing into the airport.

- *Five hours on the runway:* Between 1995 and 2000, according to BTS data for the 30 largest US airports, the number of flights that took one hour or more to taxi out from the gate before they lifted off increased 165 percent (from 17,331 to 45,993). During the same period, the number that took two hours to taxi out increased 217 percent; three-hour taxi times increased 289 percent, and the number of planes taking four hours or more to get their wheels off the ground increased by 341 percent. Finally, between 1999 and 2000, number of planes taking more than five hours to take off more than doubled (from 30 to 79).

- *Fudging the numbers:* Between 1988 and 2000, the ten major airlines tried to mask the actual growth in delays by changing their schedules. They increased their flight times tacking up to 26 minutes flying time onto approximately 83 percent (1,794 of 2,167) of their major domestic routes. If airlines' scheduled flight times had remained at their 1988 levels, the number of arrival delays in 2000 would have increased more than 28 percent, instead of the recorded 19 percent.[69]

Information, Please

A surprising amount of an air traveler's sense of helplessness and anxiety has to do with not knowing—not knowing how long a flight will be delayed, not knowing if turbulence will bounce the airplane around like a ping pong ball in a championship match, not knowing whether another passenger will explode in an unforeseen rage—and then there's the lurking fear of a terrorist incident.

Columnist and flight attendant Elliott Hester said passengers want information so they can make informed decisions. "Passengers want to know what's going on," he said. "'Why is the plane late? Why is the flight being canceled? Why have we been waiting on the runway for two hours?' People can deal with the truth. The truth, as they say, will set you free."

The truth may also "send you scampering to another airline," he said. "Consequently, management occasionally tells little white lies when the situation requires."

As an extreme example, Hester said that his (unnamed) airline had sworn up and down that a flight attendants' strike would have no impact on operations, knowing that they had almost no trained backup attendants—and that they couldn't legally

---

69   U.S. Department of Transportation, Office of the Inspector General, *Final Report on Airline Customer Service Commitment* (Report AV-2001-020), February 12, 2001, pp. 10-11, found at http://www.house.gov/transportation/aviation/issues/service.pdf.

fly passengers without them. The result on the first day of the strike was crowds of disgruntled passengers left stranded in airports.[70]

When it comes to delays, the big surprise is, the pilot may not know much either. Often pilots can't get the control tower to release the information they need. One pilot who spoke recently on condition of anonymity described his frustration at this kind of information blackout:

> As pilots, we can only pass on the information we're given. I can call our dispatchers to try to get information, but the only info we can get is from the air traffic control tower, and they don't really communicate. If you ask and try to get specific info, they bite your head off. So it comes to a point where we stop asking, because they just get mad. It's my job to try to keep the passengers at ease, and when I don't have a reason why we're delayed, I try not to lie to people.[71]

Airlines would be well advised to put a priority on getting clear and correct information to passengers. Information not only soothes impatient travelers, it also builds trust and loyalty by making the informed client feel important enough to be included "in the loop."

However, MSNBC.com travel writer Ed Hewitt says, "Airline policies seem to encourage employees to deny and dissemble instead of trying to inform and instruct, which would seem almost to be our due as paying customers." Their stonewalling is a sign of "institutional arrogance ... from the top brass to the check-in counter."[72]

One company that excels in customer service is Federal Express. Although only tangentially connected to commercial airlines, it does involve transporting things from point to point, and its legendary reputation for customer satisfaction is built largely on the methods it has adopted to include customers in the information loop. Federal Express pioneered a package scanning and tracking system to give customers hard information as well as track packages. The theory was that what customers wanted most was for their package to be delivered on time, but if there should be a delay, they wanted to know the actual location of the package. Just knowing gave them a sense of power that not only defused irritation but made them part of the delivery process. The sense of empowerment and participation in the process provided just by knowing what is going on is invaluable to the anxious airline passenger.

---

70   Elliott Neal Hester, "Out of the Blue: Lies in the Sky—An Inside Look at United Airlines' Abysmal Service," *Salon.com*, July 28, 2000, found at http://dir.salon.com/story/business/col/hest/2000/07/28/united/.

71   Terry Ward, "Confessions of an Airline Pilot: Captain 'No Name' Tells All," *AOL Travel*, 2007, found at http://information.travel.aol.com/article/air/pilot-confession.

72   Hewitt, "Why the Caged Bird Sings."

Brave New World: Information and Automation

Information Overload

While they may lack the facts they want, passengers walking into an airport are often hit with a blizzard of information they don't need. From the blur of electronic arrival and departure displays, concourse, airline and gate signs, security notices, directions at baggage kiosks, and advertisements, they must quickly find out how to process their ticket and baggage, get through security, and get to the right gate on the right concourse in the right wing of the airport fast enough to check in the required number of minutes before flight time and stand in the right line, so as not to lose their seat—all this while being assaulted by the glare of fluorescent lighting, a constant stream of announcements, the beeps and roars of vehicles taking passengers to gates, and the general roar of the crowd.[73]

Meantime, they're left to worry that their carry-on luggage isn't the right length-by-width-by-height, their tiny bottles of shampoo are too big to get through security without marking them as a terrorist, or they inadvertently packed a pair of nail scissors. As a result, in the confusion, thousands of passengers have "missed flights" because they didn't meet pre-departure gate deadlines, which can be anywhere from 10 to 30 minutes before the plane is boarded.

Automation

To save money, airlines are moving from human clerks to Passenger-Centric Equipment (PACE), an industry term for machines. Passengers will have the joy of negotiating disputes not with potentially flexible human beings, but with computers. While this system can speed passengers through the airport, Dahlberg says it assumes "that the air traveler does not suffer from fear of flying, can read, is computer literate, is physically and mentally fit, is not stressed and has a degree of situation awareness that guides him/her effortlessly through the airport."[74]

With automated ticketing, baggage check, security, and arrival and departure information, the possibilities for making a mistake are endless. Even the most computer-literate fliers may want to throw up their hands and say, "Give me a real live person to answer my questions!"

"For the global air traveler with little education and experience in such an environment—the elderly, people from third world countries, people with language problems, people whose coping mechanisms are not equipped to deal with the complexities of such an environment—the danger of alienation, mounting stress, a feeling of disorientation and incompetence is real," says Dahlberg. Facing the

---

73   Suggested by material found in Dahlberg, pp. 21–22.
74   Ibid., p. 21.

highly mechanized airport experience, they "are subjected to increased social and psychological stress."[75]

The result, she says, is greater fear, anxiety, uncertainty, and mental overload. "The accumulation of stress affects the ability to integrate the information needed to proceed to one's flight with ease," she says. We see the effects, she says, in the growing number of people who miss their flights, even though they're in the terminal.[76]

So Near Yet So Far

The worst possible outcome of a dehumanized system happened in Vancouver, Canada, in 2007. At 3:00 a.m. on October 14, 40-year-old construction worker Robert Dziekanski climbed on an airliner in Poland and flew the 15 hours to Vancouver. He'd planned for five years to emigrate to Canada and start a small business with his mother. It was the first time the would-be Canadian citizen had ever been on a plane.

When he arrived, dazed and confused from the long flight, his mom was supposed to meet Dziekanski in the baggage claim area. What neither of them knew was that baggage claims was separated from the secured customs area by a glass wall designed in such a way that they couldn't see each other. Even though his papers were fine, Dziekanski, who couldn't speak English, somehow ended up pacing around customs for ten hours, about 200 feet from his mother, as she searched everywhere on the other side of the wall, frantically trying to find him.

For six hours, his mother asked clerks in international arrivals to help her find her son; eventually they told her he hadn't arrived, and she drove the five hours home. After 15 hours of flying and ten hours of helpless waiting, Dziekanski seemed to lose his mind and began using tables to barricade himself in part of the customs hall, finally throwing a computer to the ground in frustration as a concerned passerby tried to calm him. When the computer hit the floor, airport officials were suddenly all action, calling the Mounties. Seeing the police, Dziekanski threw up his hands peacefully, but they shot him with a taser gun 24 seconds after they arrived. He fell to the ground screaming after the first blast, but was tasered again, after which a Mountie knelt on his neck and he died.

"Unbelievably," his family's lawyer said, "these people were probably no more than 150 to 200 feet apart for at least five hours, and she was unable to get any message to him. And no one on the other side (of the glass walls) thought to interview him or come outside."

"For all the high-tech stuff they have at the airport, and all the security they have, somehow a guy can sit or be in that ... immigration area for a period of nine hours," he said, "without anyone really taking much notice of him." Dziekanski

---

75 Ibid.
76 Ibid., p. 22.

had brought three suitcases with him, the *Globe and Mail* reported. Two were filled with geography books.[77]

When planes are late and connecting times are short, when passengers are trapped in a plane on a tarmac or even lost in an airport, they need information to feel a sense of mastery and control over their lives and fates; by removing this small measure of control, airlines are increasing their anxiety, adding one more stick of dynamite to the exploding levels of stress.

Sardine Seating

Once you've sprinted to your plane and gotten your baggage on board, you're faced with the next stressor: the incredible shrinking airline seat. Airlines have put smaller seats in the plane, and set them closer together, although they maintain that the legroom has not diminished because their chair backs are now three to four inches thinner than the older padded seat backs. That's hard to believe when the person in front of you leans back driving your dinner tray into your abdomen. According to Thomas, passengers are allotted less space per pound in their seats than their pets down in the hold because pets are guaranteed enough room to turn around.

Crowded seating can trigger aggressive behavior, especially in passengers who are constitutionally physically active or hyperactive, who generally have to move around frequently to work off nervous energy. They can become increasingly frustrated simply because the aisles may be blocked, the seatbelt sign might be turned on, or there may not be enough aisle space for them to move enough to be comfortable. The longer flights caused by "hub and spoke" routing through major hub airports insure that fliers will be trapped in those seats for longer periods of time, in some cases long enough to trigger the formation of life-threatening blood clots in their legs.

Not surprisingly, people will fight for the little room they're given. And the feeling of claustrophobia will put even the most mild-mannered person in a fighting mood. Psychologist Raymond Fowler can attest to that. On a flight from Bulgaria and Jordan to California, he had to sit sideways in his middle seat because the person next to him was so large. "I had about 12 inches of space," he told *USA Today*. "Luckily, I'm a peaceful guy, because by the time I got back, I was ready to pick a fight with anyone in sight."[78]

---

77   Mark Hume and Sunny Dhillon, "Questions Hang Over Taser Death," *Globe and Mail*, October 26, 2007, found at http://www.theglobeandmail.com/servlet/story/RTGAM.20071025.wtaser1026/BNStory/National/.

78   Gary Stoller, "Flight Attendants Feel the Wrath of Fliers," *USA Today*, June 10, 2007, found at http://www.usatoday.com/travel/flights/2007-06-10-air-abuse-usat_N.htm.

The Agony of the Seat

Crowding aside, the seats themselves have become acutely painful to sit in. One factor we rarely think of until we're forced to sit upright for hours on end is the "pitch" of our seat. According to an ABC.com news report, seat "pitch" is the distance between rows of seats, for example, between the front of your seat's armrest and the same spot on the armrest of the seat in front of you. In a comfortable theater, they say:

> ... you might enjoy a seat pitch of as much as 36 inches or 38 inches, and in the first-class cabin of most airliners you'll have between 38 inches and 60 inches. But the average pitch of a coach seat in the average jetliner (regardless of who builds it) has been shrinking over the years, and while many carriers still keep their pitch at 32 inches to 33 inches, others have sneaked it down to as little as 28 inches, leaving their passengers in both perceived and actual agony.[79]

But, the ABC commentator asks, "if we decide to put up with the resulting agony to keep those insanely low fares, what's wrong with that?" The answer? "In a word, safety."

First, airline safety is not served by having to deal with the type of passenger upsets that are routinely bred by discomfort. Problems can be as minor as a cabin full of sullen people or range all the way to direct, criminal assaults (verbal or otherwise) on flight attendants—incidents which at the very least distract the crew.

How do you decrease air rage incidents? By being as societally intolerant of the conditions that form a breeding ground for such incidents as we are of the air rage incidents themselves. And clearly, overcrowding and unnecessary discomfort in what is already a physiologically stressful environment of motion, low humidity and high background noise is a really bad idea.[80]

In addition, the ABC commentator said, in an emergency it might be harder to evacuate passengers wedged in Cattle Car seating. Anyone who has ever taken sardines out of a can might be able to visualize the added difficulty of hauling squashed passengers out of cramped seating areas.

The bottom line is that we don't know for certain whether shrinking seat pitches unacceptably increase potential evacuation times or not, but logic would dictate they do. But until the Federal Aviation Administration begins requiring airlines to demonstrate that tighter seat pitch arrangements do not pose a decreased

---

79 "Seat Pitch, Kneecaps and Passengers Behaving Badly," *ABC.com*, July 1, 2005 (Copyright ABC Ventures), found at http://abcnews.go.com/Business/FlyingHigh/Story?id=888873&page=1.

80 Ibid.

evacuation potential, we're just guessing, and guesswork is not the method that has made air travel the safest form of transportation.[81]

While the seating issue might seem to be a simple transaction where the passenger trades discomfort for low fares, it becomes a different matter if safety is lost along with comfort.

Illusion of Space

As the airlines have crammed more seats into a row and increased the number of rows, they've found cosmetic rather than functional ways to seem to provide more space. For example, the third generation of Boeing 737s added two inches of interior width, as well as more height overhead because airplane cabin designers have found that changing the visual perspective makes the cabin looks wider.

"A lot of the perception of comfort is visual," Boeing spokesman Sean Griffin stated.[82] After Boeing changed the contours of the overhead bins to offer more headroom and remodeled the lighting to give a perception of spaciousness, focus groups were convinced the cabin was larger, even though the seats remained the same size.[83] One doubts the focus groups made that assessment after occupying the seats during a long-haul flight.

One Size Fits Few

Discomfort, both minor and extreme, contributes to air rage. For example, obese travelers become angry about the cramped seats on planes, and their seatmates get mad about having their already small space intruded upon by the large passenger. A study conducted by a news organization and Core Data found that "Cramped seating was the leading annoyance for 68 percent of the 1,189 respondents."[84] Nearly half (48 percent) of the responses were from passengers who were offended by large people spilling over to their seating space.

Airlines have been sued by tall passengers who were injured being crammed into seats with minimal leg room, by petite passengers injured by being squashed in next to large passengers, and by large passengers publicly humiliated for their size by airline personnel and arbitrarily forced to purchase a second seat midway during a multi-leg journey.

When one six-foot-tall passenger who flew economy class on a Trans-Atlantic flight from the UK to Canada sued JMC Airlines over the "intolerable" 29-inch

---

81   Ibid.

82   Ed Hewitt, "The Shrinking Airline Seat," *The Independent Traveler.com*, found at http://www.independenttraveler.com/resources/article_print.cfm?AID=161&category=13.

83   Ibid.

84   "These Small Cracks in Your World View: Derrie Air Charging Fliers by Weight," *Johnson Lab*, June 11, 2008, found at http://johnsonlab.wordpress.com/2008/06/11/cracks-in-your-world-view-1-derrie-air-charging-fliers-by-weight/.

seat pitch, a British judge awarded him approximately $800 USD, or about the cost of a round trip ticket. The judge suggested airlines should provide plane seats with a minimum pitch of 34 inches, "to provide for people in the normal range of adult height."[85] This judgment could reflect a 2001 British government health and safety report conclusion that airlines should provide a minimum seat pitch of at least 35 inches—and that the best plan would be to provide anywhere from three to ten inches more than they do now, depending on the passenger's size.[86]

In 2000, the Tall Club of Silicon Valley, just south of San Francisco, California, sued a dozen U.S. airlines, including American and Southwest, asking them to reserve the roomier plane seats for fliers who were at least 6 feet, 2 inches tall. Their leader, 6-foot, 6-inch attorney Tom Cohen, didn't ask for money—just a reallocation of seats.[87] The case was dismissed in 2003 following a Department of Transportation recommendation that "a new seating rule would conflict with the aviation regulatory scheme," and the dismissal was upheld in 2004. "So tall people will remain squished," Cohen said.[88]

Leaders of one tall people's organization, Tall Houston, suggest another approach to the problem, joining tall groups around the United States in lawsuits over deep vein thrombosis (DVT). "Worldwide, there are now thousands of DVT cases wending their way through the courts," the Tall Houston website says. "The legal definition of an "accident" has hobbled a number of DVT cases, but the tall passengers' plight might be just what the lawyers are looking for"—especially since tall passengers often bruise their legs simply getting into and out of economy seats, and these bruises can trigger DVT.[89]

Six-foot, three-inch attorney Ira Goldman took matters into his own hands in 2003 when he invented Knee Defenders, small blocks of plastic that slip onto the legs of the tray table to prevent it from closing, and therefore, stop the seat in front from reclining. The result was a lot of unhappy would-be recliners who couldn't lean back in their seats to take a nap—which didn't please airline officials either.

---

85   R. Michael, "Anthropometry and Ergonomics in Airline Seating," *Ergonomics Today* (online magazine), November 6, 2001, found at http://www.ergoweb.com/news/detail.cfm?id=432.

86   Ibid.

87   Reynolds Holding, "Tall Folks Say Plane Seating Doesn't Fly," *SF Gate*, March 5, 2000, found at http://www.sfgate.com/cgi-bin/article.cgi?file=/chronicle/archive/2000/03/05/SC67249.DTL.

88   Moldy Peaches, "$3 for the Bathroom and $2 for the Lights," March 15, 2006, found at http://moldypeaches.blogspot.com/2006_03_01_archive.html; and Traveler, "So You Are Tall," *Airlinecrew.net* Bulletin Board, April 7, 2005, found at http://www.airlinecrew.net/vbulletin/showthread.php?t=179321.

89   "Tall Passengers May Be More Prone to Deep Vein Thrombosis," *Tall Houston* website, July 24, 2004, found at http://tall-houston.com/old-news/tall-airline-deep-vein-thrombosis.html.

"We don't believe a passenger should interfere with another passenger's ability to recline their seats," said American Airline spokesman Tim Wagner.[90]

But Goldman, a former Republican counsel to the House Intelligence Committee, was unrepentant. "This is about protection, not space," he said. In the product's first year on the market, he sold more than a thousand Knee Defenders online, promoting it as a way to avoid deep vein thrombosis by giving passengers room to move their legs. Quoting *Conde Nast Traveler*, the website brags that the device is "as devious as it is ingenious."[91]

Six-foot-tall Ann Clogherty of Vienna, Virginia said she bought a Knee Defender, because the airlines had crammed too many seats into their planes, stealing legroom from passengers. "The personal space of a passenger ends where my legs begin," she said.[92]

Goldman defended his invention by explaining that no amount of polite requests would keep travellers in front of him from reclining their seats and subtracting from his already perilously small amount of legroom. One airline, Northwest, has banned the device, but FAA spokesman Paul Takemoto told the *Washington Post* the clips were not against federal aviation rules as long as they weren't used during taxiing, takeoffs, or landings.[93]

Exceptionally tall passengers, who are almost guaranteed to fly in pain in coach due to the lack of leg room, are advised to call the airlines 48 hours before the flight (as are handicapped passengers) to arrange for the least painful seating option. Some recommend that tall passengers get a doctor's recommendation that they need space for their long legs, in hopes of turning it into a "medical" upgrade to first class.

Tall passengers are treated with relative respect in contrast to the hostile attitude some staff take toward obese passengers, which reflects the current social climate of "looking up" to tall people and casting a dim eye on those who are wide-bodied.

The Second Seat Wars

Some airlines feel free to take a punitive attitude towards obese passengers. One controversial "solution" to the problem of people who are larger than the cramped seats is the policy at Virgin, Southwest, and a few other airlines, of requiring large passengers to buy two seats. That's right. If you're large and you want to fly on these airlines you have to pay for two seats—even if two seats together aren't

90   Keith L. Alexander, "Knee Defender Keeps Passengers Upright, Uptight," *Washington Post*, October 28, 2003, E01, found at http://www.washingtonpost.com/wp-dyn/content/article/2003/10/28/AR2005033109087_pf.html.

91   Alexander and Knee Defender website at http://www.kneedefender.com/html2/buy2.htm.

92   Alexander.

93   Ibid.

available. Southwest maintains that they will refund the price of tickets if the flight is not full, but they do not reserve seats. As a result, on full flights a large passenger may be forced to buy an additional seat, even though the airline may sell that seat to another passenger; or the large passenger may be forced to buy a "second seat" that may not be located next to their own seat, which makes no sense if the goal truly is to have the large-sized passenger not impinge on another passenger's space.

A cursory examination of how Southwest in particular enforces the policy casts doubts on whether this is a physical solution to a physical problem or a social and corporate "spin" to adroitly shift blame for crowding to the obese, who are already a target of much public disapproval.

Some of the flaws in the policy of having large passengers buy a second seat are apparent in the most notorious lawsuit, which was filed against Virgin America airlines by Barbara Hewson, 63, who was sitting next to a large passenger who had to raise the armrest to fit into her seat. The large woman had bought two seats on her original flight across the Atlantic, but the option was not available on the return flight because the flight was completely booked. Hewson settled the case for damages of $20,000 (£13,000) after suffering a blood clot, torn leg muscles, and sciatica following a flight to Los Angeles in January 2001, the UK's Press Association reported.[94]

Both women were concerned about the situation during the flight, the report said:

> [Hewson] said the woman passenger was so large she had to sit with the arm rests up, but when she complained, the crew said there was nothing they could do as the plane was full. Hewson added that half-way through the flight the woman asked if she was okay, saying to her: "I'm sitting on your lap."

> "I had three sessions of sitting in the hostess seat and I stood for a little while," added Hewson.

> Virgin Atlantic said in a statement: "This was an unprecedented set of extremely unfortunate circumstances."[95]

Several lawsuits have been filed by angry large-sized passengers about the second seat policy. The main issues appear to be whether the policy is fair, consistent, and rational, since the determination of whether a large traveler needs to buy a second is at the discretion of the gate agents. It isn't clear what the criteria requiring purchase of a second seat are, since at least one passenger, Nadine Thompson,

---

94 "Woman Squashed by Plane Passenger," *BBC News*, October 22, 2002, found at http://news.bbc.co.uk/1/hi/uk_news/wales/2346319.stm.
95 Ibid.

who could fit into a Southwest seat with the arm rest down, was removed from the plane after refusing to buy a second seat. She later sued Southwest.[96]

When Lionel Bea sued Southwest over rude and arbitrary treatment, his lawyer claimed that because the requirement to buy a second seat is left up to the whim of airline employees, "It's the type of policy that can't be applied in a uniform manner."[97] In a response to an editorial about Southwest Airlines' "two seats for fat people" policy, frequent flyer Jay Early said that because some airlines like Southwest and JAL didn't allow advance seat assignments:

> … even if you buy 2 seats, there is no guarantee that you will get them both together. It is a bit hard to place one cheek on a window seat on the left side of the plane and your right cheek on the aisle seat on the right side of the aircraft. The airline offers no refund to you if this happens and is not the least bit sympathetic to your cause; after all, you do have a place to sit on the plane. On full flights, the gate agent walks the aisle counting empty seats. Immediately afterwards, a troop of people comes marching down the aisles and one plops into your purchased seat. You then have to make a big deal to defend your empty seat and try to retain it for your flight.

> … If you get bumped from a flight, you stand a very good chance of only getting a single seat on the next flight out. If you are willing to help out the airline on an oversold situation, they will not give you vouchers for both seats that you have given up. The worst part of the … policy is that it is up to the airline gate person whether you buy a second seat or not. If you leave your starting airport, not having to have bought an extra seat, why are you forced to purchase a full fare seat at the airport where you have to change planes to continue your trip, usually for more money than your whole round trip ticket cost in the first place? Are any of these practices fair for anybody?[98]

Within Kicking Range

One unintended consequence of a tight seat pitch, as many travelers have found to their dismay, is that the back of the seat is within kicking range of the toddler behind them. The Core data survey mentioned earlier found that the behavior of young children during flight annoyed 38 percent of those surveyed. Those angered by uncontrolled children may spend the whole flight seething if children of a certain age repeatedly kick the seat in front of them without being restrained by the

---

    96   "Woman Says She Was Bullied by Southwest Employee," *USA Today*, February 8, 2006, found at http://www.usatoday.com/travel/flights/2006-02-08-swa-lawsuit_x.htm.

    97   Ibid.

    98   Jay Early, "Letter Written in Response to an Editorial Supporting Southwest Airlines 'Two Seats for Fat People' Policy," 2003, found at http://www.maadwomen.com/lynnemurray/essays/southwest.html.

parents. While infants who cry throughout a flight may cause stress to passengers, they usually do not blame the parents, except perhaps for bringing the infants on the plane in the first place. But parents who let toddlers kick are another matter. Even so, it might be better to lobby for more seat room than stricter parents. As parent and author, Barbara Rowley explains:

> People without kids think—and often say out loud—how awful it is that a mother isn't doing anything to stop a child who kicks the back of your seat, but it's really important to remember that the range of what a mom can do is very limited. A mom who holds her toddler's feet (after requesting several times that he stop) may stop the kid from kicking. Or she may only succeed in replacing the kicking with full-on screaming or even a tantrum, wherein the kid manages to both scream and kick your seat.[99]

Space: "The Most Important Comfort"

According to Shirley Streshinsky, author of "Airline Seat Space, Cruel or Unusual Punishment," passengers find sitting next to an empty seat "perhaps the most important creature comfort" they can get when they fly, and of course there are precious few of them with planes flying 90 percent full. Streshinsky quotes Boeing spokesman Sean Griffin as saying having that empty middle seat has the effect of adding up to 4-1/4 inches in seat width as well as a feeling of privacy. (For long flights especially, most people prefer not to sit next to strangers.) It also puts them in a better mood. "Those lucky economy passengers who manage to have an empty seat next to them 'will also report that the delays are shorter, that the meals are hotter, and the drinks are colder,'" Streshinsky says.[100]

Added to the crowding in economy class may be one more insult—having it rubbed in the passengers' faces that the privileged people in First Class are treated far better than they are. This sense of being disrespected, when added to the crowd-induced rage, could put an already-angry or drunken passenger over the top. In his column, airline pilot Patrick Smith describes the luxurious bedrooms aboard the new A380 jets and then says:

> We hear a lot about the ever-widening gap between the rich and poor. Maybe I'm reaching too far, but airplanes have a dramatic, sometimes vulgar way of showcasing this gap. In fewer places are the demarcations of class, in a very literal sense, more plainly in view. It's difficult to say at which point comfort

---

99   Helen Baskas, "Flying with Children Doesn't Have to Get Ugly," *USA Today*, April 20, 2004, found at http://www.usatoday.com/travel/columnist/baskas/2004-04-20-baskas_x.htm.

100   Shirley Streshinsky, "Airline Seat Space, Cruel or Unusual Punishment," *Via Magazine, AAA Traveler's Companion*, found at http://www.viamagazine.com/top_stories/articles/airline_seat_space00.asp.

becomes excessive and wasteful, but there are those who'd prefer a more egalitarian layout, with improved room and service for everybody. Although an aircraft like the A380 is remarkably efficient on the whole, those 6-foot beds and private cabins are hardly an ideal use of space or an expression of the common good.[101]

Russell Rayman, director of the Aerospace Medical Association, says conditions now are ripe for more confrontations between airline workers and their customers. Planes are flying fuller as airlines slowly regain profitability, and studies have shown that crowding in a confined space can lead to aggression.[102]

Pilot Stephen Luckey agrees "Social anthropologists suggest that crowding produces increased aggression," he says "The issue of decreased personal space leading to tension and aggression is well-demonstrated through anecdotes of passenger altercations which began as a result of one person's body adjudged by another to be too close to his or her own."[103]

In one case, problems started when a passenger on a British Airways B747 flying from Lagos to London in June 2007 reclined his seat, and the passenger behind him asked him to put it back up. The first man refused, the second got up and punched him, and the fight was on. Friends of both men jumped into the fray, wielding fists, bottles, and belts up and down the airplane's narrow aisle. By the time the crew handcuffed two of the men, as many as 20 people had joined the fight and a female flight attendant and a male passenger had gashes on their heads. Police arrested the two instigators when the plane landed.[104]

One study indicates that overcrowding not only produces aggression, it produces pointless aggression, fighting for fighting's sake with no end in view.

Mouse Rage: When Good Mice Go Bad

John B. Calhoun, MD, who conducted some well-known experiments on the impact of overcrowding on mouse colonies in 1973, said he was painfully concerned about the implications of their results for human beings. His research convinced him that, because of the growing need for high-density living, humanity was "on a knife-edge." Dr Calhoun may have conducted the only scientific study to begin

---

101   Patrick Smith, "Ask the Pilot," *Salon.com*, November 9, 2007, found at http:// www.salon.com/tech/col/smith/2007/11/02/askthepilot252/ or http://www.salon.com/tech/ col/smith/2007/11/09/askthepilot253/.

102   Stoller, 2007.

103   Statement of Captain Stephen Luckey, Chairman, National Security Committee, Air Line Pilots Association, Before the Subcommittee on Aviation, Committee on Transportation and Infrastructure, U.S. House of Representatives, Passenger Interference with Flight Crews and the Carry-on Baggage Reduction Act of 1997, June 11, 1998, found at http://cf.alpa.org/Internet/TM/tm061198.htm.

104   "24th June 2007—London, UK" incident cited in AD Aerospace.

with a quotation from the Book of Revelations and a table based on the text that begins: "I saw ... a pale horse, and its rider's name was Death ..." (Revelations 9:7).[105]

Calhoun found that dense populations of mice trapped and unable to migrate away from the social stress suffer social breakdowns, including random aggression very similar to the crime in crowded human populations. The aggression exhibited by the irritable mice was not directed to any goal such as seeking a mate or defending a territory. Indeed, overcrowding and the lack of new territory to move into shattered their social structures. Calhoun may never have experienced air rage, but his penned-in mice seem to have duplicated the experience.[106]

Jean-Paul Sartre dramatized his vision of hell in the play *No Exit* as three people imprisoned forever at close quarters in a small space, unable to leave and doomed to harass one another for all eternity. Some frequent flyers may think they've lived his nightmare when they're stuck on a long-haul flight, crammed into a tiny airline seat next to an obnoxious fellow passenger. Fear and stress can be ratcheted up to the breaking point at the thought that the hostile stranger sitting in the next seat—possibly actually touching one's knees in coach seating—may be ready to explode with rage.

In the last few years, more and more planeloads of passengers have gotten to live something even worse.

No Exit: False Imprisonment

Recently a new kind of stress has been added to air travel. In the first seven months of 2007 there were suddenly hundreds of reports of passengers trapped on parked airplanes for 6, 8, and even 12 hours, with food and water running low and toilets becoming filthy. For extra frustration, many of them were within easy walking distance of the airport terminal, but were not allowed off the plane.

This was a stunning increase over the 30 planes nationwide that sat on the runway five hours or more in 1999, and even the 79 that were stuck that long the following year.

The wave of strandings seemed to start on December 29, 2006, when passengers on American Airlines flight 1348 from San Francisco to Dallas were stranded for 12 hours on the tarmac in Austin, Texas, because of bad weather in Dallas, which caused the cancellation of nearly all flights going through that hub city. The passengers were trapped in the plane with no food, no information, overflowing toilets, and rising frustration levels as they watched the planes outside their windows take off and land.

---

105   John B. Calhoun, "Death Squared: The Explosive Growth and Demise of a Mouse Population," *Journal of the Royal Society of Medicine*, January 1973, 566, found at http://www.pubmedcentral.nih.gov/articlerender.fcgi?artid=1644264.

106   Ibid.

The American Airlines pilot couldn't let people off the plane because the slides could be used only for emergencies, and the Transportation Safety Administration has strict guidelines about the use of stairs. "You know, we've got kids here. My 5-year-old daughter has been on here for 11 hours," Tom Dickson, 44, of Los Altos, California, told *Dallas Morning News* reporter Claire Cummings by cell phone from the grounded plane. "And there's younger kids on here than her. We've been told several things, and none of it has happened. Even when they tell us something, we can't have any faith in it." Passengers tried to stay calm, Cummings wrote, but confusion reigned.

"The bathrooms have gone from a gas station to, 'What's the last concert you've been to?'" said Andy Welch, 53, of Linn Creek, Missouri. "Think about that. It's probably about that." One of the passengers explained that since the plane left Dallas early in the day, many passengers hadn't gotten much sleep or had any breakfast. All they had was the memory of the previous night's dinner.[107]

Official airline policies may not include humane treatment of people, but sometimes a crew member's humanity will kick in. At about 8:15 p.m. the pilot took it upon himself to taxi the plane toward the terminal. Passengers were able to get off at 9:04 p.m.—nearly 12 hours after they'd arrived in Austin.[108] A little over a month later, a Jet Blue flight was stuck on the tarmac at New York's Kennedy airport for 11 hours. Both stories were highly publicized, as was the earlier stranding of a Northwest Airlines jet in Minneapolis in 1999. Since then, there seems to have been an epidemic of stranded and gridlocked planes, and passengers can add to their other stresses the worry that they'll be trapped in a planeload of airport inmates.

The 1999 stranding caused a storm of bad publicity, followed by a flurry of "Customer Service Initiatives" from airlines, "a document of cheery promises and pledges that each airline was obliged to draw up," said Ed Hewitt. But, he said:

> … as almost every industry pundit and expert noted at the time, the initiatives were in fact little more than a PR-savvy repackaging of the existing airline "Contract of Carriage," a document that does its level best to absolve the issuer of responsibility. Sure it was in nice sugary language, and the airlines ate a bit of crow for effect, but the new initiatives had almost no teeth. The whole thing amounted to Congress forcing the airlines to take a pledge to do better, and when the TV cameras went away, it was business as usual for the airlines, with a few big checks cut to lobbyists and public relations firms. Whew.[109]

---

107 Claire Cummings, "Passengers Stuck on Plane Over 8 Hours," *Dallas Morning News*, December 30, 2006, found at http://www.dallasnews.com/sharedcontent/dws/bus/industries/airlines/stories/123006dntswstranded.331dc32.html.

108 Ibid.

109 Ed Hewitt, "The Airline Passenger's Bill of Rights," *MSNBC.com*, February 16, 2007, found at http://www.msnbc.msn.com/id/17173370/.

"The current Customer Service Initiative mostly says, 'we'll try our best, but we don't really promise anything,'" says Hewitt. "It's all squish and slip."[110] However, after a woman named Kate Hanni was trapped on American flight 1348 in Austin, she started the Coalition for an Airline Passenger's Bill of Rights, which is calling for a passenger's bill of rights to be written into law. As of March 2009, the bill was still under consideration.

Cabin Air Quality: "Is It Dizzy in Here?"

One cause of air rage may lie out of passengers' control: the impact of airplane air on brain chemistry. No matter where in the world you fly, says air rage expert Andrew Thomas, "the air quality inside the cabin will invariably seem poor."[111]

But the problem can be far more significant than the stuffy, germy dryness of recycled air. In recent years, pilots and flight attendants have complained that toxic engine fumes leaking into their air supply have triggered nausea, headaches, memory loss, confusion, neurological problems, and even temporary paralysis serious enough to keep them from flying safely.[112] According to Dr Sarah Myhill, an expert on this "aerotoxic syndrome," chemicals in airline air can also cause "destabilisation of mood (mood swings)," including "increased tearfulness, irritability and aggression, impulsive suicidal thoughts," and "rage."[113]

In one report, two Swedish pilots suddenly became nauseated, confused, and nearly paralyzed during a landing because of toxic air. Luckily, they got their oxygen masks on in time to land the plane, but, according to *The Daily Telegraph*, "many of the 73 passengers on the flight were so deeply asleep that it was difficult to wake them up—a fact confirmed by the accident investigator who noted that passengers were in a 'zombie-like condition.'"[114]

Former British Airways pilot Tristan Loraine said he had made an emergency landing at London's Heathrow Airport in an oxygen mask because fumes in the cockpit had left him feeling "like I'd been hit by a baseball bat." Two hours later he was still so disoriented, he couldn't find his keys to start his car. They were hanging in the car door. The long-term health problems that resulted from the

---

110 Ibid.

111 Anonymous and Thomas, p. 26.

112 Tristan Loraine, "Toxic Airlines: Is Your Plane Trip Poisoning You?" *Daily Mail online*, February 8, 2008, found at http://www.dailymail.co.uk/news/article-513209/Toxic-airlines-is-plane-trip-poisoning-you.html.

113 Sarah Myhill, "Aerotoxic Syndrome: The Poisoning of Airline Pilots, Cabin Crew, and Passengers that Is Possible in Any Air Flight," found at http://www.aerotoxic.org (in right margin, click on "Dr Sarah Myhill's briefing sheet") or http://www.aerotoxic.org/articles/20071118_3.

114 Charles Starmer-Smith, "Is Cabin Air Making Us Sick?" *Telegraph.co.uk*, Travel section, first appeared February 23, 2008, (last updated May 29, 2008), paragraph 15, found at http://www.telegraph.co.uk/travel/759562/Is-cabin-air-making-us-sick.html#continue.

exposure, including numbness in his fingers and feet, nausea and heart palpitations, eventually forced him to quit flying.[115]

Why are passengers and pilots exposed to toxic engine fumes? The air at high altitudes has too little oxygen for passengers to breathe safely. Until 1962 airlines dealt with that problem by pumping planes full of clean outside air that had been treated with compressors to make it breathable. Then airline executives realized it was cheaper to recycle the air that was already *in* the plane than to treat the air from outside. Airlines can save tens of thousands of dollars every year for each plane that recycles cabin air.[116] As a result, about 50 percent of the air on board is continually recirculated cabin air, passed through filters that may or may not be clean (raising fears of catching flu or tuberculosis from that passenger hacking and wheezing in the back row).[117]

But what most passengers don't realize is that in the interest of cutting costs, the other 50 percent of the plane's air is "bled off" the engines and pumped directly into the cabin without being filtered in any way. As it passes over "the blisteringly hot heart" of those engines, says Tristan Loraine, the air can easily pick up leaked engine oil or hydraulic fuel if the seals aren't working perfectly, before being cooled and pumped into the cabin.[118] Observers say that engine oil or hydraulic fuel is more likely to leak in some planes because of design flaws. (According to *The Telegraph*, British CAA records show that the British Aerospace 146, Boeing 757, Airbus A319, and Embraer 145 seem to be particularly susceptible to this problem.)[119] When that happens, passengers and flight attendants are not only given a second, third and fourth shot at breathing each other's germs, they're also inhaling a dollop of jet fuel byproducts. (While British government statistics suggest this "only" happens once every 2,000 flights, airline activists suspect that figure is much higher.)[120]

Airline employees are especially concerned about a carcinogenic chemical called tricresyl phosphate (TCP). "Exposure to TCP can cause brain damage that may take weeks or months to fully develop," said an Association of Flight Attendants Safety and Health Alert. "Also, when oils (and hydraulic fluids) are heated in the air supply system, carbon monoxide gas can be generated. Carbon monoxide basically robs your body of necessary oxygen. This is especially serious

115   Loraine, 2008.

116   Excerpted from International Air Transport Association, "Carriage of Passengers," as cited in Anonymous and Thomas, p. 94.

117   Loraine, 2008.

118   Ibid.

119   Starmer-Smith, 2008.

120   "Where Do Aerotoxic Fumes Come From?" *www.aerotoxic.org*, found at www. aerotoxic.org or http://www.aerotoxic.org/categories/20070829_2.

in-flight because the air you are breathing *already* has less oxygen than does the air at ground level."[121]

Airline representatives defend the quality of the air passengers breathe. Compared to an office building, "the airplane has far more air exchanges per hour," said Cris Bisgard of Delta Airlines, "…and the air that comes into the aircraft cabin is sterile."[122] But Association of Flight Attendants industrial hygienist Judith Andersen Murawski disagreed, said air rage expert Andrew Thomas. She told him airlines reduce the amount of fresh air, "just because they want to save money."[123]

"Aerotoxic Syndrome" Goes Public

As a result of the growing awareness of cabin air problems, airlines and airplane manufacturers were already being "hit with a flurry of 'toxic air' related lawsuits" by 2001, said the online newsletter, Power-of-Attorneys.com. Thousands of Alaska Air flight attendants had filed a class action suit against Monsanto, the maker of Skydrol hydraulic fluid.[124] Also that year a group of Alaska Airlines flight attendants sued the airline, claiming they had become ill from toxic fumes in the airline cabin. Without admitting responsibility, Alaska Airlines paid a $725,000 out-of-court settlement to the flight attendants. The following year, twenty-six Alaska Airlines flight attendants sued Boeing and Honeywell for the impact of contaminated air on their health.[125]

By October of 2007, questions about air quality were expanding, as flight crews on Australian airliners found themselves overcome by toxic fumes. Newspapers throughout Australia carried a *Sun Herald* report that a Qantas flight engineer was off work for a week after inhaling toxic fumes on the flight deck of a Boeing 747 flying from Los Angeles to Auckland, New Zealand, in July 2007.

WorkCover, South Australia's workplace safety agency, ordered the airline to fix the problem, but the newspaper said, "Senior pilots have warned that crew and regular passengers could suffer serious long-term illnesses unless the

---

121 Association of Flight Attendants, AFL-CIO, "Oil Switch on the B737 Fleet," Safety and Health Alert, November 2002, found at http://ashsd.afacwa.org/docs/291to254. pdf.

122 Excerpted from International Air Transport Association, "Carriage of Passengers with Infectious Diseases," IATA Passenger Services Conference Resolution Manual, Recommendations PSC (19) 1798, June 1, 1998, as cited in Anonymous and Thomas, p. 94.

123 Nancy Keates, "Something's in the Air," *Chicago Tribune*, July 30, 2000, page 7, as cited in Anonymous and Thomas, p. 94.

124 "Flying the Unfriendly Skies," *Power of Attorneys* online newsletter, (no date given), found at http://www.power-of-attorneys.com/unfriendly_skies.htm.

125 Byron Acohido, "Verdict expected soon on toxic air aboard jets," *USA Today*, May 9, 2002, found at http://www.usatoday.com/travel/news/2002/2002-05-09-cabin-air. htm.

aviation industry admits jet airliners worldwide have a critical design flaw."[126] The newspaper said the toxic fume problem was "not a one-off incident" and that flight crews feared there would be a disaster if both pilots on an airplane were overcome by fumes during a flight.

"People don't need to stop flying," said Australian and International Pilots Association general manager Peter Somerville, "but there is a problem and it needs to be fixed." The newspaper reported:

> If the engine has an oil leak, [Somerville] said, the warm air that enters the cabin is laced with a chemical called tricresyl phosphate, as well as carcinogens and organophosphates that attack the nervous system and can result in brain damage.
>
> Air crew are now so concerned about the issue that they have covertly taken swabs from the walls inside commercial airliners on three continents including Australia and in 85 per cent of cases found positive traces of the chemicals.
>
> "It affects the flight crew the most because they receive a lot more oxygen and they fly more often," Mr Somerville said.
>
> His organisation is funding a project with the RAAF and aircraft engineers to measure the long-term effects of the toxic fumes on flight crew.
>
> But Australian Federation of Air Pilots spokesman Lawrie Cox said the short-term effects could be worse.
>
> "If we get a major incident where two pilots are affected, the outcome would be a disaster," he said.[127]

In the same month as the 747 incident, one Qantas crew refused to fly a 767 because they noticed fumes on the flight deck, the *Sun Herald* reported. When Qantas asked another crew to fly the plane, they also refused.

"Instances such as these are extremely rare and we take them seriously," a Qantas spokesman said, adding that the company was "reviewing our occupational health and safety procedures and are in the process of discussing these procedures with our people. WorkCover fully supports this approach."

"There is no evidence to suggest that cabin air quality is an issue in any of our aircraft," he said.[128]

---

126   "Australian Flight Crews Overcome by Toxic Fumes," *Sydney Morning Herald*, October 22, 2007, found at http://www.smh.com.au/articles/2007/10/22/1192940945399. html.

127   Ibid.

128   Ibid.

On many flights, there's also another kind of poison in the air—neurotoxins from pesticides that flight attendants are required to spray on airplanes while the passengers are in their seats prior to arrival in many countries. In addition they spray empty aircraft between flights in other countries—a practice that has left many passengers and crew members literally reeling.[129]

Finally, there's the unknown effect of synergy, the multiplier effect that makes two chemicals working together more than twice as damaging as each one alone. As one pharmacist described it, this is the chemical reaction in which "one + one = three,"[130] and it's the reason passengers who are drinking or taking prescription medicines that alter their brain chemistry may react more strongly to pesticides in the cabin, especially if they are mixed with hydraulic fluid fumes and low cabin pressure.

However, there is some good news for cabin air activists. The new Boeing 787, due to come into service in 2009, won't use air "bled" from the engines at all, but will replenish its cabin air from the cool clean air outside.[131]

Source of the Problem: Oxygen Deprivation

Many of the effects caused by high altitude, drinking, smoking and toxic chemicals on our bodies seem to be due to a single problem—oxygen deprivation. To work properly, our brains need a certain amount of usable oxygen in our bloodstreams. Unfortunately altitude, alcohol, smoking, and toxic chemicals all reduce that usable oxygen level, which can leave passengers with a form of oxygen deprivation called "hypoxia." The symptoms of hypoxia range from headaches, nausea, thirst, irritability, rage, sexual excitability, and loss of judgment and control to, at the extreme, seizures, paralysis, coma and death.

In the early days of commercial flying, scientists were already recommending that pilots be required to inhale extra oxygen because a 1940 study showed breathing the thin air at 10,000 feet caused headache, dizziness, poor memory and judgment, inability to concentrate, irritability, and poor performance on psychological tests. In some people with previously existing emotional problems, they found it also caused lack of inhibition, "frank sexual advances" and threatening behavior.[132]

---

129   Linda Bonvie and Bill Bonvie, "Airline's Insecticide May Be Affecting More than Bugs, Australia and New Zealand Demand That All Incoming Planes (and People) Be Sprayed with Pesticides Before Debarking," *www.safe2use.com*, March 4, 2001, found at http://www.safe2use.com/ca-ipm/01-03-04.htm.

130   Sal Nassar, Pharm.D., Pharmaca Pharmacy, Solano Ave., Berkeley, California, Interview by email with the author on February 1, 2008.

131   Loraine, 2008.

132   Alvan L. Barach and Julia Kagan, "Disorders of Mental Functioning Produced by Varying the Oxygen Tension of the Atmosphere," *Psychosomatic Medicine,* 2(1), January, 1940, 54 and 64–66, found at http://www.psychosomaticmedicine.org/cgi/reprint/2/1/53.pdf.

Today, airplane air is treated to simulate air found at 8,000 feet—but alcohol, nicotine, and any toxic chemicals in the air further reduce our bodies' ability to use the oxygen in that air. For example, drinking one drink adds the equivalent of 2,000 feet to our bodies' experience of altitude—meaning that as you toss back that third beer, your body has started breathing as if you were at 14,000 feet.[133] For many drinkers, this causes "headache and lassitude"; for others, excitability and loss of inhibition.[134] The effects of alcohol and altitude are compounded because any toxic fumes in the cabin also bind with oxygen, making our bodies unable to use it.

According to Dr Ross Lee Graham at Linkoping University in Sweden, the resulting hypoxia causes "temporary environmental anemia" that might be more likely to cause air rage in passengers who were already prone to anemia at sea level.[135] In his paper, "Environmental Anemia, a Basis for Sky-Rage," he said temporary anemia causes "irritability that can amplify into rage," which might help explain "the many cases of rage where no alcohol is involved."[136] Because environmental anemia "can override the desire to control one's image in public," Graham said, passengers accused of air rage "should be given blood tests and metabolism tests to establish whether their oxygenation levels were sufficient to resist the imposed aircraft cabin anemia effects. This could help the authorities decide whether they are dealing with criminals or people who are victims of environmental anemia."[137]

Oxygen, Low Blood Sugar and Rage

Low blood oxygen also aggravates low blood sugar, or hypoglycemia, Dr Graham said. When blood sugar is low, hypoglycemic people are irritable and quick to anger. They usually blame their flashes of rage on something happening around them, having no idea that a sugar crash made them do it. They also don't realize that the loss of temper momentarily relieves the headache, fatigue, confusion, and dizziness caused by plummeting blood sugar. "Losing one's temper sends an adrenaline shock to the liver that stimulates the liver to release sugar into the blood," Graham said. "The hypoglycemic person who is focused enough to lose temper can thus gain an immediate relief from the sugar released into the blood." However, repeated loss of temper can set up a downward cycle: The blood sugar

---

133   Joe Pilot (online identifier), "How Does Alcohol and Smoking Contribute to Hypoxia for Pilots Flying Aircraft?" *Yahoo Answers,* found at http://answers.yahoo.com/question/index?qid=20070720230014AAGxaB1.

134   Barach and Kagan, pp. 64–66.

135   Ross Lee Graham, "Environmental Anemia, A Basis for Sky-Rage," Linkoping University, Sweden, found at http://www.rosslg.com/works/WebNotes/Systems/skyrage01.html.

136   Ibid.

137   Ibid.

drops and the person becomes enraged, triggering relief from the adrenaline and sugar rush—that in turn creates the next sugar crash.[138]

For many hypoglycemic passengers, low blood sugar is aggravated when they dash out of the house without eating in the morning to make their plane. If their no-frills, no-food flight sits on the runway for hours before finally taking off as poor cabin air and low air pressure make them hungrier and less rational, there's not much they can do about it but brood about the flight attendant's shortcomings.

The combination of altitude-induced oxygen deprivation, toxic chemicals, and rage caused by plummeting blood sugar on long, food-free flights might help explain why someone like Jonathan Burton, who was killed by fellow passengers on a Southwest Airlines flight in 2000, suddenly turned from "a mellow, easygoing, consistently happy person" who wasn't drunk, hadn't done drugs, and had no history of mental illness, into a raving maniac. It could help explain why, having cheerfully kissed his mother goodbye at the gate an hour and a half earlier, he suddenly became agitated, jumped up, and bolted to the front of the cabin yelling, "Everybody just sit down!" with eyes that "revealed his hysteria" as he exploded in an incoherent, adrenaline-fueled drive to escape the plane.[139]

Otherwise, there is no explanation. Without a prior history of mental illness or evidence of extreme psychological stress, Burton was unlikely to have had a complete psychotic break, said Houston University research psychologist and schizophrenia specialist Dr Gordon Paul. "Something like that happening out of the blue is so rare, I really question whether it ever happens," he said.[140]

Alcohol and Altitude: "The Drink's on Us!"

The way altitude and toxic air exacerbate the effects of alcohol on the human body might help explain the following event:

In October 1995, wealthy and well-respected investment banker Gerard Finneran of Greenwich, Connecticut, reached a new low in air rage. When a United Airlines flight attendant refused to serve the inebriated executive another drink on his international flight, he allegedly went on a rampage, assaulting a flight attendant, terrorizing the passengers, and pouring liquor on himself. But what made him notorious was his finale; he climbed up on the first class food cart, said something rude, and relieved himself, using linen napkins as toilet paper, after which he walked down the aisle of the plane, tracking the evidence with him.[141]

---

138   Ibid.

139   Timothy Roche, "Homicide in the Sky," *Time*, October 2, 2000, found at http://www.time.com/time/magazine/article/0,9171,998079,00.html.

140   Gordon Paul, interview by email with the author, October 6, 2008.

141   Eric D'Amato, "Mystery of Disgust," *Psychology Today*, January/February 1998, found at http://www.psychologytoday.com/articles/pto-19980201-000032.html.

Finneran was ordered to pay more than $49,000 to cover cleanup costs and reimburse his fellow passengers, headlines about the "Jet-Mess Exec" went national, and one assumes his career was over.[142] One also assumes that it would take a powerful mix of scrambled brain chemistry and alcohol to inspire an executive, who was described as otherwise "mild mannered," to act out in such a humiliating way.

In July of 2001, flight attendants fanned out to airports across the country, distributing leaflets calling for stronger air rage policies and better training to deal with air rage. A major problem, they said, was airlines' alcohol policies, which amounted to "the sky's the limit." Airlines' reluctance to offend customers and customers' near constant access to in-flight liquor had contributed to a dramatic increase in air rage incidents.[143]

"The airlines are providing champagne and hard liquor to passengers before the plane ever leaves the gate," flight attendant Dawn Marie Bader told the San Francisco Chronicle. "They're drinking before breakfast, before dinner. They're drinking during dinner, after dinner and during the movie. Passengers are drinking all the time."[144]

Captain Stephen Luckey told the congressional subcommittee on Aviation, Transportation and Infrastructure that some airlines promoted drinking by having flight attendants offer passengers more alcohol before their glasses were empty, and offer drinks before they're requested. The effect of in-flight drinking on the body is well known, Luckey said: People get drunker faster when cabin pressure is decreased. "Combine that fact with the reality that passengers often drink on empty stomachs," he said, and you have a set up for an ugly situation.[145]

An IAS report confirms this:

> Alcohol has a pronounced effect on fliers. Due to cabin pressure and oxygen deprivation, "one drink in the air may equal two on ground." Its effects can be compounded by lack of food/delays in foodservice and high concentrations of carbon monoxide in recycled cabin air. The result, according to Muir and Moyle of the College of Aeronautics at Cranfield, (in the UK), is an increase in "aggression, confusion, poor judgment, loss of inhibitions, lack of insight and delayed reaction time."

> Alcohol is widely available and promoted in airports and on board aircraft. Some airlines use alcohol to mollify travelers who have been stranded, bumped

---

142   "The Drunken Defecator," *That's Plane Funny* (no date) found at http://www.thatsplanefunny.com/cornecopia.html.

143   Steve Rubenstein, "Flight Attendants Fight 'Air Rage,'" *San Francisco Chronicle*, July 7, 2007, found at http://www.sfgate.com/cgi-bin/article.cgi?file=/chronicle/archive/2000/07/07/MN99774.DTL.

144   Ibid.

145   Statement of Captain Stephen Luckey.

or inconvenienced. In some cases, free alcohol is promoted as a service element, competitive advantage, perk for frequent flyers or a travel package bonus. Once expectations (of alcohol service) are raised it is difficult to reduce service, particularly when problems such as flight delays occur. An additional temptation, particularly to international passengers, is the duty-free shop. Despite being cut off, some inebriated passengers continue to drink from their stash of purchased liquor, albeit illegally.[146]

Anyone who's ever dealt with a drunk knows it's like trying to reason with an avalanche. They're going to do what they want to do, and have no shame about doing it. The only thing that can make the "corralling a drunk" scenario worse is playing it out in a small, poorly ventilated cabin at 30,000 feet. "A plane is not a bar," says former flight attendant Elliott Hester. "If someone drinks too much at my favorite tavern, we can push him out the door and call him a cab. Try doing that at 30,000 feet."[147]

In addition, people who normally smoke several cigarettes an hour may use extra drinks as a replacement for their cigarettes, Luckey told the Congressional committee, leaving attendants to deal with someone who's suffering from nicotine withdrawal while drunk.[148]

"To nobody's amazement," said pilot Patrick Smith in 2004, "studies reveal that alcohol plays a central role in about 90 percent of air rage incidents."[149] In fact, estimates of the percentage of incidents brought on by alcohol have ranged from 20 to 90 percent, but most seem to be settling at around 40 percent.[150] It may be the drama of alcohol-related events that convinces people they cause virtually all air rage problems, but no one knows exactly how often alcohol is involved. The *Daily Telegraph* reported that air rage incidents doubled between 2003 and 2006; 80 percent of the culprits were male, and "more than a third" of the incidents were alcohol related.[151]

---

146   "Zeroing in on Air Rage," International Transport Workers' Federation (ITF), 2000 (quoted by Agent Premium News [APN], 2001), found at http://www.itfglobal.org/transport-international/airrage.cfm

147   Elliott Neal Hester, "The Passenger from Hell," *Salon.com*, August 17, 1999, found at http://dir.salon.com/story/travel/diary/hest/1999/08/17/passenger/.

148   Statement of Captain Stephen Luckey.

149   Patrick Smith, "Ask the Pilot," *Salon.com*, June 11, 2004, found at http://dir.salon.com/story/tech/col/smith/2004/06/11/askthepilot89/index.html.

150   Statement of Captain Stephen Luckey.

151   "Air-Rage Incidents Double in Two Years," *Daily Telegraph*, November 25, 2006, found at http://www.telegraph.co.uk/travel/737102/Air-rage-incidents-double-in-two-years.html.

In 2004, an article in the *Journal of Primary Prevention* reported that alcohol caused 40 percent of air rage incidents,[152] echoing a 1999 Aviation Safety Reporting System report that put that number at 43 percent.[153]

"The number of alcohol-related incidents was thought to be much higher," said pilot Steve Luckey in *Air Line Pilot* magazine, "but air travelers have been drinking on airplanes since people began flying without an epidemic of serious behavior problems. Granted, drugs and alcohol are enabling factors in many cases, but most people who consume alcohol have a drink or two, lean back, and take a nap."[154]

Sadly many air rage episodes are perpetrated by passengers who are drinking because they are afraid of flying. Drinking alcohol on top of consuming prescription medication might exacerbate the problem even further. The flight attendant serving alcohol to a passenger has no way of knowing if they are self-medicating with prescription medicine or, indeed, illegal drugs that should never be mixed with alcohol.

In response to flight attendants' 2001 protest against lax air rage policies, Air Transport Association (ATA) spokesman Michael Wascom said the accusation of improper training procedures was "patently false," adding that airlines did provide conflict resolution training.[155] The flight attendants countered that a three-hour class was not enough to deal with the issue.[156]

AFA president Patricia Friend said that the current airline alcohol policy amounted to this: "There is no such thing as too much alcohol, and an empty wine glass is a bad thing."[157] Captain Luckey agreed that a more conservative alcohol service program would greatly alleviate air rage. He also specifically recommended that airlines support flight attendants who refuse to serve alcohol to someone who's drunk. "Flight attendants have been disciplined, suspended and even fired for not serving alcohol to intoxicated passengers," he said.[158]

He described a case in which an airline was sued for serving a passenger later arrested for drunk driving, "eleven, I repeat, eleven drinks in one and a half hours while seated in first class." The airline disputed the claim for five years,

---

152   Lisa Anglin, Paula Neves, Norman Giesbrecht, and Marianne Kobus-Matthews, "Alcohol-Related Air Rage: From Damage Control to Primary Prevention," *Journal of Primary Prevention*, March 2003, 23(3), found at http://www.springerlink.com/content/u1338427v01282h1/.

153   Aviation Safety Reporting System report, 1999, as cited in Luckey, "*Air Rage.*"

154   Luckey, "*Air Rage.*"

155   "Airlines Reject AFA Attacks on Air Rage, Alcohol Policies," *World Airline News*, July 13, 2001, found at http://findarticles.com/p/articles/mi_m0ZCK/is_28_11/ai_76547444.

156   Ibid.; and Michael McConnell, "Air Rage Takes Back Seat in Our Post–9-11 World," *Detroit Metro Connections*, September 19–October 2, 2002, found at http://metro.heritage.com/dtw100202/story3.htm.

157   Rubenstein.

158   Statement of Captain Stephen Luckey, p. 8.

until an investigator taking the same flight was served 12 drinks in the same time period.[159]

Columnist and pilot Patrick Smith, who estimated that liquor was involved in 90 percent of air rage incidents, said when the risk is so high, "it seems an easy call: lock away the liquor and episodes of airborne assault are cut by nine-tenths. Except it's never so simple. In the absence of alcohol, a portion of those predisposed to belligerence will find other excuses to rant, rave and break things."

In the meantime, he says, "airlines make money from those bottles and cans, and the vast majority of passengers who indulge do so peacefully. Neither consumer nor server is eager to do away this mainstay of in-flight service."[160] That's especially true, says air rage expert Andrew Thomas, because on many long distance flights, it's possible to cover the entire cost of the flight crew by selling alcohol in the back of the plane.[161]

Smoking

"An overwhelming amount of physiological and psychological research suggests that barring smoking for nicotine-addicted passengers can easily lead to higher levels of stress and increase the likelihood of an air rage incident," says Andrew Thomas.[162] One reason many passengers are drinking more now on planes is that they no longer can light up a cigarette. In France, where the entire country is a smoking area, the need for a fix is so strong, flight attendants scamper down plane aisles passing out nicotine tablets.[163]

Most air rage incidents reported by the Aviation System Reporting System are alcohol-abuse and smoking-related. On a Thomas Cook flight in Europe in March 2007, Stephen Robinson of Darlington, UK, must have really needed a smoke, because when he was asked to put out his cigarette he clambered over other passengers and assaulted an air steward, damaging his teeth. The flight was diverted to Frankfurt, and Robinson was ejected and later sentenced to 12 months in jail.[164]

---

159   Ibid.

160   Smith, *"Ask the Pilot,"* June 11, 2004.

161   Andrew Thomas (Interview), *Court TV*, April 3, 2002, found at http://www.courttv.com/talk/chat_transcripts/2002/0403safety-airrage.html.

162   Anonymous and Thomas, p. 60.

163   "Comfort for Smokers," *GlobeLife Travel section of Globeandmail.com*, November 8, 2000, found at http://www.theglobeandmail.com/servlet/Page/document/v5/templates/hub?hub=Travel&subhub=activities&activity=smoking.

164   "Air Rage Passenger Faces Prison," *BBC News*, September 5, 2007, found at http://news.bbc.co.uk/2/hi/uk_news/england/6980172.stm; and "28th September 2007—Newcastle, UK" incident cited in AD Aerospace.

In April of that year, a woman flying on Delta from Cincinnati to Honolulu started fighting with flight attendants after she was caught smoking in the lavatory. When the pilot, who'd left the cockpit to help calm her down, threatened to handcuff her, she punched him in the chest, and the plane was diverted to San Francisco. She had "a complete meltdown freak-out," said another passenger who called the Associated Press from her cell phone. She "appeared to be out of her mind." The smoker was given oxygen during the rest of the flight and taken to hospital on landing.[165]

"Like It or Lump It" Service: Processing the Passenger

In his newsletter, *Hot Flash*,[166] Michael Boyd, president of Airline Services Training Inc, said customers feel airlines have contempt for them. He challenged airline CEOs to go through what the average businessman making an unscheduled midweek business trip halfway across the country would endure, walking his hypothetical CEO through an average trip.

To buy a ticket the week he was flying, the CEO would most likely pay a nonrefundable "special fare" of $2,000 for a mediocre seat in coach. That $2,000 would buy him the chance to stand in long lines at a ticket counter or gate, Boyd said, before being:

> ... summoned to the position with the word "next"—if he's lucky. Often it's just a wave of the agent's hand. Saying "may I help you" is something that the CEO's middle management apparently feels would be too stressful for front line staff. Our CEO/consumer then finds he has to answer very stupid questions that do nothing to improve security, but which will confirm that he does not employ a butler to pack his bags, and he's not moonlighting as a mule for the PLO.

Even though the agent demands to see picture ID to match against the name on the ticket, he'll never take time to call the customer by name, Boyd said, though he will take the time to finish a bag of Fritos or slurp his coffee while working with passengers. Then he'll hand over the CEO's boarding pass, "often with all the courtesy of an East German border guard condescendingly allowing a refugee to cross the frontier." After giving the airline $2,000 in business, he said, the CEO will find his chances are "less than 50 percent that the airline employee will end

---

165   Associated Press, "Hawaii-Bound Flight Diverted after Unruly Passenger Strikes Pilot," *USA Today*, April 3, 2007, found at http://www.usatoday.com/travel/flights/2007-04-03-passenger-strikes-pilot_N.htm.

166   Michael Boyd, "The Airline CEO Challenge: Experience What You Put Your Passengers Through," *Hot Flash,* July 23, 2001, found at http://www.aviationplanning.com/airline1.htm#CEO.

the transaction by actually saying 'thank you' or 'we appreciate your business' (they don't, unfortunately) or 'have a nice flight.'"

After listening to a laundry list of rules, the CEO would slog on board, where he'd find his $2,000 had bought him a meal "consisting of a bag of stuff he has to dig out of a mini-dumpster, giving passengers the homeless person experience" and one pass at the beverage cart. "Maybe another offer of coffee. But that's it. The CEO is alone with his sacked lunch. Often, he may be thrilled by the fact that his company is saving money by cleaning aircraft cabins only every other Leap Year. The tray table, the headliners, and the ceiling vents might have been untouched by any form of cleaning solutions for months or maybe years."

If, as is likely, the flight is a bit late, "the CEO will experience something his customers face every day, the dreaded *will-I-make-my-connection* anxiety attack."

> Deplaning, he anxiously asks the agent inside the terminal, "what gate for flight 54 to Portland?" "Gate 19, terminal B," is the response. "If you run, you might make it."

> Galloping just in time up to Gate 19, in the process flirting with a coronary, he's stopped cold. "The overheads are all full," he's brusquely informed. "You'll havta check that carry-on. Oh, and you're late and we've gone to open seating. Take any seat that's empty." The CEO will then experience the joy of trying to wedge his frame into 26E between two people from a culture that doesn't use any form of soap.

Nonetheless, Boyd said, when he lands, the CEO may well find that after all, his airline has done what it promised: gotten him and his luggage to their destination on time. But he'll also feel that the $2,000 fare he paid was a bad bargain because, "He was *processed*, not served. He was *tolerated*, not valued." He'll feel he's been put through a meat grinder, like the rest of his passengers, most of which would rather not ever fly his airline again, "and many of which are cheering on the bloodthirsty clowns in Congress who, they hope, will punish the CEO and his entire airline."

"This experience, in whole or in part takes place every day, and many airlines' senior management is oblivious," Boyd said. "When it comes to why consumers dislike airlines, we'll be blunt: too many airlines have not bothered to try to identify what makes air passengers go bonkers."[167]

---

167   Ibid.

Carry-on Bags: "The Other Airline Let Me Bring It!"

An estimated 15 percent of all air rage incidents start as fights over carry-on luggage. Many passengers try to stretch the limits of what they can carry and fight to the death to keep bags with them because they're afraid that's the only way to guarantee the contents won't be lost, stolen, or broken. It's a reasonable fear: In just two months, from May to July of 2007, more than one million pieces of luggage (eight of every 1,000 pieces) were lost, damaged, delayed, or stolen by US airlines, according to the Bureau of Transportation Statistics.[168] So many bags were separated from their owners, the airlines were running out of places to put them, said CBS reporter Nancy Cordes.[169] These lost bags become a major anger trigger for travelers. Airlines do not pay the full amount of every claim received and can completely deny a claim, forcing passengers to bicker over the value of their lost luggage.

In addition, more and more passengers are using E-tickets, which only require them to show up at the departure gate. As a result, many busy travelers prefer to take their bags with them. Not surprisingly, they're showing up at the gate with more and larger bags. Thomas says it's amazing what people try to bring on board. Either he or his coauthor saw passengers trying to stuff everything from elk antlers to a used camel saddle in their overhead compartments. It takes time to check carry-on bags at the last minute, especially when the process includes an argument between the aggrieved passenger and an airline clerk. The ITF estimates that the biggest cause of flight delays is the time wasted transferring extra carry-on bags to the cargo hold or making sure luggage is safely stowed on board—and flight delays are another major cause of air rage.[170]

Adding to the confusion, conflict and delay, different airlines allow different sized carry-on bags. The size of carry-on luggage is partially determined by how much money an airline wants to spend on sturdy overhead bins, and how much cabin room they want to give over to storage. In an editorial calling for a consistent carry-on policy, *USA Today* said, "The best course would be for airlines to agree on a common standard. ... By failing to take action, the FAA has once again shown that it is more inclined to follow the industry it is supposed to regulate than to lead it."[171]

Spitting Mad

The news that you can't take a bag with you that other airlines have allowed on board puts many passengers over the edge. The ITF estimates that questions about

---

168 "Travel: Lose Your Cares, Luggage, Sanity."
169 Ibid.
170 Anonymous and Thomas, p. 92.
171 Ibid., p. 93.

cabin baggage trigger approximately 10 to 15 percent of air rage incidents, and they can get nasty.[172]

When flight attendant Jackie Hamilton prevented passenger Vicki Smith from bringing her carry-on bag on board, Smith, a 56-year-old horse farmer from Addison, Vermont, spouted racial epithets and spat on Hamilton's shoe. Smith, who said she'd been able to take the bag on all her previous flights, said that Hamilton had screamed at her when she asked questions about checking the bag and that she'd taken it on other airplanes during the day. While admitting she "did not say happy things" to Hamilton, Smith said she was under a lot of stress during her previous flight because her seat was small, a passenger in the next seat crowded her, she was diabetic, and she was "severely dehydrated" because she didn't get enough to drink.[173]

In many cases, overhead bins aren't as strong as they should be; worldwide, says Andrew Thomas, it's estimated that baggage falling from overhead compartments causes an average of one injury an hour. About the time Continental Airlines spent more than $12 million to install overhead bins that could hold larger bags, United Airlines set up sizing templates at security checkpoints that only fit smaller bags. Continental sued United, fearing that by making passengers think all airlines required the smaller bags, United would rob Continental of its competitive advantage.

In ruling for Continental, the judge wrote the suit had shown that "some airlines are not able (or willing) to provide onboard storage capacity and carry-on baggage policies the flying public wants."[174]

The Last Straw: Hidden Fees

Many passengers feel they can just barely tolerate the constant hum of low-level abuse that is no-frills air travel in return for their low-cost ticket. However, after standing in a long line, dragging and pushing their suitcases, laptops, and backpacks towards a ticket agent, passengers at many airlines are now being surprised with the news that they have to pay an added $10 to $100 to check their bags. And starting in 2006, choosing certain seats could cost an extra $15 at some airlines. Of course everyone's gotten used to paying for food and drinks on the plane, but in 2006 some airlines started charging $2 a suitcase (before the expected tip) for curbside check-in.[175]

Suddenly that cheap ticket isn't looking so cheap. Finding that out at the gate is enough to make a passenger snap—especially if the reason they have to pay $50

---

172 Ibid., p. 92.

173 Stoller.

174 Anonymous and Thomas, pp. 93–94.

175 Donna Rosato, "Airlines Pile on the Fees," *CNNMoney.com*, April 30, 2007, found at http://money.cnn.com/2007/04/30/pf/airline_fees.moneymag/index.htm.

to $100 to check that "excess bag" is because the gate agent says their carry-on is too big to go in the cabin.[176]

Flight attendant Elliot Neal Hester described such a moment. He was boarding passengers on a flight to Barbados when an angry linebacker-sized woman found out about the airlines' new $50 fee for extra carryon luggage:

> For one nerve-rattling moment it seemed as though she might actually snatch my head with her massive paws and squeeze until it burst like a grape. Instead, the woman made a nonviolent, albeit equally intimidating gesture. Lips pursed, nostrils flaring, she brought her face to within a few inches of my own and thrust her hands upon hips that jiggled like huge jello molds in an earthquake. Then she sort of growled. That's the best way to describe it. She took one deep breath after another and growled.

> Despite a nervous twitching in my upper lip, I stood in front of the boarding gate like a true airline professional: a phony smile pasted across my face, fingers locked behind my back, shoulders back, chin up, chest thrust forward like an army recruit in the face of a maniacal drill instructor. I was dauntless. Unflappable. Quite capable of handling the situation. But as the hulking passenger loomed before me, growing angrier with each blink of her eyes, I felt the first pangs of vulnerability.

> "How can you charge so much for extra baggage?" the woman demanded. "How can you!" When I opened my mouth to answer, she waved one hand, compelling me to silence. The barrage of questions continued as if I was the subject of an FBI interrogation. "Why did you change the checked baggage rates? Huh? Why are you making it so difficult for me to carry my belongings on your airplane? Do you have any idea how expensive this is? Huh? Do you? Why are you so inflexible? Why?"[177]

As will be seen later, her rant continued to escalate from there. Passengers don't like being hit with hidden fees. Most airlines allow you to check two bags weighing no more than 50 pounds each. Because of fuller flights and smaller planes, they're cracking down on people who bring more. You'll pay an average of $25 for any bag that's heavier than 50 pounds, and as much as $100 extra for checking a third bag.[178] A regional officer who looks after workers at Stansted Airport near London said that long lines and being charged for excess luggage were two common

---

176   Ibid.

177   Elliott Neal Hester, "When Passengers Rage," *Salon.com*, October 20, 2000, found at http://dir.salon.com/story/business/col/hest/2000/10/20/rage/.

178   Rosato, 2007.

causes of passenger rage. He said if someone was mad on the ground, their abusive behavior would most likely continue on the plane.[179]

Being "nickeled and dimed" by these hidden fees is especially galling because air fares were set at the highest level in 2007 that they'd been since 2000. One woman was so angry about a $150 round trip "unaccompanied minor" fee to send her 14-year-old daughter from Virginia to Florida, she called her blog post about it "Delta is a Thief!" For a bonus, passengers will find themselves paying "fuel surcharges" that are likely to keep rising with the rising cost of oil. In 2007, British Airways started charging a fuel fee of $66 each way on flights that were longer than nine hours.[180]

As a final insult, some airlines are out to make a few dollars extra by charging passengers for speaking to a ticket agent, either on the telephone or in person. Far from offering service with a smile, this sends the message, "If we are forced to talk to you it's going to cost you."

According to the online magazine *Travel Industry Review*, US Airways is "the greediest on this count."[181] They charge $35 to book over the phone, or $45 to book at the airport or at a city ticket office.[182] "Can it possibly cost the airline that much for a simple, 10-minute call?" the reporter asks. "Surely it doesn't pay its reservationists that much. United levies $15 for the privilege of speaking to a human. American, JetBlue, and Southwest charge $10 (for Internet-only fares in Southwest's case, but it does make exceptions, we were told). Northwest and Virgin America charge just $5."[183]

Imagine the customer's joy at finding this little fee unexpectedly tacked onto the ticket price. At the very least consumers should know that they will be subject to this extra charge before they make the call. Informing the traveler of these charges beforehand may not make them like the airline more, but it will at least make them feel that they are not being blatantly cheated.

---

179   Julie Clothier, "When Cabin Fever Turns to Air Rage," *CNN.com*, August 8, 2006, found at http://www.cnn.com/2006/TRAVEL/08/08/air.rage/index.html.

180   Leanna621 (online identifier) posting on *IndependentTraveler.com*, August 2, 2007, found at http://boards.independenttraveler.com/showthread.php?t=10863.

181   George Hobica (of Aviation.com), "10 Most Obnoxious Airline Fees," *MSNBC.com*, December 2, 2007, found at http://www.msnbc.msn.com/id/22041918/.

182   George Hobica and Kim Liang Tan, *Daily Herald* correspondence, 2007, found at http://www.scribd.com/doc/2116568/tag1210047pagenews1tExamining-those-annoying-hidden-airline-feesd25.

183   George Hobica (of Aviation.com), "10 Most Obnoxious Airline Fees," *MSNBC.com*, December 2, 2007, found at http://www.msnbc.msn.com/id/22041918/.

One Final Insult: Creating Former Customers

After running the gauntlet to their planes and paying a series of unexpected fees, many passengers are surprised to find themselves trapped in their seats in midair listening to commercials for the duration of their flight. That's right; in their quest for profit over service, airlines have turned many flights into sales pitches for products being marketed to what literally amounts to a captive audience.

US Airways passenger David Meerman Scott was trying to relax and enjoy his flight when he was jolted by frequent announcements over the loudspeaker promoting free flights and Airways Signature Visa cards. When the flight attendants followed up on the announcements by passing out a card about services being marketed during the flight, it was the last straw. On the card he announced, "I'm naming US Airways to receive a Lifetime Achievement [in the] Marketing Hall of Shame."[184]

A basic principle of anger management is to try to calm a negative or a stressful situation by offering the angry person some encouragement, but when a Mr Putnam was stranded on an American Airlines plane for three hours, the customer service was so poor that he made a decision that should concern the airline. "I do not fly with American Airlines any more because of the way my wife and I were treated," he said. "We needed to be treated better than a herd of cattle. We are human and if it means a little more cost ... we need some sort of regulation."[185]

Airline passengers say they're paying more and getting less. Many airlines are charging extra for snacks and there are some discussions that their next move will be to charge for soft drinks and juices. A humorous commercial run by Southwest could be a sign of things to come. It shows a passenger inserting a coin into a slot to use the overhead compartment.[186]

Security-Related Stress

By adding long lines and inconvenience to the flying experience and reminding fliers that they might be subject to terrorism, increased security measures have multiplied the stress and tension of flying. "Some travelers cited a sour atmosphere perceptible from curbside to cabin," the *New York Times* reported. "'All the pressure

184 David Meerman Scott, "US Airways Flight Attendants Paid $50 Commission to Interrupt Us in Flight," *Weblink*, September 2007, found at http://www.welinknow.com/2007/09/us-airways-flig.html.

185 Gene Putman, "Coalition for an Airline Passengers' Bill of Rights," August 17, 2007, found at http:// strandedpassengers.blogspot.com/2007/06/flight-attendants-advocate-for.html.

186 Dan Reed, "Are Extra Fees in Southwest Airlines' Future?" *USA Today*, March 26, 2007, found at http://www.usatoday.com/travel/flights/2007-03-25-southwest-fees_N.htm.

of the extra security has made people working here more snippy,'" Edith Logan of Exton, Pa., said as she waited to meet her daughter at Philadelphia International Airport. 'You always feel on edge.'"[187]

Because of new security requirements that passengers arrive earlier at airports, travelers with a lot of time to kill may be consuming more alcohol at airport bars or drinking too much in-flight. During this extra time, smokers' agitation generally builds because they're not allowed to smoke inside many airports.

And depending on their politics, some passengers see some security measures as needless, political grandstanding, or both. In reaction to a foiled terrorist plot, said left-wing columnist Alexander Cockburn, British Home Secretary John Reid "decided to keep his name on the front pages by banning all carry-on bags at Heathrow, thus instantly paralyzing the busiest airport in Europe." Even after very small bags were allowed back onboard, he said, "the walk-in closets that passengers routinely drag onto planes had to be loaded into the belly of the plane ... and Heathrow remained paralyzed."[188]

To some, being screened for security reasons is taken as either an insult or a needless delay. One German tourist flying through Manila showed his irritation fairly directly. Having been asked to go through the X-ray machine twice, the man didn't say anything—he just did a striptease, taking off his pants and handing them to the screener.

"Authorities were not amused," the Associated Press reported. He faced as much as six years in a Philippine jail.[189]

Problems in the Terminal? Kick Them Upstairs!

Before they board their planes, more and more passengers are drunk or angry—most often about long lines, flight delays and cancellations, lost bags, and being charged for excess luggage. Many are both. Passengers who are angry in the terminal are likely to be angrier by the time they step on the plane.[190] And rather than take the time to confront them at check in, Andrew Thomas says, an untrained underpaid 18-year-old ticket clerk is likely to pass them on, making them the flight attendants' problem. The result is trouble for passengers and crew when they get on the plane.[191] In March 2005, a 35-year-old man was heard swearing as he stumbled onto a flight from Denver to Anchorage, and the pilot notified him that he would not be served any more alcohol during the flight. When the flight

---

187   Mansnerus, 2004.

188   Alexander Cockburn, "In Transports of Horror and Delight," *The Nation,* December 3, 2007, p. 9.

189   "Today in the Sky," blog posted on February 12, 2007, *USA Today,* found at http://blogs.usatoday.com/sky/2007/02/manila.html.

190   Clothier, 2006.

191   Anonymous and Thomas, p. 114.

attendant later refused to give him a drink, he went on a rampage through the plane, urinating on the floors and breaking trays. He was arrested when the flight landed in Anchorage.[192]

Training ground personnel to recognize and screen angry or intoxicated passengers off the plane can drastically cut the rate of air rage:

> The air rage problem may begin on the ground, with a failure to note observable symptoms manifested by potentially disruptive passengers as harried check-in and gate agents process passengers and get the flight off the gate on time. Gulf Air added a one-day training course last year for its ground staff and has seen a 50 percent decline in cases of air rage, according to a Gulf Air official.

> To reduce the pressure on gate agents to board passengers of doubtful conduct in order to meet on-time performance, KLM is now using a special reporting code to cover cases of drunk, agitated passengers who delay boarding, according to KLM management instructor Ben van Ernich. "We may refuse up to 10 people per day from boarding," he added.[193]

Carrying Deportees

In Britain, 1,173 attempts to return asylum seekers in Britain to their home countries failed between 2005 and 2007 because these individuals became so aggressive they threatened passengers' safety, reported the *Scotsman* newspaper. Would-be deportees regularly "scream and lash out, attack cabin crew, and even strip naked on planes in a desperate bid to delay the end of their dreams of staying in the UK," the newspaper reported.

Planes apparently turned around and dropped them back in Britain. Home Secretary John Reid admitted the rate of aborted removals had reached an all-time high, with more than 10 failed asylum seekers every week dodging deportation. The detainees were returned to detention until they could be sent home with in-flight escorts.[194]

According to Andrew Thomas, 70,000 illegal immigrants—about half of whom had been indicted for criminal acts or involved in criminal activity—were deported from the United States on commercial airplanes in the year 2000.[195] In all but a

---

192   "10th March 2005—Anchorage" incident cited in AD Aerospace.

193   "Training Can Reduce and Defuse Disruptive Passenger Incidents," *Air Safety Week,* March 11, 2002, found at http://findarticles.com/p/articles/mi_m0UBT/is_10_16/ai_83681236.

194   "Air Rage Stops 1173 UK Deportations," *Scotsman.com,* May 16, 2007, originally found on Scotsman site but more recently found at http://frontexwatch.wordpress.com/2007/05/16/air-rage-stops-1173-uk-deportations/.

195   Anonymous and Thomas, p. 95.

very few cases, when they got on the airplane, groups of ten or fewer deportees traveled without any escort. The Immigration and Naturalization Service (INS) required that while being driven to the airport, they would always be handcuffed and often in leg irons, with two guards watching them. The guards would put them on the plane, wait until everyone was boarded and the airplane door was about to close, remove their handcuffs and leg irons, and leave.[196]

In pilot Stephen Luckey's words, "These vehicles are allowed to pull up along side of our air craft and unload deportees, who moments before were in handcuffs, to ride unescorted in the seat next to Grandma."[197]

"This becomes an accident waiting to happen,"[198] adds Thomas:

> The simple fact that deportees are being forced to go against their will to a place they wanted to get away from automatically puts them in the category of potential air rage offender—regardless of whether they have a criminal background… Many illegal immigrants have risked life and limb to enter a new country and are understandably quite upset when they are compelled to return to their home country. Some may face prison or political retribution, or worse. Others might simply not want to face the shame of coming home a failure. As a result these passengers may feel they have little or nothing to lose.[199]

"The INS won't even discuss this issue," Thomas said in 2002. "They refused to testify before Congress during the debate on the Aviation Security Act passed last year. We find since 9/11, more and more incidents of unruliness and air rage involving deportees."[200] On top of that, he said, because they had sneaked into the country without the usual inoculations, they were likely to spread disease, including tuberculosis, which was staging a comeback in the Third World, as they traveled in poorly ventilated airport cabins.[201]

In 2002, INS spokesman Russ Bergeron said that there had been no change in the escort policy since Sept. 11, 2001, and that commercial airlines would still be used to carry deportees, including those going home to Arab countries.[202]

---

196   Statement of Captain Stephen Luckey.
197   Ibid.
198   Anonymous and Thomas, p. 96.
199   Ibid., p. 97.
200   Andrew Thomas (Interview).
201   Anonymous and Thomas, p. 98.
202   Paul Sperry, "INS to Deport Arab Aliens on Airliners," *Worldnetdaily.com*, August 1, 2002, found at http://www.worldnetdaily.com/news/article.asp?ARTICLE_ ID=28474.

Fanning the Flames: Crew Reaction Increases Rage

When raging passengers start to lose it, they usually find themselves surrounded by crew members and passengers determined to make them sit down and shut up. This sudden flurry of threats and restraints, the feeling of being totally hemmed in by hands and bodies and rules, only amplifies the fight-or-flight reflex, making the unruly passenger feel more controlled, more panicked, more attacked, and more enraged.

Experts say the key to reducing anger is to get away from the source, but these overwhelmed ragers are immediately faced with the exact opposite experience, as the source of their irritation seems to close in on them, determined to get them under control. Their minds can't think, but a super-jolt of adrenalin is telling their bodies to do two things—flee (no great hope on a plane, though that explains the many attempts to open exit doors at 30,000 feet) and fight to the death. They have the strength of ten, because their heart is fueled by stress hormones. Lots of luck wrestling them to the ground.

What can be done? Try a non-confrontational approach, says Dr August Dragt, Ph.D., a social psychologist at the KLM Wings Academy. "The more you repeat 'we have rules' the more you can aggravate the situation," he said. Telling angry people they have to obey "can provoke people into behavior."[203]

Airline Response to Complaints

"There is little evidence that those with power to change the system are addressing these questions," says Angela Dahlberg. They don't seem to have a vision for taking care of the psychological needs of the harassed traveler, she said. "What does the stressed air traveler do with built up anger without the opportunity of early intervention by an airline professional?" If the airlines' only response to travelers' stress is to bar more inebriated passengers from taking their flights, said Dahlberg, the situation will only become more explosive.[204]

Travel writer Ed Hewitt agreed. "In no way do I condone [passengers'] 'flipping out' to the point of violence," he said. However, airlines need to recognize that "frustration and powerlessness combine to make people feel helpless and cornered, without sensible recourse, and that's a bad place to put anyone."[205]

Consumers are filing more complaints than ever before about communication, overbooking, fares, cancellations, crowded cabins, personnel rudeness, and bad service, Dahlberg said. "At a time when the rift between consumers and the airlines

203   "Training Can Reduce and Defuse Disruptive Passenger Incidents."
204   Dahlberg, p. 23.
205   Ed Hewitt, "Air Rage: Readers Speak Out," *The Independent Traveler.com*, found at http://www.independenttraveler.com/resources/article.cfm?AID=165&category=13.

widens," she said, "airlines demand that the consumer follow strict behavior codes when in their care or else."[206]

This is when push comes to shove. And that is when air rage happens.

---

206   Dahlberg, p. 23.

Chapter 3

Personnel Policies that Cause Air Rage

or

Why Unhappy Workers = Angry Passengers

On July 13, 2007, when a toddler on a flight from Atlanta to Oklahoma wouldn't stop saying, "Bye-bye, plane!" the flight attendant ordered the mother to give him drugs to shut him up. When the mother refused, the attendant kicked her and her baby off the plane.[1]

****

On a flight to Denver, a flight attendant barged into one passenger's locked lavatory and then refused to apologize, after which a baggage delay made the passenger miss his connection, leaving him stranded in Chicago. There the ticket agent responded by outlining all the ways he couldn't help and all the reasons he shouldn't have to. A quick call to the passenger's travel agent finally got him on the next flight home. He mentioned that to the agent, who snapped, "Well then you've wasted my time."[2]

****

After Hartford, Connecticut, passenger Peter Bennett discovered his plane to Chicago had been cancelled, he asked if the airline could get him to Chicago on another carrier. The ticket agent sneered, "Those days are over. We're going bankrupt. That's your problem."[3]

"Hey, I understand people are stressed," Bennet said. "It's tough, obviously, to give bad news to lots of people. But that's no excuse for the whole attitude."[4]

---

1   William Marra, "'Bye-Bye' Baby: Mother, Son Booted from Plane," *ABC News*, July 13, 2007, found at http://abcnews.go.com/GMA/story?id=3371901.

2   Bill Staudt, blog post from billstaudt, Zip Code 19425, on *Denver Post* "Neighbors" website, September 17, 2007, found at http://neighbors.denverpost.com/viewtopic. php?t=6913089.

3   Laura Mansnerus, "Turbulent Manners Unsettle Fliers," *New York Times,* February 15, 2004, found at http://query.nytimes.com/gst/fullpage.html?res=9805E2D9173AF936A 25751C0A9629C8B63.

4   Ibid.

****

From Glamorous to Grim

If customer complaints are any measure, airline personnel are suffering from a bit of air rage themselves. That's not surprising. Working for an airline has lost its luster in the last 15 years. Before the era of price wars and cost cutting, said an airline professional who wrote for ABC on condition of anonymity, "Working for an airline had panache and style, some glamour and a lot of action, and for people who loved working with and for other people, it was heaven."

"And today?" he said:

> With overcrowded airplanes, little civility in dress or demeanor of passengers, few meals, fewer amenities, industry-wide salary cuts of epic proportions, and (the worst sin of all) airlines canceling pension plans because they've robbed the fund of hundreds of millions, far too many of America's airline employees are shell shocked, depressed, disillusioned and resentful. In effect, we're now an industry full of employees going through post-traumatic stress and wondering why we ever thought it was fun.

> And that, in a nutshell, equates to bad and inattentive service with a "who cares" attitude. Morale, in other words, is the key, and it's in precious short supply today.[5]

Corey Caldwell, a spokeswoman for the national Association of Flight Attendants in the United States, says it's "a very troublesome time" for flight attendants. Packed planes, flight delays, security hassles and other factors already have made flying more unpleasant. Airline bankruptcy reorganizations became "the industry norm" after 9/11, so flight attendants have had to cope with pay, benefit, and work-rule concessions, she says. They're not only working more hours, they've taken on their fired co-workers' duties, too, working harder than a few years ago for less money. The resulting fatigue, stress, and frustration could be making workers more aggressive with customers.[6]

Coffee, Tea, or Mean?

Flight attendants and ticket agents are the public face of an airline, the people who represent the company to its customers. Yet, to save money, many companies treat

---

5   "Why Airline Service Suffers," *ABC News,* April 4, 2006, found at http://abcnews.go.com/print?id=1800726.

6   Gary Stoller, "Flight Attendants Feel the Wrath of Fliers," *USA Today,* June 10, 2007, found at http://www.usatoday.com/travel/flights/2007-06-10-air-abuse-usat_N.htm.

these front line employees (FLEs) so badly that some are snapping under pressure and taking their anger and fatigue out on passengers—who in turn vow never to fly their airlines again.

Customers want to feel valued, employees want to feel valued—and airline management wants to drive profits. Airlines often act as if these were mutually exclusive goals, as if the only way to make a profit were to demean and undervalue their staff. "They told us the reason we were losing money was because we were rude to passengers," a flight attendant said bitterly.[7] One company ordered flight attendants to attend "Commitment to Courtesy" courses—on their own time, without pay.[8] Blaming underpaid, overworked employees for falling profits doesn't inspire hard work and loyalty; it just inspires rage.

Abuse Becomes a Two-Way Street

Not only are front line employees under fire from their airlines, they're also taking abuse from angry passengers. In one case, a man on a flight from Seattle to Honolulu pinned a flight attendant to the floor and spat in her face again and again.[9] Employees say abuse is a two-way street, with passengers dishing out every bit as much as they take. The tension between front line employees and passengers is rising as outraged passengers become more rude and volatile and workers respond in kind. The result is an upward spiral of hostility.

Veteran flight attendant Elliot Hester described how one flight attendant was pushed beyond her breaking point. She was serving dinner when a female passenger thrust a small fragrant bundle of trash toward her, saying, "Take this." Realizing the trash was actually a used baby diaper, Hester said:

> ... the attendant instructed the passenger to take it to the lavatory herself and dispose of it. "No," the passenger replied. "You take it!" The attendant explained that she couldn't dispose of the dirty diaper because she was serving food— handling the diaper would be unsanitary. But that wasn't a good enough answer for the passenger. Angered by her refusal, the passenger hurled the diaper at the flight attendant. It struck her square in the head, depositing chunks of baby dung that clung to her blond locks. The infuriated attendant leapt upon the passenger, strangling her until passengers could separate the two.[10]

---

7   Jim Clemmer, "Blame Management for Poor Service," *Expert Magazine*, January 9, 2006, p. 1, found at http://www.expertmagazine.com/artman/publish/article_818.shtml.

8   Ibid.

9   "17th November 2004—Seattle, USA" incident cited in AD Aerospace, "Is FlightVu the Answer?" found at http://www.ad-aero.com/products_witness_news.php.

10   Elliott Neal Hester, "Bad Passenger, Bad!" Out of the Blue, *Salon.com,* April 13, 1999, found at http://archive.salon.com/travel/diary/hest/1999/04/13/passenger/index. html.

Alin Boswell, union president of the Washington, D.C., local that represents 350 US Airways flight attendants, says that right after the Sept. 11, 2001 terrorist attacks, passengers sympathized with flight attendants, but "that had a very short life span." Now, he said, "We're back to pre-9/11 passenger attitudes. Flight attendants are bearing the brunt of passengers' anger."[11]

Enforcing Heartless Policies

Adding insult to injury, these demoralized employees are required by their bosses to enforce policies that passengers find heartless and dehumanizing. They are the ones at the front lines where painful policies meet angry passengers, where a harried mother finds out it will cost an extra $50 to take her child's baby seat on the plane or when the family delayed by a snowstorm finds out their seats have been given away because they've arrived two minutes past an arbitrary deadline. Some observers say executives enact infuriating policies and then leave their front line employees to deal with the fallout—while remaining unfailingly cheerful and upbeat.

This is hard to do moments after being verbally abused by a customer, said flight attendant Hester. When he told a large angry woman she'd be charged an extra $50 at the gate to check her carry-on bag, he said she paused, "gathering her hostility in one great exhalation. 'You people are so ...so ...ughhh!'"[12]

"Am I the one responsible for charging passengers for extra baggage?" Hester asked. "Am I the one to blame for a change in rates? Is my goal in life to make it difficult for passengers to carry belongings onto my airplane?"[13] He continued:

> Because flight attendants spend more time with passengers than do other employee groups, we're often hit by the crap passengers want to throw at less reachable targets: baggage handlers, catering chefs, aircraft cabin designers and airline CEOs with $10 million salaries and golden parachutes that make them twice as rich upon retirement—even if the airline goes belly-up in the interim.
>
> We aren't the ones who design tiny overhead bins that can scarcely accommodate a tote bag, yet we get yelled at when there's not enough room for a carry-on bag the size of an Amana fridge. We don't establish short connection times, though we bear the brunt of passenger rage when they come stumbling onto an aircraft, clutching at their chests due to the 30-minute sprint from gate Z-29. We don't determine seat pitch, the boarding hierarchy or whether passengers should be served peanuts or lobster thermidor on a three-hour flight. And we most

11   Stoller, 2007.

12   Elliott Neal Hester, "When Passengers Rage," *Salon.com,* October 20, 2000, found at http://dir.salon.com/story/business/col/hest/2000/10/20/rage/.

13   Ibid.

certainly don't create the pricing structure for additional checked baggage. All this is left up to some bonus-motivated number cruncher sitting at a computer in an ergonomic airline office (far away from seething, fist-clenching, flight attendant-hating passengers), creating policies that give shareholders a more profitable bottom line.

As for the female passenger who ached to put me in a headlock, she never gave me a chance to say what I'd been trained to say: We're sorry for any inconvenience the change in rates may have caused, ma'am. The increases were necessary due to blah, blah, blah in the blah, blah, blah because of blah-blah. She went on and on, refusing to let me speak, while lashing my ears with her ceaseless rant about unfair baggage rates.

"This is ridiculous," she continued, spraying me with spittle as she spoke. "You should be ashamed."... she gave me an "I'll never fly your f——ing airline again" tirade that ranked among the best I've ever heard. "You people are the worst. The very worst!" she screamed. "I never have this problem when I fly other airlines."

I looked straight into her eyes, unable to quell the anger that had been bubbling inside. "When you fly other airlines, ma'am," I said, "I never have this problem either."[14]

At that the woman began to shout, showering him with more spit and morning breath, punctuating her points by tapping her ticket on his nose. How many incidents like that would it take to erode an employee's good manners?

Research shows that when told by an authority figure to hurt someone else, most people will do it. Taken to its extreme, Yale University researcher Stanley Milgrim found that ordinary people would take actions that were opposed to their values if an authority figure ordered them to—even if they thought their actions were causing physical pain.[15]

Not surprising, then, that underpaid, overworked airline personnel enforce their airlines' less humane policies. Obviously airline employees aren't usually inflicting pain, but they are carrying out policies they may not like or think are fair. What is less publicized about the Milgrim experiment and similar follow-up experiments is the devastating effect on people of the forced departure from their values.[16] It's not known what happens over time to underpaid and disillusioned

---

14 Ibid.

15 Stanley Milgram, *Obedience to Authority: An Experimental View* (New York, NY: HarperPerennial, div. of Harper Collins Publisher, 1974).

16 Philip Zimbardo, *National Public Radio* discussion in May 2007 of experiments described in his book, *The Lucifer Effect: Understanding How Good People Turn Evil* (New York, NY: Random House, 2007).

front line employees when their job requires them to inflict inconvenient policies on helpless customers.

Revenge of the Ticket Agents

We do know that the upward spiral of hostility between employees and passengers can erupt into sabotage. In his online article, "Revenge of the Ticket Agents," MSNBC reporter Christopher Elliott tells how some rogue ground personnel are known to take revenge on passengers they feel have inconvenienced them by mis-tagging their luggage so it gets sent to the wrong city, re-seating them by the bathroom, or in a worst-case scenario, getting them kicked off their flights.[17]

An "innocuous-looking grandmother" named Barbara Arbani, who ran a bed and breakfast in New Hope, Pennsylvania, found herself branded a potential security risk when she crossed a ticket agent. Her crime? Asking for seats closer to the front of the plane.

"The agent had been speaking with a co-worker," she told Elliott. "It was just a social conversation, not work-related, and she felt we had interrupted her." The irritated agent slotted Arbani in two random seats up front, but they were worse than the originals, so Arbani asked to be moved back.

"The agent then harrumphed, rolled her eyes at her co-worker, and reprinted the original seat," Arbani told Elliott, handing her new boarding passes—with a line of red SSS's stamped across the top, indicating she would undergo extra security screening. Although airline spokespeople said ticket agents wouldn't seek this kind of revenge, a security agent confirmed it was the agent who designated Arbani a selectee, adding, "This sometimes happens."

Most airline employees aren't vindictive, Elliott stressed, but you never know if you're going to meet a "rogue agent," or just rub someone the wrong way. If you find yourself a selectee, he added, don't fight it because the security line sometimes moves faster than the regular one.[18]

How About a Seat by the Bathroom?

A former airline ticket agent told Elliott that moving passengers to a bad seat is a favorite tactic, because it's hard to prove the passenger was moved for the wrong reasons. The only time an agent gets in trouble is when a displaced traveler is either "very angry or very important," she said. If you get moved, either ask to talk to a supervisor or, to avoid confrontation, wait and see if you can be moved to a better seat when you arrive at the gate.

---

    17   Christopher Elliott, "Revenge of the Ticket Agents," *MSNBC.com,* October 1, 2007, found at http://www.msnbc.msn.com/id/21080989/.
    18   Ibid.

Suitcase Skullduggery

Some agents pay back problem passengers by enforcing rules as rigidly as possible—for example, forcing them to squeeze their carry-ons in the sizing box at the counter. "They usually succeed when it is placed standing upright on all wheels," one ticket agent said. "But will that suffice? Of course not. It must lie on its side, which usually never works out for the customer." You're stuck checking bags that may contain valuables or electronics, knowing the airline won't pay if they're damaged or lost.

The agent can also mis-tag your bag, sending it to the wrong airport and possibly losing it forever, or rigidly enforce weight limits, making you pay extra fees for your belongings.

Ellen Simonetti, a former Delta Air Lines flight attendant who wrote the *Queen of the Sky* blog, told Elliott that agents stooped to this kind of payback because they felt so powerless, and this was the only way they could vent their frustration. "It's a really crummy job," she says. "So I guess they have to get their revenge once in a while."[19]

"See Ya!" Tossed Off the Flight

A ticket agent for a major airline told Elliott, "My airline actually tells its agents and supervisors to scan the gate areas for passengers with too many carry-ons, oversized luggage, oversized passengers and anyone who looks inebriated—which, if you've flown lately, could be half of the flight." As a result, if you've had one drink and argue with an agent, the agent can recommend you take the next flight—even if that leaves you stranded for a day. The agent added that some folks get "quite a kick" out of denying someone boarding for the smallest infractions. To avoid any kind of retaliation, he recommended flying "stone-cold sober," obeying every regulation to a T, and being kind to the agents.[20]

Elliott wasn't the only travel writer telling flyers how to dodge angry airline employees. By 2007, they had gotten such a bad reputation that MSNBC travel writer Ed Hewitt had this advice for flyers who wanted to get out of the airport unscathed:

> Avoid human contact. Like some kung fu master, your skills of evasion and avoidance will trump debating. … If you don't interact with anyone who can mistreat you, you can't be mistreated. Check in online, check your bags at a kiosk for minimal exposure, board swiftly and silently, and BYO whatever it is that will get you through the flight.[21]

---

19   Ibid.
20   Ibid.
21   Ed Hewitt, "Air Rage: Why the Caged Bird Sings," *MSNBC.com*, October 30, 2007, found at http://www.msnbc.msn.com/id/21384567/.

In other words, if you can slip past those big bad ogres at check-in, you might just make it to Grandma's. We've come a long way from the friendly skies.

After the *Denver Post* reported on air rage in 2007, many readers wrote their website to complain that ticket agents for one major airline used their power to "play God," giving rude answers and refusing to meet reasonable requests, do their job, or even help when missed connections were caused by their airline.

One blogger said that when he tried to get help buying a ticket, an airline employee "told an airport police officer that she had been 'threatened and assaulted' and tried to have my wife and I arrested for the crime of complaining to her and not just leaving her alone and using the automated check-in machines."

"It seems that [the airline], and its contractors, have a 'customer be damned' attitude which is at least allowed—if not fostered—by their management," he said. "Anyone who actually does assault an airline employee needs to be dealt with appropriately by law enforcement—but creating a blacklist of fliers looks ripe for abuse with the current attitude of [the airline] towards its customers."[22]

Another blogger laid the blame at the feet of airline management, saying, "it can be frustrating when you *know* the [airline] agent can help you and simply refuses to do so or views you as someone who is getting in the way of them 'doing their job' ... It does start at the top and [the airline] does need to show its employees some loyalty, financially."[23]

Plummeting Morale: From Flying High to Flying Hungry

A serious change in airline employee attitudes has been seen over the last decade, and the airlines are trying to counter the extreme resentment that some employees feel. Many of these employees have worked for a carrier for at least 15 years. They, more than most, feel overworked, underpaid, under-appreciated, and unsure about their futures.[24] The best-selling customer-service book, *It's Not My Department* by Peter Glen, says that by affecting morale, management's treatment of airline personnel affects their treatment of customers.[25]

---

22   Scotty (online identifier), blog post from gryphon99, on *Denver Post* "Neighbors" website, September 17, 2007, found at http://neighbors.denverpost.com/viewtopic. php?t=6913089.

23   Rich Street (online identifier), blog post from Denverstreetcar, Zip Code 32828, on *Denver Post* "Neighbors" website, September 17, 2007, found at http://neighbors. denverpost.com/viewtopic.php?t=6913089.

24   Barbara De Lollis, "Job Stress Beginning to Take Toll on Some Airline Workers," *USA Today,* November 19, 2004, found at http://www.usatoday.com/travel/news/2004-11-29-unhappyair_x.htm.

25   R. Spector and P.D. McCarthy, *The Nordstrom Way: The Inside Story of America's #1 Customer Service Company* (New York, NY: John Wiley & Sons, Inc., 1995), p. 119.

Little marks of contempt chip away at staff morale. For example, airlines must serve meals to pilots, says flight attendant Elliott Hester, but quite often will not feed cabin crew, even those working a 14-hour day. Some foresighted flight attendants who make time in their hectic multi-country schedules to pack a lunch bag still may not eat because fresh food is often confiscated on international flights when they go through customs.[26]

In airlines' salad days, flight attendants would just eat leftover passenger meals, but times are tighter now and computerized records have eliminated most extra meals. As a result, according to Hester, hungry crew members often hover like vultures in the galley after meal trays are collected to scavenge any leftovers from the more generous first class meals.[27]

Some airlines have started providing a "snack bag" for the cabin crew containing maybe a shrink-wrapped peanut butter sandwich and a bag of chips—hardly enough to sustain workers who are on their feet non-stop and don't have time to eat between flights.

To add hunger to the many assaults on airline attendants' health seems to set the stage for a little staff air rage, or at best to minimize their alertness and effectiveness in a crisis.

How well respected do crew members feel when they have to either graze through the scraps on passengers' trays in hope of snagging an untouched roll or fly hungry?

Front line employees report that it's extremely stressful to maintain a mask of pleasantry while working under extreme pressure and taking insults and verbal abuse daily. They cope with both external stressors, like enraged customers, while hiding internal stressors like management pressure to maintain sometimes-unreasonable policies. These workers complain that no matter what the stress, they're expected to express positive emotion when interacting with customers and act in a way that builds trust, demonstrates promptness and reliability, and gives each passenger the sense that he's getting personal attention.

The result can be poor employee job performance that is most apparent in the treatment of airline customers. It is clear that customer service on the airlines is not what it used to be, due primarily to growth. A pleasant appearance, a caring attitude, and good manners may not be so easy to come by.[28] Employees' behavior is critical because it has a strong impact on the organization's image, customers' expectations, and their reaction to any perceived service failures.

Although flight attendants and crew members are responsible for the safety of passengers, they are human and under even more pressure than passengers. They're exposed to the cabin's environmental climate that is often poor, stuffy, and

---

26 Elliott Neal Hester, "Eating on the Fly," *Salon.com,* May 16, 2000, found at http://archive.salon.com/travel/diary/hest/2000/05/16/eating/print.html.

27 Ibid.

28 Anonymous and Andrew R. Thomas, *Air Rage: Crisis in the Skies* (Amherst, NY: Prometheus Books, 2001), p. 34.

physically upsetting for longer hours at a stretch than passengers, and if they feel rage on the inside, they can't let it show on the surface. One of the challenges and burdens of an airline crew member's job is to maintain a professional demeanor at all times, even in the face of great workplace stress. The tragic 9/11 attacks left airline employees suffering post-traumatic stress disorder, but it's easy to see how such stress-related illness can occur even without a major disaster.

The Troubled 10 Percent: New Hiring Policies

In spite of all the stress and provocation, it turns out that most airline personnel keep their heads and at least maintain civility, if not politeness. In fact, according to a report in Air Safety Week on the 19th Annual International Aircraft Cabin Safety Symposium in San Diego in 2002, only an estimated 2 to 10 percent of all cabin staff are involved in 90 percent of the incidents of passenger misconduct. If these particular employees were identified and trained, the incidence of air rage might be reduced.[29]

However, the article's unnamed author listed one caveat. Although these personnel might benefit from extra and intense training, their airlines might also need to change their hiring standards to avoid hiring people who can snap.[30]

Air rage author and expert Angela Dahlberg told the conference:

> "Training by itself does not fix anything. An integrated management approach is needed, with a long-term requirement for defining new flight attendant selection criteria."

> "The flight attendant job, attracting a large number of applicants for life style reasons rather than professional skills and management, is now on the verge of becoming a true profession," she said. "Airlines need to rethink their service product design and aircraft cabin environment. This includes a new profile of flight attendants to meet the changed reality of air travel," she said.[31]

The article's author concluded that "more focused training directed at the minority of cabin staff who seem to be involved in the majority of cases could further reduce the incident rate. Updating cabin staff employment criteria could further mitigate the problem over the long term."[32]

---

29   "Training Can Reduce and Defuse Disruptive Passenger Incidents," *Air Safety Week,* March 11, 2002, found at http://findarticles.com/p/articles/mi_m0UBT/is_10_16/ai_83681236.

30   Ibid.

31   Ibid.

32   Ibid.

It is difficult to peg a precise reduction in the number of incidents from a particular training policy. Dr August Dragt, a social psychologist at the KLM Wings Academy, said one of the challenges in measuring the effectiveness of training is that "you hardly know if people apply the techniques." However, he said uniform application of the policy can yield a 30 percent reduction in passenger incidents. Lodewijk Oosthoek, manager of flight safety and quality assurance for KLM, seconded that estimate. "We are down 30 percent" as a result of the program, he said, "but that's only what is reported."[33]

No Backup: Facing Attackers Alone

For a flight attendant or ticket agent, a day's worth of spit and invective is bad, but even worse is never knowing when verbal abuse will suddenly erupt into violence. On December 16, 1997, on a US Airways flight from Los Angeles to Baltimore, a 200-pound football player named Dean Trammel began walking down the aisle telling passengers, "We're all going to go to heaven." Recognizing the signs of a psychotic episode, flight attendant Renee Sheffer, a former psychiatric nurse, calmly guided Trammel, who'd begun announcing that he was Jesus Christ, to the back of the plane, away from passengers who were becoming upset.

As Sheffer spoke to the muscular 200-pound man in a soothing voice, he seemed to relax, kneel down, and begin to pray. Then he grabbed Sheffer's breast, apologized, and then raced up the aisle to "bless the pilots." After a scuffle at the cockpit door that left one flight attendant on the floor, Sheffer got Trammel back in the back galley—where he suddenly became enraged and hurled the 114-pound Sheffer across three rows of seats. After crashing into the wall, she slid limply to the airplane floor. Several passengers and two off-duty pilots finally wrestled Trammel to the ground and tied him up with seatbelt extensions and handcuffs—but not before Trammel had kicked Sheffer into an exit door and bitten the men restraining him, scattering blood in all directions. When the plane landed, Sheffer was rushed by ambulance to the hospital. She was suffering from internal bleeding, kidney and bladder trauma, spinal damage, a separated shoulder, a torn meniscus in her right knee, bruises all over, cuts, and—in time—post traumatic stress. She underwent three operations, and it was two years before she could return to work.[34]

---

33   Ibid.
34   Elliott Neal Hester, "Flying in the Age of Air Rage," *Salon.com*, September 7, 1999, about para. 24, found at www.salon.com/travel/diary/hest/1999/09/97/rage/print. html.

Fighting Back: Sky Rage

Though Trammel admitted that he'd taken LSD before the flight, his only punishment was a $1,500 fine, probation, community service, and mandatory psychiatric treatment. Although he could have brought the plane down, he was declared not criminally responsible for his actions because he was "mentally ill." Renee Sheffer's husband Mike founded Sky Rage Foundation, a watchdog organization whose website documents air rage incidents, posts information about court proceedings, and gives passengers advice on how to handle or prevent air rage.[35]

In other incidents, flight attendants have been hit over the head with liquor bottles, choked, punched, and stabbed. When they were verbally or physically abused by a customer, these front line airline employees said that their airline managers discouraged them from pressing charges or reporting the incident. According to Andrew Thomas, "International aviation organizations, deeply anxious about maintaining the integrity of their industry, become understandably upset when they hear how air rage negatively influences the public's perception of air travel."[36]

That might explain what happened when American Eagle flight attendant Christa Tess was attacked in 1997 by a passenger who was obviously drunk. "I was beaten up pretty bad," Tess said. Although the attacker had to be strapped down by other passengers and the flight crew, "the company refused to prosecute because he didn't do any damage to the airplane." Tess said she was disappointed by her co-workers' lack of support and the airline's lack of understanding of what she'd gone through. Saying she loved her work—"It was all I ever wanted to do"—Tess quit her job after the incident.[37]

The International Workers' Federation, which represents air crews, says that only half the airlines have a policy to tackle air rage—and two thirds do not provide any training for cabin crew in how to deal with disruptive passengers.

Many airline employees feel that they are standing on the front lines, frequently meeting air rage head on, with little back up from the airlines. At an Australian Services Union (ASU) meeting with Qantas in May, 2004, the airline personnel union representative said:

> It's also ironic that if someone jokingly, although wrongly, says "I should blow this place up," or "I've got a bomb in my bag" the reaction is immediate, people start appearing from everywhere, and rightfully so. However if someone pushes

---

35   Ibid.

36   Anonymous and Thomas, p. 35.

37   K. Tyler, "Afraid to Fly and It Shows. Air Rage Is an Escalating Problem. So, Why Don't Airlines Adequately Train Their Employees for This?" *HR Magazine,* 2001, 46(9), p. 3, found at http://www.shrm.org/hrmagazine/articles/0901.

you, punches you, threatens you, stalks you, more often than not nothing seems to happen.[38]

Inconsistent Enforcement

In the 2002 Safety Symposium, KLM Wings Academy social psychologist Dragt said it was important that personnel be more consistent in upholding policies, even with the enlightened, non-confrontational approach he recommends. "If you enforce policies more uniformly, we've seen a decrease in incidents," he said, adding that he's aware of many cases "where the pursers did not support the flight attendants."[39]

In one famous incident, this disconnect between crew members' need for support and top management went far higher and quite public. Shortly after police took rock singer Courtney Love into custody for swearing wildly, abusing the cabin crew, refusing to sit down, and, according to some reports, stripping to her underwear on a Virgin Airlines flight, Richard Branson, the President of Virgin Airlines, hosted the rock singer at a party and joked that the airline's new slogan should be, "Rock stars swear by us!"

Flight attendants were not amused.

"We were surprised at Richard Branson's comments," a spokesman for the British Airline Pilots Association said. "Air rage should be taken much more seriously. She was arrested and should have been charged. Rock star or not, she should have ended up in the dock."[40]

Love had lost her temper when a companion in economy class wasn't allowed to sit with her. A spokesman for the Transport and General Workers Union, which represents some cabin crew, said, "It matters not whether you're a rock star or a celebrity or whoever," the industry needs to "stamp out this modern-day scourge."[41]

In Britain, a turning point in the way air rage incidents are dealt with by the authorities came about on October 30, 1998, when stewardess Fiona Weir was assaulted on an Airtours flight. On a flight from Spain, Weir asked British passenger Steve Handy to stop smoking. He responded by smashing a broken vodka bottle across her head and dragging it across her body, scarring her for life. Weir is suing

---

38 Australian Services Union, "Qantas to Act on Rage at Airports," *ASU National Net,* May 13, 2004, found at http://www.asu.asn.au/media/airlines_general/20040513_ airrage.html.

39 "Training Can Reduce and Defuse Disruptive Passenger Incidents."

40 Karen McVeigh, "Branson All Kisses But No Love Lost for Crew," *Scotsman. com,* February 7, 2003, found at http://www.scotsman.com/uk/Branson-all-kisses-but-no.2400125.jp.

41 Ibid.

Airtours, arguing that the attack could have been prevented, because the passenger had been creating trouble for hours before he attacked.[42]

Since then, countries outside the United States have taken a hard line on air rage. The United Kingdom, which doesn't have the jurisdictional problems that exist in the United States, has become a leader in prosecuting violent passengers. By 1999, British courts were routinely dispensing three-year jail terms for air ragers. One passenger was sentenced to a year in jail for refusing to turn off a cell phone. Judge Anthony Ensor said, "Any sentence must not only punish you, but act as a warning to others who might be inclined to behave similarly."[43]

In 2003, MPs considered a bill that would raise the maximum sentence for "endangering the safety of an aircraft" to five years. Liberal Democrat Malcolm Bruce backed the bill. "The lack of punishment has perhaps made people think it is a joke, a bit of fun, it's a laugh," he said. "Yet we have seen incidents where clearly crew and passengers have been put into a very serious state of fear and alarm."[44]

And several United States airlines, including United, TWA, and Northwest, instituted "Zero Tolerance" policies, permanently banning abusive customers from the airlines for life. United's in-house attorneys give free legal advice to victims of passenger rage, and give them time off with pay if they need to testify against a defendant. One spokeswoman said, "Employees have the right to be safe at work."[45]

In 2000, the Association of Flight Attendants issued a report card that gave the FAA, Department of Justice, and airline industry a failing grade in protecting flight attendants and the public and discouraging air rage. A *USA Today* investigation in December of 2001 found that FAA officials did not press charges in most of the 1,500 cases of air rage they reviewed. Although many of the 1,500 cases in the *USA Today* report preceded the September 11 attacks, some had similar elements; in more than a dozen cases between 1990 and 2000, an out-of-control passenger gained access to the cockpit or tried to.[46,47]

In a *New York Times* article, a US Airways customer service agent and union local president said, "Sometimes it seems like the enemy is not the passengers but senior management. On the issue of passenger disrespect, management does not

---

42   Elliott Neal Hester, "Flying in the Age of Air Rage."

43   Ibid.

44   "Air Rage Crackdown Backed," *BBC News,* May 16, 2003, found at http://news.bbc.co.uk/2/hi/uk_news/politics/3034889.stm.

45   Hester, "Flying in the Age of Air Rage."

46   Michael McConnell, "Air Rage Takes a Back Seat in our Post-9-11 World," *Detroit Metro Connections*, September 19, 2002, found at: http://metro.heritage.com/dtw100202/story3.htm.

47   Blake Morrison, "FAA Seldom Punished Violence," *USA Today,* December 5, 2001, found at http://www.usatoday.com/news/sept11/2001/12/05/air-violence.htm.

want to support us. They prefer to avoid conflict and possible litigation and put their heads in the sand."[48]

Airline spokeswoman Amy Kudwa denied that. "We have had a history of supporting both our ground agents and our flight crews when it comes to instances of air rage," she said.[49] Employees are especially upset when airlines don't pursue cases because, since November 1, 2001, there has been a federal law providing for a maximum sentence of 10 years in prison for passengers who interfere with the performance of an airline employee's duties. But the law has never been applied, according to Rick Braswell, administrative assistant to the president of the Communications Workers of America. In December 2003, Senators John F. Kerry of Massachusetts and Ernest F. Hollings of South Carolina, both Democrats and sponsors of the 2001 bill, urged Secretary of Transportation Norman Y. Mineta to raise awareness of the law.[50]

If airport police do march a violent passenger off the plane, what happens next? In the United States, the answer has often been, "nothing."

"This is where the real rage occurs," Andrew Thomas said in 2002:

> That is, the penalties for the vast majorities of aberrant, abnormal or abusive behaviors is almost non-existent. The federal government, in its infinite wisdom, has instituted a paltry $1,100 civil penalty for perpetrators of air rage, in most cases. Even more incredible, the most extreme cases that really threaten security of crew and passengers, are often plea-bargained to where no penalty at all is ever levied. You are the least protected by the criminal code when you are traveling in an aircraft at 35,000 feet—less protected than almost any other place in our society today.[51]

Lack of Air Rage Training

Research has shown that education about air rage can reduce the problem, but the subject doesn't get much attention in travel education programs. The Barron study of air rage conducted at the University of Queensland focuses on the significant role that higher education can play in combating air rage. A survey of 24 higher education institutions in Australia offering degrees in tourism and travel management found "no evidence" that air rage was included in 12 of the

---

48   Barry Estabrook, "A Paycheck Weekly, Insults Daily," *New York Times*, February 15, 2004, found at http://query.nytimes.com/gst/fullpage.html?sec=travel&res=9C0CE3D9 173AF936A25751C0A9629C8B63&fta=y.

49   Ibid.

50   Ibid.

51   Andrew Thomas (Interview), *Court TV*, April 3, 2002, found at http://www.courttv. com/talk/chat_transcripts/2002/0403safety-airrage.html.

programs.[52] None of these 12 respondents had definite plans to introduce air rage into their curriculum in the near future, and when asked if the topic was worthy of inclusion, only five said that it might be considered when subjects were reviewed.[53]

Yet when an air rage incident erupts, it takes special skills to quell it. Dealing with explosive outbursts effectively, using just enough force when necessary to control a violent individual without crippling or killing them, is skill learned through training, experience, and a measure of maturity. The line between controlling a violent person and damaging him or her is not always clear, and if the airline cabin crew has lost control of the situation or is unable to exercise leadership, the situation is that much worse. Asking untrained crew to be able, suddenly and magically, to deal with violence is dangerous in the extreme, and naively thinking that air rage will never happen again borders on the delusional.

In addition, since the September 11 attacks, passengers are likely to overreact to anything that looks like violence on a plane in ways that can turn them to vigilantes in the blink of an eye. "The threat of uncalled-for passenger involvement is real and needs to be controlled," said *Air Rage* author Angela Dahlberg at the 2002 Air Safety Week conference. "It's very important for everyone to keep a cool calm head."[54] The death of violently disruptive Jonathan Burton at the hands of terrified fellow passengers on Southwest Flight 1763 on August 11, 2000, described at the beginning of this book, is a classic example of how defensive intervention and righteous indignation can tip over into mob violence.

At the time of the incident, Southwest spokeswoman Linda Rutherford said that flight attendants were not trained for situations like the Burton incident, but were trained to deal with general emergencies. "We feel our flight crew did exactly what they needed to do to get that plane on the ground, and that the passengers who were restraining Mr Burton did what they thought they had to do to keep him from moving again."[55]

An unfortunate choice of words, since Burton certainly was not capable of moving again. He died about an hour after being removed from the plane, and some observers wonder whether better flight crew preparation could have kept him alive. While the Southwest crew and passengers made many right moves, they made mistakes too. Passenger Anne Crawford, who was sitting two rows behind Burton, said that passengers had succeeded in getting Burton into his seat and calming him down when the flight attendant announced loudly that an off-duty

---

52   Paul E. Barron, "Air Rage: An Emerging Challenge for the Airline Industry," *Asia Pacific Journal of Transport*, Summer 2006, 4, pp. 39–44.

53   Ibid.

54   Dahlberg, as cited in *"Training Can Reduce and Defuse Disruptive Passenger Incidents."*

55   L. Anne Newell, "Crew 'Antagonized' Agitated Air Passenger, Police Report Indicates," *Seattle Times,* September 29, 2000, found at http://community.seattletimes.nwsource.com/archive/?date=20000929&slug=TTN11026L.

police officer on the plane would take charge of the situation. Crawford felt certain that was a mistake.

"She was standing next to me when she was making the announcement and I was just cringing in my seat because they had pretty much calmed him down," she said. As she feared, Burton lashed out, hitting the police officer in the face. "He was calm, he seemed like he was going to relax, but then he went into this fit again," she said. "I was just wondering how much training Southwest gives to help deal with these situations."[56]

It's a valid question. The post-mortem showed Burton had been effectively strangled and died of asphyxiation. His body had multiple bruises and contusions on the chest, legs, arms and face, the result of being struck with blunt objects, fists and feet.[57] Most American reports of the incident emphasized Burton's height and muscular appearance and the explosive violence of his attacks that threatened the safety of everyone on board, and most agreed that the passengers who subdued him acted in self-defense. British and Canadian reports mentioned other chilling aspects:

> A few days after the post-mortem results were announced a passenger on the flight told a very different story. Dean Harvey, a Canadian, told his local newspaper that one man jumped off a chair and on to Burton several times while other passengers held him down on his back, arms outstretched.

> "I asked him to stop," Harvey explained. "I said, 'you've got the guy subdued. What more do you want? You don't have to pound his head in.' It wasn't self-defence. No way." The man had been hit by Burton and, according to Harvey, was out for revenge.

> "It doesn't make sense. Couldn't they have restrained him without standing on his neck and choking the life out of him? Couldn't the flight attendants see that the guy was unable to breathe?"[58]

Shortly afterwards *Time* magazine in America asked similar questions. "Was [Burton's] killing a horrible accident or a case of vigilante malice?" the reporter wrote. "And what are the lessons for airlines dealing with the growing incidence of air rage?"

---

56   L. Anne Newell, "Was Killed Air Rage Passenger Provoked?" *ABC News.com,* September 29, 2000, found at http://abcnews.go.com/Travel/story?id=118734&page=1.

57   "A Death on Descent," *CBS News*, September 21, 2000, found at http://www.cbsnews.com/stories/2000/09/21/national/printable235154.shtml.

58   David Usborne, "Murder debate on air-rage killing," *The London Independent*, September 24, 2000, found at http://findarticles.com/p/articles/mi_qn4158/is_20000924/ai_n14324057.

"The question to ask," California aviation lawyer Phillip Kolczynski told *Time* magazine, "is whether the flight attendants attempted to restrict the Good Samaritans from using undue force. Are we reaching the point where we need police officers on board, or do we need to start arming crew members with Mace or Taser guns?"[59]

No one could question the right of passengers to defend their lives. But at what point and how does one stop a continuing violent attack when the threat has been removed? Perhaps no flight attendant could have done anything to stop the men from continuing to hit the unconscious Burton. But it is also certain that the flight attendants had no training to even begin to address this kind of situation. That lack of training is only beginning to be remedied.

The Burton incident took place in 2000, and aside from the tremendous focus on preventing terrorism, the main change in the cabin crew's arsenal against air rage in the intervening years appears to be the issuance of plastic handcuffs. Still, even that small measure might have saved Burton's life by eliminating the need for the passengers to stand on his body to restrain him.

"No Respect": The Status Problem

Author Barbara McCuen inadvertently reflects one underlying cause of poor passenger behavior when she says, "It is no more acceptable to assault a flight attendant in the air because your plane was delayed than it would be to strike your waiter because your lunch was delayed."[60] While she's right that it's never acceptable to attack a flight attendant, by discussing waiters and flight attendants in the same breath she reflects the dangerous status perception problem that hobbles flight attendants as they deal with air rage.

A flight attendant may serve coffee, meals, and drinks, but he or she is not and has never been simply a waiter or waitress, and when the passenger is allowed or encouraged to make that assumption, everyone's safety is at risk. Captain Steven Luckey explains why in his statement to the United States Congress:

> Some disruptive business executives, who are used to being in control of others and in positions of authority, resent even minor kinds of requests from the cabin crew. A request to turn off a laptop computer or not to make a cellular phone call during takeoff were given as examples of such requests which have provoked outbursts from upper echelon airline clientele. These individuals, it was noted,

---

59   Timothy Roche, "Homicide in the Sky," *Time*, October 2, 2000, found at http://www.time.com/time/magazine/article/0,9171,55721,00.html.

60   Barbara McCuen, "Are Airlines to Blame for Passenger 'Air Rage?'" *SpeakOut. com*, June 15, 2000, p. 2, found at http://www.speakout.com/activism/issue_briefs/1340b-1.html.

may not take well to receiving such requests from some person beneath them in social rank.[61]

Arrogant business executives are not the only ones who scorn a request to comply with rules from staff members they consider servants. As we'll see in the next chapter, anyone from self-styled princesses and pop stars to socialites and TV evangelists think they're too important to take orders from "the help." They don't realize that flight attendants have never been flying waitresses. From the earliest days of commercial flying, cabin crews have been trained to handle medical emergencies and mechanical malfunctions in highly technical equipment.

Flying on Illusions

It's partly because the flight crew does its job so well that passengers can cruise along at 30,000 feet thinking flight attendants aren't doing anything but serving food. But that illusion of normalcy can be dangerous if it lulls people into thinking disrupting the routine in flight has no consequences.

The commercial air travel industry has succeeded perhaps too well at making air travel seem routine and easy. Passengers are familiar with the basics of flying to the point where, even when they are stressed by delays or squashed by a small seat, they often are able to tune out the safety announcements and forget that they're isolated in a small vessel that is quite literally up in the air. Passengers on an ocean liner can look out at the vast sea around them to get a sense of being isolated and literally "all in the same boat" with everyone else onboard. But airline passengers have limited visibility through a necessarily thick window, and are insulated from most of the sounds and sense impressions of flight that buffeted earlier passengers in smaller airplanes. The skills of pilots, airplane designers and cabin crews have created a padded, shielded airline environment that allows passengers to exist in a kind of cocoon for the duration of the flight. What is gained is a certain calm, particularly for nervous flyers; but what is lost is the understanding that passengers are isolated from the rest of the world, and getting along with the flight crew and fellow passengers is essential.

Air rage is so dangerous because one unchecked episode could sufficiently interfere with the airplane's functioning enough to cause a crash. Flight attendants are the employees on the frontlines defending against this possibility.

So much of the cabin crew's job involves making passengers comfortable, serving food and drink, and in recent years, marketing duty free goods and other

---

61   Statement of Captain Stephen Luckey, Chairman, National Security Committee, Air Line Pilots Association, Before the Subcommittee on Aviation, Committee on Transportation and Infrastructure, U.S. House of Representatives, Passenger Interference with Flight Crews and the Carry-on Baggage Reduction Act of 1997, June 11, 1998, found at http://cf.alpa.org/Internet/TM/tm061198.htm.

merchandise, that it is easy to forget how responsible the cabin crew is for the safety of the airplane. Their most important skills are only on view as they cope heroically with serious emergencies, like this one in Charlotte, North Carolina on July 2, 1994. Reporting on the crash of USAir Flight 1016, Flight Attendant Richard DeMary said:

> It happened so fast. Initially it was disbelief, and then just the terrifying feeling that we're crashing.
>
> My recollection was that there were two impacts ... The first impact with the ground, the sound of trees breaking, at that point knowing you were crashing— just the force of the impact was extremely violent, almost takes your breath away when you're crashing like that. Then immediately after the first impact, the second [and] most violent impact, to me, is when I think we hit a tree, basically peeled back [that] one side of the airplane—broke the airplane apart into three sections. The nose section, with a few passenger seats, went off to the left.
>
> I was in that section, the nose section. One part of the airplane—and I believed it was the center part of the airplane—from the first class seats back to just past the emergency exit rows ... it was basically wrapped around a tree ... We hit a tree [and the aircraft broke into separate sections] and then the tail section proceeded to go into [the carport of a house].
>
> I remember just after we hit the tree, the feeling of the rain hitting us, the wind, the noise, because we were in a darkened, enclosed cabin as we were coming in to land and then all of a sudden we were opened up to all of the elements and I remember feeling the rain hit me and the noise—screeching of metal, hearing the rain hit the airplane, feeling it hit me ... Probably the loudness came from the scratching of the airplane on the ground and on the pavement because the section I was in slid down a street.
>
> I remember sitting in my jump seat, not seeing anything once the airplane came to a stop, and at that point knowing we were in a crash, knowing that it's time to get out, it's time to evacuate, and I immediately went for my seatbelt [and] started yelling, "Release seatbelts and get out! Release seatbelts and get out!" which is the first command that we would yell upon coming to a stop, and at that point Shelly [Markwith, a flight attendant sitting in the jump seat beside DeMary] ... was yelling her commands, "Release seatbelts and get out! Release seatbelts and get out!" and trying to get her seatbelt unbuckled. Shelly told me, "I can't get out. My legs are broken. I can't get out."
>
> [At that point, DeMary half carried, half dragged Markwith to safety].

I don't have a memory of little bits of what I did ... But I remember ending up by the tail section and it was very quiet. I didn't hear anybody, didn't see anybody. There was a break in the fuselage, and at that point, I thought, "Well, I have to do something!" and I started yelling my commands. I thought, "... If [people are] in shock, if they hear, 'Release seatbelts and get out!' it's going to give them the starting point!"

So I started yelling....as I'm walking, as I'm looking for somebody, looking...

I had really given up at one point ... I remember how hot it was, the fire was tremendously hot.

Then a woman appeared at that break with a baby. She was able to get out of her seatbelt and this was probably some time after the accident [before any rescue squads had arrived on the scene] ... It seemed like an eternity but she came toward my voice.

... She appeared at the small opening and I reached in and I grabbed the baby ... and grabbed her arm and pulled her ... I just grabbed [this woman with the baby] ...

There was a small shed in the backyard ... and I took them back there to safety.

[DeMary returned to the airplane and managed to pull another woman from the burning plane and to point rescuers toward the carport that the plane had hit where another passenger was trapped.]

So the fire and rescue trucks were arriving. [I] helped [the firefighters] pull out some hose [from a fire truck] and then was asked to get away. I was told ... "Your job's done. Just get away."[62]

Knowing that flight attendants are prepared to function at this level might change arrogant passengers' willingness to follow their instructions. Of course, it is not in the interests of the airlines to scare passengers who might already have some fear of flying by reminding them of their cabin crew's lifesaving skills. So airline advertising focuses on flight attendants' pampering functions, painting a picture of air travel so unrealistic that no cabin crew could ever approach that level of service. The image of a traveler snoozing in a cozy armchair while being plied with snacks by a charming flight attendant is a recipe for disappointment that provokes infantile expectations in passengers and puts impossible demands on

---

62 Richard DeMary (Interview), in "Sudden Impact—A Flight Attendant's Story of Courage and Survival," *Cabin Crew Safety*, March/April and May/June 1995, found at http://www.flightsafety.aero/ccs/ccs_mar_june95.pdf.

attendants, who must also fulfill management's demands that they sell duty-free items during the flight, while catering to the needs of passengers in all kinds of situations and fielding complaints from those whose needs aren't being met. As a result, the cabin crew often becomes the target of rage, even though they have very little control over most of what is angering the passenger.

A major step towards empowering flight attendants will be to redefine their role away from the server role and toward that of the staff in charge of the cabin. FAA Flight Attendant Certification, which was signed into law in the fall of 2003 to take effect in 2004, is intended to do that:

> The Federal Aviation Administration (FAA) currently requires that flight attendants be on board transport category aircraft (20 seats or more) to perform routine safety and security tasks, as well as to respond to safety emergencies and security threats. Flight attendant training and responsibilities include fire control, first aid, aircraft evacuation and other emergency procedures—making flight attendants the first line of defense for safety/security in the aircraft. Additionally, flight attendants are considered safety/security sensitive employees and thus must be drug/alcohol tested, are required by regulation to have rest limitations which stipulate duty time limits and mandatory rest periods, and are now subject to criminal background checks.
>
> In recognition of these responsibilities, in the fall of 2003, Congress incorporated a flight attendant certification requirement under the Vision 100-Century of Aviation Reauthorization Act. Although flight attendants perform safety- and security-related functions, they previously had never been certificated like pilots, mechanics, aircraft dispatchers, parachute riggers, and others.[63]

Hospitality won't suffer if flight attendants are given the respect they deserve as safety and security experts, and reinforcing the flight attendants' authority to make safety decision may help some status-conscious passengers to follow security instructions that they would ignore if they felt they were being ordered around by a waiter or waitress.

No Support for the Angry Flight Attendant: Is Anyone Listening?

Flight attendants are trapped between unhappy passengers and demanding employers. Because airlines don't welcome negative feedback and employees fear losing their jobs if they speak out, it is hard to know how angry flight attendants are. However, anonymous responses to the ASU survey on passenger rage testify

---

63   Association of Flight Attendants–CWA, Flight Attendant Certification, posted November 11, 2004, found at http://ashsd.afacwa.org/print_article.cfm?homeID=10814.

to the depth of staff frustration. When asked, "What else could be done at your airport to improve security?" flight attendants' answers included:

• "All we want is to be treated with respect at all times. This campaign is long overdue,"
• "[We want] more training for staff to handle conflict/rage situation and staff rights," and
• "Qantas couldn't give a rats arse about air rage. They care about making money!"[64]

Indeed, many flight attendants are exploding with anger, but they're expressing it in anonymous blogs. One wrote in 2007, "If you want a plane with air conditioning, PAY MORE! You want HAPPY FLIGHT ATTENDANTS—PAY MORE so that we can make a decent living. I've been in this industry for 7 years and [I] make $15,000 a year. So, if you want better service (be) willing to pay for it!"[65] This explicit statement reflects ongoing rage in an underpaid flight attendant that could well affect her everyday dealings with passengers.

These anonymous flight attendants' voices clearly outline the airline industry's failures. "Management hired and trained us and should therefore give us the ability to make decisions outside the box when it would be in the best interest of customer service," one said. "There needs to be better communication among all employees—from pilots to cleaners—and we should all be working as a team."[66]

Some of the most important questions about front line employee attitudes and performance have gone unasked. They include: Are airlines setting realistic work targets for flight attendants? Is the ratio of one flight attendant for every 50 passengers workable? Do flight attendants have an adequate infrastructure in place to give feedback on flight operations, or are their concerns and opinions largely ignored? Like airline passengers, flight attendants see the in-flight experience from their own perspective. Unfortunately the two groups have no agreed-upon standard of what they have a right to expect during a flight. A common understanding of how flight attendants should serve passengers and how passengers should relate to flight attendants could evolve from a customer service model designed to enhance their joint experience.

---

64   Australian Services Union National Office, "'Zero Air Rage' Survey, Preliminary Survey Results," October 20, 2003, found at http://www.aph.gov.au/house/committee/jpaa/aviation_security/submissions/sub62a.pdf.

65   Anonymous, blog comment about "Flight Attendants Advocate for Legislation and Join Coalition in Passenger Rights Fight!" *Coalition for Airlines Bill of Rights Hotline*, posted June 22, 2007, found at http://strandedpassengers.blogspot.com/2007/06/flight-attendants-advocate-for.html.

66   Bill McGee. "Readers Weigh in on Airline Passenger Rights," *USA Today*, March 27, 2007, p. 2, found at http://www.usatoday.com/travel/columnist/mcgee/2007-03-27-passenger-rights_N.htm.

The distance between the flight attendant and passenger at this point is apparent in an Amazon.com online review of flight attendant JoAnn Kuzma Deveny's book, *99 Ways to Make a Flight Attendant Fly Off the Handle*. According to reviewer J.K. Kelley, Deveny's advice can best be summed up this way:

1. Have no emotions except gratitude to your sainted flight attendants for choosing to serve you. Strive for your own form of sainthood, which amounts to never having needs or feelings except the foregoing.
2. You are not here to get from point A to point B. You are here to monitor your every action to improve the flight attendants' convenience. Now you know.
3. Flight attendants basically do not like you, so watch it, lest you receive the Dreaded Eye Roll and the Stony Ignore.[67]

When flight attendants write books about how much they dislike their job, and passengers respond by writing how much they hate flight attendants, it is time to make some major changes in the airline industry.

Obviously passenger problems are the front line employees' responsibility, but when working conditions are so bad the worker is angry before reaching the customer, the airline's customer service model isn't working. Even Kelley's Amazon.com review of *99 Ways* concluded that people shouldn't hate the flight attendant. "Focus your anger where it is deserved," she said, "[on] the airline industry executives and the immense bonuses they get, all because flight attendants and passengers are the ones jointly taking a hosing."[68]

Most "Bang for Your Buck": A Little Courtesy Goes a Long Way

In the airline industry, "stuff happens," and given the nature of the business, they are always going to happen. In the midst of the challenges, passengers depend on frontline staff not to add to the misery. "Airlines underestimate the power of simple courtesy," one passenger wrote.[69]

In a recent flight with AirTran, ticket agents were making jokes, handing out little freebie coupons and small flight discount certificates. This was a two-hour delay whereas 12-hour flight delays with Northwest and United have offered no

---

67   J.K. Kelley, "Review of JoAnn Kuzma Deveny's *99 Ways to Make a Flight Attendant Fly off the Handle* (2003)" *Amazon.com*, November 8, 2007, found at http://www.amazon.com/review/R3RSDAYGEEV6AE/ref=cm_cr_pr_viewpnt#R3RSDAYGEEV6AE.

68   Ibid., p. 2.

69   Diane (online identifier, St. Paul, MN), "Frustrations on a Plane," blog comment posted August 21, 2007, in response to "Peeved Passengers Want Answers from Airlines," summary by Kathleen Schalch for Blog of the Nation, *National Public Radio*, August 21, 2007, found at http://www.npr.org/templates/story/story.php?storyId=13831847.

niceties at all, but instead, curt, info-withholding agents who seem like they'd as soon hit you as look at you.[70]

On hearing airline employees grouse about passengers who wanted champagne service but didn't want to pay for it, one passenger said, "I didn't know that we had to pay for politeness from airline employees."[71] Airline top management can improve the infrastructure of the industry, and flight attendants and other crew members can recognize the power of these simple courtesies.

The airline industry's front line employees can make or break their company. They are the voices that communicate with customers, effectively or not. They can win customers over or alienate them forever. They can defuse a potential explosive anger incident or fan the fires of rage. Brower, Shannon, and Berger suggest that front line employees function as their airline's ambassadors and have a strong negative or positive impact on the customers' perceptions of the air travel experience.[72] Last century's customer service skills training model will not suffice for today's industry's challenges, these authors say. "Ensuring that employees are adequately prepared to fulfill their responsibilities," they say, "is a recurrent process that begins during the hiring phase and continues through the initial training, monitoring, and evaluation by management as well as in the ongoing provision of refresher training."[73] As airlines remodel staff training programs, they'll uncover the need to revisit their philosophical approach to management and the goals of their customer service policies.

Every airline passenger has some degree of relationship with the airline's front line employees. If passengers think they're dealing with waiters, waitresses, and clerks while airline employees know they're trained as safety engineers, health monitors, and trip administrators, it raises the potential for anger in the air. However, the staff can help defuse this tension if they are trained in a customer-centric or customer-oriented service model and focus their efforts on the customers' needs.

"Humanity Fatigue": As Dangerous as Metal Fatigue

One of the most insidious effects of the air rage phenomenon is its propensity to cause a kind of "humanity fatigue" that weakens the bonds between people as surely

---

70   Ibid.

71   Terry Moses, blog comment posted August 21, 2007, in response to "Peeved Passengers Want Answers from Airlines," summary by Kathleen Schalch for Blog of the Nation, *National Public Radio*, August 21, 2007, found at http://www.npr.org/templates/story/story.php?storyId=13831847.

72   Katherine Brower, Ellyn Shannon, and Karyl Berger, Permanent Citizens Advisory Committee to the MTA, "Best Foot Forward: Training Front Line Personnel to Provide Quality Customer Service," November 2003, found at http://pcac.org/reports/pdf/Best%20Foot%20ExecSumm.pdf.

73   Ibid.

as corrosion and rust weaken metal. When the normal human bonds of cordiality and cooperation disintegrate, just saying airline employees are "supposed" to fix it doesn't make them able to do it. Worse yet, their fatigue factor will be multiplied if management simply throws the problem back on them without giving them the training, equipment and backup to deal effectively with air rage situations.

Just as anger is contagious, so is professionalism. Properly motivated employees can offer service with a smile, perform miracles for the customer, and be proud to do so.

Airlines may think hiring "disposable" employees saves money, but the cost of poor quality work and constantly reinventing the wheel by training new staff and getting them up to speed is high in the long run. Safety must be the first priority of the airline industry, and employees who deal with abuse from the public and demands from management can become so stressed, or feel so abused, that their own exhaustion and/or rage will not allow them to concentrate sufficiently to do their jobs correctly.

At this point flight attendants and gate attendants have taken the full responsibility for connecting with passengers, and management at most airlines are reluctant to engage with either the flight attendants or the passengers on the issue of customer service. This highly questionable "see no evil" style of management has consequences; but whether or not those are addressed, the airline employees who actually interact with passengers are in dire need of backup from management. Front line staff members need emotional intelligence training in stress management to learn techniques for managing their own anger that they can use while helping passengers control their feelings of neglect, fear, anger, or disappointment.

Airline customer service needs to improve soon, because our ceiling for disenchantment has been reached. Understanding the psychology of anger can contribute to this reform and improvement process. When facing situations that might trigger anger, flight attendants can become skilled at implementing strategies for changing the way passengers perceive the situation. They can use calming voice tones, smiles, and body language that support the passengers' own efforts to cope. Agitated passengers can be persuaded to relax, once they believe that the flight attendant is working with them to solve the problem.

It's of paramount importance to retrain the frontline staff, giving them a customer-centric model that highlights the importance of the simple courtesies. A smile from a flight attendant can go a long way. Politeness means so much, and the non-verbal message speaks volumes. There really are times when "A soft answer turneth away wrath: but grievous words stir up anger."[74]

---

74   *Proverbs* 15:1, King James version.

Chapter 4

Passengers' Emotional Baggage: Addicted, Crazy or Just Plain Rude?

On a flight carrying 143 passengers to the Canary Islands from Germany in March 2000, an apparently intoxicated German man named Oliver-Jan Westphal broke into the cockpit, announced the plane was being attacked by terrorists, and began punching, kicking, and choking the 59-year-old pilot. He grabbed the controls and the plane started to dive before the co-pilot stabilized it. "Help, we need strong men, we need strong men!" the pilot announced. For the next 14 minutes he and the co-pilot grappled with the deranged man until four passengers broke down the door and helped wrestle him to the ground.[1]

****

When the pilot on a Ted flight to Denver announced that the plane from Phoenix would be delayed five minutes until one woman's oxygen tank arrived, most of the passengers were surprised to hear screams filling the cabin. It was an outraged traveler, hollering that he would miss his connection and asking why this woman was so important.[2]

****

On one 14-hour flight, two highly inebriated business-class passengers who had not known each other previously became romantically involved, kissing and fondling each other in their seats. Eventually their public passion built to sexual intercourse as unnerved passengers and flight attendants pleaded with them to stop. The airborne lovemaking continued until the captain physically separated

---

1   Paul Redfern (in London) and David Mugonyi (in Nairobi), "Air Drama Man Was a Student," *Daily Nation on the Web*, December 21, 2000, found in paragraph 31 of http://www.nationaudio.com/News/DailyNation/31122000/News/News72.html; and Elliott Neal Hester, "Cockpit Assault," *Salon.com*, April 8, 2000, found in paragraphs 3 and 4 of http://dir.salon.com/story/travel/diary/hest/2000/04/08/cockpits/.

2   Jane L. Levere, "Flying in a Snit," *New York Times*, January 2, 2006, found at http://www.nytimes.com/2006/01/24/business/24rude.html?_r=1&oref=slogin.

the two. After being arrested when the plane landed, the passengers, both of whom were married, said the liquor made them do it.[3]

****

As a flight from Sweden to Finland was taxiing to the runway, a British man leapt from his seat, screaming that he had to get off the plane. When the crew tried to calm him down he yelled obscenities, tried to break into the cockpit and then opened an emergency exit. That caused the inflatable exit slide to deploy, which would have caused a serious accident if the slide had been sucked into an engine. Luckily, the pilot was able to stop the plane while the cabin crew overpowered the man. Afterwards, the man said he had no memory of the event, and blood tests revealed traces of buphenorphine, a treatment for drug addicts, in his system.[4]

****

Destined to Blow

In the cases above, nothing the airlines had done had caused the passenger meltdowns. They were destined to behave badly no matter how well they were treated. Unless toxic cabin air had totally scrambled their brain chemistry, they'd brought their tendency to make a scene with them when they left home.

Though infuriating airline policies contribute to the growth in air rage, passengers' brain chemistry and learned attitudes—everything from bad manners and a sense of entitlement to alcoholism and "rage addiction"—can also trigger outbursts. When it comes to air rage, passengers bring their own mental problems, addictions, habits, and training to the party.

This chapter will examine the impact of alcoholism, drug addiction, nicotine withdrawal, mental illness, and plain bad manners on air rage. In Chapters 5 and 6, we'll look at how passengers' emotional problems contribute to air rage and examine the growing phenomenon of "rage addiction," including how rage is triggered, its effects on the body, and the history of rage. In Chapter 7 we'll outline potential solutions to the problem of air rage.

---

3   Elliott Neal Hester, "Bad Passenger, Bad!" *Salon.com,* April 13, 2008, found at http://www.salon.com/travel/diary/hest/1999/04/13/passenger/; and Anonymous and Andrew R. Thomas, *Air Rage: Crisis in the Skies,* (Amherst, NY: Prometheus Books, 2001), p. 51.

4   "28th June 2007—Arlanda, Sweden" incident cited in AD Aerospace, "Is FlightVu the Answer?" found at www.ad-aero.com/products_witness_news.php.

Change in Flying Population

In the past two decades, the values and attitudes of the general public have changed dramatically. Airline employees have had to deal with a flying population that is less polite and well-mannered than ever before, as well as specific subgroups of passengers—from drug addicts, alcoholics and desperate deportees to rageaholocs and the mentally ill—who can be accidents waiting to happen. After considering the various kinds of customers airline personnel are dealing with, we'll consider what can be done to prevent them from "losing it" in the air.

Brash New World: The Decline of Manners

Airline personnel agree that the general public has become less polite in the last few decades. "When I started in the business, flying was glamorous. It was a luxury," said Nancy Sargent, who had been a flight attendant for Delta Air Lines for 34 years. "Men wouldn't think of boarding a flight unless they were wearing a coat and tie. I can remember standing in the aisle carving a rib roast."

"Now all that has changed, and we are dealing with a very different group of passengers," she told the *New York Times*. "There's not the level of sophistication and understanding, so you have passengers getting on the plane, dropping their bag at your feet and saying, 'Find a place for this.'"[5]

In a Travelocity online survey of 1,000 members, two thirds said rudeness and disrespectful behavior were a serious problem in travel. The most likely cause, after the strain on tempers caused by long lines and crowds, was that "too many parents are failing to teach respect to their kids" and "values and morality are in decline in our society."

"We're a lot more comfortable in public than the society of the 50's," said Amy Ziff, Travelocity's editor at large in New York. "Along with that is a breaking down of certain boundaries."[6]

But there's such a thing as too comfortable. Many people interviewed at airports said they'd seen travelers cut into lines, talk loudly on cell phones, abruptly recline their seats into other people's laps and throw tantrums. At Hartsfield-Jackson Atlanta International Airport, an agent talked about passengers who insisted on dragging overnight bags aboard. "It's very common for people to flat-out refuse

---

5   Barry Estabrook, "A Paycheck Weekly, Insults Daily," *New York Times*, February 15, 2004, found at http://query.nytimes.com/gst/fullpage.html?res=9C0CE3D9173AF936 A25751C0A9629C8B63.

6   Laura Mansnerus, "Turbulent Manners Unsettle Flyers," *New York Times*, February 14, 2004, found at http://query.nytimes.com/gst/fullpage.html?res=9805E2D9173AF936A 25751C0A9629C8B63.

to check these rollers, as if making a big-enough scene will cause additional space to appear," he said.[7]

"As a society, our manners are simply getting worse," said Pam Terry, who has been a passenger service agent for US Airways at Reagan National Airport in Washington since 1992. "We don't have as many controls on our behavior as we used to. We don't think we have to respect authority." Though she'd never been physically assaulted, Terry told the *New York Times*, one passenger threw a cup of soda with ice cubes at her when she insisted he check his oversized bag, and another who arrived at the gate too late for his flight told her, "I hope you get cancer and die. Slowly." She'd also seen a passenger slam a gate agent's hand in a Jetway's heavy steel door. Throwing staplers, she said, is a particularly common way for unruly passengers to vent.[8]

"I don't know what gets into people's heads when they travel," another airline worker told the *Times*. "Could you even imagine someone swearing at or assaulting a department store clerk if they had run out of the right size pants? You'd say the customer was mentally unstable. But in airports, such behavior is almost viewed as normal."[9]

Passengers themselves admit to bouts of rudeness. In a study by a group called Public Agenda, while most passengers give travel personnel high marks for overall courtesy, 67 percent say that when they have a run-in with rude travel employees, they are likely to be rude in return. Respondents to the Public Agenda survey cited several causes for passengers' rudeness. Nearly 70 percent of workers said that a general decline in values and morals has led customers to be less polite and respectful.[10]

Cell phones users are prone to a special oblivious rudeness, as they force bystanders to become unwilling witnesses to their social lives. On a trip to Seattle, a New York executive named Jonathan Yarmis found a clever way to get revenge on an obnoxious caller after finding himself stuck in United's Red Carpet Club at LaGuardia Airport listening to a young man who was obviously on his first business trip and talking to "everyone he knew." After the man ignored passengers' repeated pleas that he quiet down or move somewhere else, Yarmis wrote down the talker's phone number (repeated at top volume during the calls). Then Yarmis called him at 2:00 a.m. in the morning.

"You must think it's pretty rude getting a phone call at 2 a.m.," he told the budding executive. "It's certainly less rude than the behavior you exhibited in the Red Carpet Club this afternoon."[11]

Bill Lareau, an Indianapolis-based consultant and author, attributes the epidemic of bad manners to more than just the stresses of the road. He thinks the

---

7   Ibid.
8   Estabrook, 2004.
9   Ibid.
10   Ibid.
11   Levere, 2006.

inexperience of young executives plays a big role too, because they "don't know how to behave when they travel and are not used to it."[12]

According to the *New York Times*, etiquette in the air took a turn for the worse after 9/11, "as travelers' frustrations over long lines and intrusive security checks boiled over, and it sank even further last year as planes grew as crowded as cattle cars."

"Before September 11, air travel was a reasonably good experience," Robert W. Coggin, a former executive vice president for marketing at Delta Air Lines, told the *Times* in 2006. Since then the percentage of occupied seats on most flights had skyrocketed, he said. "Five years ago, load factors in the '60's (percent of seats filled) were good, but today they're in the '80's," he said. At times during 2007, the average flight was 90 percent full.[13]

Workers in all forms of transportation say travelers are ruder. In a survey of 875 airline, bus, train, and highway employees late last year, the nonpartisan public opinion organization Public Agenda found that 54 percent of travel workers feel that passenger rudeness is a top cause of job-related stress and tension. Nearly half said they had seen a situation where disrespectful behavior threatened to escalate into a physical confrontation, and 19 percent said they had observed violent acts. "Rudeness can definitely ruin your day," said Terry, who is president of her local of the Communications Workers of America, which represents about 6,000 US Airways agents. "And it doesn't have to involve violence. When a passenger becomes vocal or menacing, you get gun shy knowing that there's a chance they might go over the edge. It causes me enormous stress even when they don't get physical."[14]

Influx of New, Less Sophisticated Flyers

Along with the general decline in manners in society, airline workers have been dealing with a large new, less sophisticated population of flyers who came on board as lower fares became available. Since tickets have gotten cheaper, author Andrew Thomas said, "air travel has brought all the elements of society closer to us. Unfortunately, some of those elements are not the best intentioned, brightest, or most considerate." These included many who used garbage bags as suitcases and shouted into the air vents trying to reach flight attendants, some who packed loaded guns, and one who, on being told to put her baby carrier in the overhead bin, did so—with the baby strapped in.[15]

"The lack of common courtesy and decency also are on the rise," Thomas said. "It's unnerving sometimes to witness the audacity of some passengers who feel the

---

12   Ibid.
13   Ibid.
14   Estabrook, 2004.
15   Anonymous and Thomas.

rules don't apply to them and are only in place as an inconvenience, violating their rights as Americans."[16] In general, passengers who engage in air rage share a "me first" mentality and a sense of entitlement. Some overtly ignore airline rules and many have a "looking for a fight" attitude.

The results can be disturbing or dangerous, especially when liquor is involved. After a flight attendant refused to serve the Denver Barbarians rugby club members more liquor on a flight home from a tournament in August of 2005, they became disruptive and urinated in the plane's galley and on the walls of the lavatory.[17]

In May 2007, six Scottish travelers went on a drunken rampage on a Thomas Cook flight from Glasgow to Spain, drinking vodka, smoking in the lavatories, swearing at the staff, sexually assaulting stewardesses, and biting one on the arm. On arriving in the Catalonian city of Reuson, they were arrested and released by Spanish police, then rearrested for "running amok" at their hotel, thrown out of the hotel, and barred from ever flying with Thomas Cook again. The travel firm asked British authorities to press charges against the men.[18]

After flight attendants on a flight from England to Tenerife refused to serve one "rude and aggressive" drunken passenger any more drinks, he found himself paying a steep price for refusing to calm down. The captain landed the plane on a tiny desert island off the coast of Africa called Porto Santo (population 4,500) and left the passenger to fend for himself. He was stuck walking the beach on the nine-kilometer long island for a few days, until he could book a seat on a German charter flight.[19]

The Arrogant Elite

The bad behavior of less sophisticated passengers is more than matched by that of travelers at the other end of the social scale—the rock stars, executives and socialites who are used to getting their way—now. First-class and business-class passengers can be especially aggressive and demanding, as they have a higher expectation of service.

"But I'm famous! I need to go on first!" *American Idol* judge Paula Abdul cried when she wasn't allowed to board her Southwest Airlines flight before anyone else. (Referring to an eccentric *American Idol* contestant, someone in the crowd yelled "You're no Sanjaya! You have to board like everyone else.") It was reported that

---

16   Ibid., p. 86.

17   "Barbarians Apologize," *ABC, Channel 7 in Denver* online, August 23, 2005, found at http://www.thedenverchannel.com/news/4885984/detail.html.

18   "Tourists Rampage on Holiday Plane," *BBC News,* May 23, 2007, found at http://news.bbc.co.uk/2/hi/uk_news/scotland/glasgow_and_west/6685197.stm.

19   Simon Freeman and Russell Jenkins, "Air-Rage Passenger Dumped on Paradise Island," *Times Online,* December 29, 2005, found at http://www.timesonline.co.uk/tol/news/uk/article783301.ece.

she ignored crew members' instructions, pushed her way past the other passengers to get on first, and then tried unsuccessfully to keep the seat next to her empty.[20]

In May 2007, a United Air Lines flight from Los Angeles to Florida was about to leave the gate when pop diva Britney Spears threw a temper tantrum, saying she couldn't stay on the plane because "it doesn't have leather seats." Furious passengers waited an hour as the walk-on tunnel was brought back, Spears' party deplaned, and their bags were found in the hold and taken off the plane.[21]

Flying First Class on a United Air Lines flight to New York City in 1997, upscale televangelist Robert Schuller, founder of the $20 million glass-walled "Crystal Cathedral" in Garden Grove, California, became upset when a steward wouldn't hang up his garment bag, didn't bring dessert fast enough, and brought him fruit and cheese when he'd only asked for fruit. Fuming, he strode back to the galley, grabbed the steward by the shoulders and shook him "violently," causing serious whiplash to his neck. Schuller eventually paid a $1,100 fine and underwent a six-month diversion program. "I am innocent," the mega-church minister told the press. "I have not broken a single one of the Ten Commandments. I have not broken any of the teachings of Jesus Christ."[22]

In addition to feeling entitled to special treatment, many upper-class passengers don't take kindly to being told what to do by people they consider beneath them socially. One flight attendant told the *New York Times* that rude passengers "sneer and say, 'You're nothing but a flight attendant, don't get uppity with me.'"[23]

Andrew Thomas agreed. "Now so many of the frequent fliers are business people who aren't used to being told what to do when asked to turn off their phones, computers or Blackberrys," he said. "They also aren't used to hearing the word 'no' when they ask for something."[24] In one case, a woman identified only as a "royal princess" went into a rage and attacked a crew member who told her to fasten her seat belt.[25]

---

20 "Today in the Sky" blog posted on April 19, 2007, *USA Today*, found at http://blogs.usatoday.com/sky/unruly_passengers/index.html.

21 "Britney Demands to Leave Plane Minutes Before Takeoff," *Celebitchy*, May 21, 2007, found at http://www.celebitchy.com/3935/britney_demands_to_leave_plane_minutes_before_takeoff/.

22 "Robert Schuller," Notable Names Database (NNDB), *Soylent Communications*, 2008, found at http://www.nndb.com/people/603/000022537/; and Dana Parsons, "Heresy! Pulling for Flight Attendant Over Rev. Schuller," *Los Angeles Times*, Orange County edition, July 4, 1994, found (and for sale) at http://pqasb.pqarchiver.com/latimes/access/12801059.html?dids=12801059:12801059&FMT=CITE&FMTS=CITE:FT&date=Jul+04%2C+1997&author=DANA+PARSONS&pub=Los+Angeles+Times&desc=Heresy!+Pulling+for+Flight+Attendant+Over+Rev.+Schuller&pqatl=google.

23 Estabrook, 2004.

24 Anonymous and Thomas.

25 H. Franken, "The Friendly Skies Falling Victim to 'Air Rage,'" *Central Ohio Source*, March 1999, found at http://centralohio.thesource.net/Franken/99/Mar11/tag.html.

Most people want respect and feel angry if they don't get it. The socially elite are used to getting what they want immediately. They see any refusal or slow service as a sign of disrespect, a failure to recognize their value. Their response to a "no" is often some variation on, "Do you know who I *am?*"

On the other hand, people at the lower end of the social scale may expect poorer treatment. For that reason, they might react to neutral treatment as though they were being disrespected or "dissed." The anger that results is some variation on, "You'd do it for Britney Spears, why not for me?" reflected in the defensive response, "my money's as good as anyone's!"

People also get angry because anger works—it can inspire people to do what you want.[26] And for some people, panic can turn to anger because it's more comfortable to feel angry and blame the anger on someone else, than to live with the fear.

Alcohol and Drug Users

After describing what may be the most legendary act of air rage, the defecation on a First Class beverage cart by a Connecticut investment banker, former flight attendant Hester asks:

> What makes people lose control in such a manner? Three things: alcohol, liquor and booze. In most high-profile cases of passenger misconduct, drunkenness lies at the root of the problem. So why not eliminate booze on all commercial flights? For one thing, the majority of passengers have a drink or two or three, and behave in a perfectly respectable manner. Besides, eliminating alcohol from the cabin would create a whole new category of misbehaving passengers: fearful flyers who rely on a vodka tonic to prevent them from screaming bloody murder during turbulence.[27]

"After a drink or two, most of us have been known to say a little bit more than is necessary," said Andrew Thomas. "We exaggerate ideas and movements, and we can get a little bit more irate. Some people become violent. [In an airplane] the violent ones are Molotov cocktails just waiting to explode."[28] That's especially true because the lower air pressure in the airplane cabin, Thomas says, "eases the process by which alcohol is absorbed into the bloodstream. It is, therefore, a lot easier to get more drunk, more quickly in the air than on the ground."[29] It's

26   "Anger: What Causes Anger?" *Yahoo Geocities*, 1997, found at http://www. geocities.com/Athens/Acropolis/6729/anger2.htm.

27   Elliott Hester, *Plane Insanity: A Flight Attendant's Tales of Sex, Rage, and Queasiness* (New York, NY: MacMillan, 2003), p. 58.

28   Anonymous and Thomas, p. 43.

29   Ibid., p. 48.

generally agreed that one drink in the air is as potent as two on the ground. Alcohol also keeps cells from using oxygen effectively, an effect called cytotoxic hypoxia, which is why drinking one ounce of alcohol has the same effect on the body as adding an additional 2,000 feet of altitude.[30]

During a flight, many passengers are stuck in an uncomfortable space with little or no food as they grapple with stress and fear of flying. They have all they want to drink, nothing to do but drink, and each drink hits them twice as hard. Under these conditions, some passengers are guaranteed to get drunker than they normally would.

No surprise then that most air rage stories start, "When a flight attendant refused to serve him more liquor. ..." At least 40 percent of all air rage incidents are the result of a passenger getting drunk.

A passenger flying from Glasgow to Cyprus may have been blindsided by the high altitude effect when he staged a "Full Monty" for his fellow-passengers. The incident started when flight attendants noticed him downing vodka from a bottle. Easing the bottle out of his hands, they guided him to an area of the plane where the seats were empty to sleep it off. Later, he returned to his original seat, began taking off his wet T-shirt, and suddenly stripped off his pants and boxer shorts too, exposing himself to children nearby. He later told a judge he was disgusted with himself, but couldn't remember any part of the incident because he'd been too drunk.[31]

Of course, some fliers are alcoholics struggling with their own demons that happen to break loose on a plane. This could have been the case with Paul Randall Burns, who began drinking vodka in the Oslo airport before boarding his plane to Newark, New Jersey. When a flight attendant refused to serve him more drinks midway through the flight, he began hitting two other passengers, whereupon six passengers helped the plane crew handcuff him to his seat. The plane made an emergency landing in Labrador and Burns continued trying to deck the Canadian Mounties who dragged him from the plane. Somewhat poignantly, it was reported that he hadn't had a drink for years before the incident. Lacking the $12,000 to pay the fine, he remained in the Labrador jail. Continental Airlines was considering suing him for an additional $13,000 in restitution.[32]

An unruly self-described alcoholic was kicked off a flight from Orlando, Florida, to Washington, D.C., after he lit up a cigarette, was told to put it out, and expressed his displeasure by urinating in the aisle. In court, he said he was a homeless lawyer scheduled to check into a rehabilitation center the week of his arrest. Though licensed to practice law in Illinois, he said he was down to his last

---

30   Joe Pilot (online identifier), "How Does Alcohol and Smoking Contribute to Hypoxia for Pilots Flying Aircraft?" *Yahoo Answers*, found at http://answers.yahoo.com/question/index?qid=20070720230014AAGxaB1.

31   Anonymous and Thomas, pp. 51–52.

32   "Airplane Rage Costs Fla. Man $12,000," *CBC News*, March 28, 2007, found at http://www.cbc.ca/canada/newfoundland-labrador/story/2007/03/28/airplane-rage.html.

$85. Charged with creating a disturbance and interfering with a flight crew, he faced a potential sentence of five years in jail and a $250,000 fine. People this far gone are probably not going to be persuaded into good behavior by cheerful flight attendants.[33]

Acting on Impulse: Lowered Impulse Control

Both air rage and heavy alcohol consumption are associated with lack of impulse control, and this inability to control one's impulses may well be triggered by changes in brain chemistry. Some are prone to hair-trigger rage because early emotional or physical traumas have "rewired" their brains to be overly sensitive to stress. As a result, they often see the most neutral events as threats that send them into "fight-or-flight" mode, upping the odds that they'll act on aggressive impulses. When this tendency towards aggression is coupled with alcohol or substance abuse, air rage may well result.[34]

Substances that change neurological activity—including psychotropic medications, alcohol, and illegal drugs—can heighten the reaction to stress and remove inhibitions that ordinarily prevent people from acting aggressive. If someone is using, overusing, or withdrawing from these substances, their behavior may be far from normal.[35] The majority of air rage incidents are, in fact, associated with the use of mind-altering substances, particularly alcohol.[36]

If the passenger is also dealing with low air pressure, toxic cabin air and fear of flying, bad service can easily become the final spark that causes this brain-chemistry time bomb to explode. While exceptionally good service might just keep addled and agitated drinkers who are already teetering on the edge of anger from tipping over to rage—bad service can't be said to have caused any rage they exhibit.

Got a Light? Nicotine Withdrawal

Heavy smokers—especially those used to smoking several cigarettes an hour—find themselves in serious withdrawal during long flights. Since they've also been

---

33   "Unruly Passenger: 'I'm Homeless,'" *USAToday.com*, November 28, 2005, found at http://blogs.usatoday.com/sky/unruly_passengers/index.html.

34   S.L. McElroy, Recognition and Treatment of DSM-IV Intermittent Explosive Disorder, paper presented at the Closed Symposium Phenomenology and Treatment of Aggression Across Psychiatric Illnesses held in Chicago, Illinois, August 1998, found at http://www.grandrounds.com/supplenet/v60s15.htm.

35   Ibid.

36   Statement of Captain Stephen Luckey, Chairman, National Security Committee, Air Line Pilots Association, Before the Subcommittee on Aviation, Committee on Transportation and Infrastructure, U.S. House of Representatives, Passenger Interference with Flight Crews and the Carry-on Baggage Reduction Act of 1997, June 11, 1998, found at http://www.worldnetdaily.com/news/article.asp?ARTICLE_ID=28474.

forbidden to light up during their long wait in the airport, they may be in nicotine withdrawal before they even reach the plane.

The nicotine in cigarettes is a mind-altering drug that soothes and pacifies its users. While it's a boon to fly without secondhand smoke, the smoking ban creates a subset of passengers who are abruptly, unwillingly, and without help, being thrown into a detox situation at 30,000 feet, when their brain chemistry may already be scrambled and their head already aching from the lack of oxygen, high altitude, and bad cabin air.

In addition, said Clive Phillips, a member of an Australian airline cabin safety working group, smoking restrictions can lead to even more alcohol consumption. "Smoking is a particular factor on long-haul flights where you have people who normally smoke several cigarettes an hour," he said. When they can't do that, "they substitute by drinking more alcohol and you end up with a twin problem: people suffering from cigarette withdrawal and too much alcohol."[37]

The resulting meltdown can be ugly. On a packed flight from Antalya, Turkey, to Newcastle, England, 53-year-old Stephen Robinson was already drunk and angry about not being able to buy more liquor. When he ignored all the no smoking signs and lit up a cigarette, air steward Philip Miles told him to put it out. Clambering over seats and passengers, the enraged Robinson launched himself at the steward, punching him in the face and damaging eight teeth. Cabin crew and passengers held him down and handcuffed him while the pilot diverted the flight to Frankfurt, Germany. "I have never witnessed any behaviour like this before when I have flown," one passenger said, while another reported, "An elderly lady was visibly upset and trembling, with tears in her eyes." At a hearing the judge said, "He is the sort of person I think should never go on an aircraft again." Later he sentenced Robinson to 12 months in jail, saying, "You terrified the people who were about you."[38]

Even smokers who do not self-medicate with alcohol may find themselves more likely to be affected by hypoxia, which means lack of oxygen, than their fellow passengers, because the carbon monoxide in tobacco smoke has diminished their blood's ability to carry oxygen. As one pilot explained it, the carbon monoxide "sticks to hemoglobin much easier than oxygen. This reduces the hemoglobin available for transporting oxygen to the brain causing Hypemic Hypoxia—which is the inability of blood to carry oxygen."[39]

The resulting lack of oxygen can cause headache, irritability, nausea, muscle weakness, fatigue, blurred vision, and shallow breathing. Adding hypoxia to the symptoms of nicotine withdrawal can leave a cigarette-deprived smoker at high

---

37   Ibid.

38   "Air Rage Passenger Faces Prison," *BBC News*, September 5, 2007, found at http://news.bbc.co.uk/2/hi/uk_news/england/6980172.stm; and "Jet Passenger Jailed Over Air Rage," *Sky News*, September 28, 2007, found at http://news.sky.com/skynews/article/0,,70131-1286214,00.html?f=rss.

39   Joe Pilot.

altitudes ready to explode.[40] Not surprising, then, a 2006 Civil Aviation Authority study describes the average passenger in an air rage incident as "a thirty something male who is furious about not being allowed to smoke."[41]

As a result, though they're usually less dramatic than alcohol- and drug-fueled incidents, the largest number of reports of air rage to the Aviation Safety Reporting System (ASRS) are related to alcohol abuse and smoking. According to Ben van Ernich, a cabin management instructor at the KLM Wings Academy in The Netherlands, a training subsidiary of KLM Royal Dutch Airlines (KLM), about 1,400 reports of smoking in the lavatory are filed annually. "The real number is probably ten times higher," van Ernich said, at the 19th Annual International Aircraft Cabin Safety Symposium in Los Angeles in March of 2002.[42]

Illegal Drug Use

About 90 minutes into an America West flight from Las Vegas to Florida, a sleeping passenger woke up with a start, turned to the passenger next to him, raised a clenched fist to his shoulder as if he were about to hit him, then swiveled and punched out the interior pane of the plane's window. Ryan J. Marchione, 24, shattered the inner plastic shield covering the glass window and disconnected its frame, but the plane did not depressurize because the outer window was not damaged. The best excuse his lawyer could come up with for the outburst was that Marchione might have had a psychotic episode caused by drug abuse. He faced up to 20 years in prison.[43]

This burst of air rage was clearly unrelated to airline service or policies, unless the impact of drugs was exacerbated by low cabin air pressure, hypoxia, and toxic chemicals in recycled cabin air having a synergistic effect on the illegal drugs in the passenger's system. But whether they're mixed with bad cabin air or not, drugs create a problem that flight attendants can't predict, they can only hope to manage.

Flight attendants are also called on to cope with the fallout from illegal drug trafficking. After a flight from Vietnam to Australia had been airborne for an hour, it was forced to turn back after a male passenger became ill and vomited up a bag of white powder suspected to be heroin. On landing at Tan Son Nhat Airport, the

---

40   Ibid.

41   Catherine Reiley, "Air Rage? Try This Nicotine Gel, Sir," *Times Online*, November 11, 2006, found at http://travel.timesonline.co.uk/tol/life_and_style/travel/news/article1086958.ece.

42   "Training Can Reduce and Defuse Disruptive Passenger Incidents," *Air Safety Week,* March 11, 2002, found at http://findarticles.com/p/articles/mi_m0UBT/is_10_16/ai_83681236.

43   Associated Press, "Florida Man Charged with Punching Out Airplane Window in Flight," *USA Today,* October 14, 2005, found at http://www.usatoday.com/travel/news/2005-10-14-window-punch_x.htm.

man produced two more bags of powder and, according to reports, he had 30 more in his stomach. Several Australians have been arrested in Vietnam in recent years for drug trafficking, and at least four were sentenced to death.[44]

Mental Illness

In Australia in 2004, a man suffering from paranoid schizophrenia thought he was on a mission from God to crash the plane into the walls of Jerusalem National Park and rid the world of the devil. To that end tried to hijack a plane flying from Melbourne to Launceston with wooden stakes and aerosol cans. He was found not guilty of attempted hijacking, attempted murder, and intentionally causing grievous bodily harm, because of mental impairment.[45]

As a Continental Airlines plane sat on the ground in Ft Lauderdale, 28-year-old Troy Rigby began complaining loudly that he was claustrophobic and had to get off the plane. As the flight finally taxied towards the runway, he fought with crew members and passengers, bit a man, jumped out of the moving plane, and started running towards the terminal, at which point police brought him down by shooting him four times with a Taser. Rigby's sister said her brother was schizophrenic and had recently stopped taking his medication. "He called our mother yesterday and said he was going to commit suicide," she told the *New York Daily News*, adding that their uncle put Rigby on the plane against her wishes. "I told him he needed psychiatric care first." Rigby had a heart attack shortly after being taken to jail and died two weeks later.[46]

Aerotoxic Syndrome Increases Risk

According to Dr Sarah Myhill, an expert on "aerotoxic syndrome," chemicals leaking into airline air can also cause violent mood swings, including tearfulness, irritability, aggression, impulsive suicidal thoughts, and rage. Combined with the effects of oxygen deprivation at high altitudes, aerotoxic syndrome may well be triggering temporary mental breakdowns and bizarre behavior on planes.[47]

---

44   "7th May 2007—Ho Chi Minh City, Vietnam," incident cited in AD Aerospace.

45   "Hijacker Wanted to Crash Plane," *Fairfax Digital*, July 12, 2004, found at http://www.smh.com.au/articles/2004/07/12/1089484298190.html?oneclick=true.

46   "Man Bites Passenger, Jumps from Moving Jetliner onto Tarmac," *USA Today*, January 24, 2006, found at http://blogs.usatoday.com/sky/unruly_passengers/index.html; "Man Who Jumped Aircraft in Fort Lauderdale Suffers Heart Attack," *Airline Industry Information*, January 30, 2006, found at http://www.allbusiness.com/operations/shipping-air-freight/859245-1.html; and Dave Reynolds, "No Clear Answers Yet on Inmate's Death," *Inclusion Daily Express*, June 26, 2006, found at http://www.inclusiondaily.com/archives/06/06/26/062606flrigby.htm.

47   Sarah Myhill, "Aerotoxic Syndrome: The Poisoning of Airline Pilots, Cabin Crew, and Passengers that Is Possible in Any Air Flight," found at http://www.aerotoxic.org (in

Many cases seem to confirm this theory. On one flight from Dubai, United Arab Emirates, to Chennai, India, a man named Pannatta Mesuwan stripped to his underwear and started to dance around the cabin. When asked to sit down and behave, he took his underwear off and continued dancing. Flight attendants and passengers overpowered him and threw clothes over him. When he was arrested, he said he had no memory of the incident.[48]

In 1998, Dr S.L. McElroy said that physical problems could also trigger an air rage episode. According to Dr McElroy, an individual suffering from Alzheimer's disease, closed-head trauma, post-stroke disorders, or pancreatic disorders like diabetes that affect glucose levels, would have a greater reaction to stress, and could be unable to control their impulses.[49] In one case, on Alaska Airlines Flight 259 in 2000, a passenger named Peter Bradley threatened passengers, attacked a flight attendant with a knife, and tried to take over the plane from the pilot before passengers finally tackled him. Later it was learned that Mr. Bradley had encephalitis, which caused delirium.[50]

As war continues in the Middle East, airline personnel may be dealing with more veterans suffering from post-traumatic stress syndrome. In July of 2006, an Iraq war veteran on a Delta flight from New York City to Tampa, Florida, became agitated shortly before the plane was due to land, refusing to sit down. Suddenly he ran towards the cockpit door and tried twice to knock it down and break into the cockpit. Three passengers were able to subdue him until the flight landed. He was later identified as a 24-year-old soldier with "mental problems" whose active duty was about to end the following week.[51]

Finally, well-known, well-researched mental illnesses can cause the most dangerous mid-air situations of all.

Paging Dr. Jekyll

Instantly the spirit of hell awoke in me and raged.

—Robert Louis Stevenson

This is how Robert Louis Stevenson describes the transformation of the brilliant, mild-mannered scientist Dr Henry Jekyll into the debauched and murderous Mr Edward Hyde in his famous novel, *Dr. Jekyll and Mr. Hyde*. The title has become shorthand used to describe the wildly differing behavior of people suffering mental

---

right margin, click on "Dr Sarah Myhill's briefing sheet") or http://www.aerotoxic.org/articles/20071118_3.

48   "June 21st 2007—Chennai, India" incident cited in AD Aerospace.

49   Blake Morrison, "FAA Seldom Punished Violence," *USA Today*, December 5, 2001, found at http://www.usatoday.com/news/sept11/2001/12/05/air-violence.htm.

50   Elliott Neal Hester, "*Cockpit Assault*"; and Morrison.

51   "Passenger Detained After Trying to Break into Delta Cockpit," *USA Today*, July 7, 2006, found at http://blogs.usatoday.com/sky/unruly_passengers/index.html.

conditions from bipolar disorder (manic depression) to the highly controversial Dissociative Identity Disorder (originally named Multiple Personality Disorder). In such people, a sudden explosion of violent behavior can seem to come out of the blue, wrote Dr Kay Redfield Jamison, as if a different person had suddenly surfaced:

> Manic-depression distorts moods and thoughts, incites dreadful behaviors, destroys the basis of rational thought, and too often erodes the desire and will to live. It is an illness that is biological in its origins, yet one that feels psychological in the experience of it; an illness that is unique in conferring advantage and pleasure, yet one that brings in its wake almost unendurable suffering and, not infrequently, suicide.[52]

Indeed, mental illness of one sort or another is implicated in many cases of road rage or air rage. Very few flight attendants are trained to handle passengers who are this seriously mentally ill. As shown in Chapter 3, even flight attendant Renee Sheffer, a former psychiatric nurse, wasn't able to talk down football player Dean Trammel when he had his LSD-induced psychotic break in 1997. She ended up with internal bleeding, kidney and bladder trauma, spinal damage, a separated shoulder, and a torn meniscus in her right knee, after which she underwent three operations and was unable to work for two years. And the crew on the famous "8/11" Southwest Airlines flight was even less well equipped to deal with the seemingly deranged Jonathan Burton when he tried to break into the cockpit—an episode that ended with Burton dead at the passengers' hands.

Fear of Flying

Another cause of air rage that passengers bring to the airport with them is fear of flying. At an Aircraft Cabin Safety Symposium in 2002, Angela Dahlberg said, "We know from research that approximately 50–60 percent of passengers suffer some form of fear of flying, with 30–40 percent of these suffering additional phobia. The majority of this group tends to use alcohol and drugs to cope with their condition." Add to this, "the general frustration with airport generated stress," she said, and it's clear that flight attendants are asked to deal with, "an emotionally volatile group of strangers who would rather be elsewhere."[53]

In his statement to the United States congress on air rage, Captain Luckey told the United States congress that fear of flying plays a role in many flight rage incidents, and, like nicotine withdrawal, it can drive fliers to drink too much. Quoting Dr Gerald Post, who'd treated many patients for aerophobia, Luckey said

---

52   Kay Redfield Jamison, *An Unquiet Mind* (New York, NY: Alfred A. Knopf, div. of Random House, Inc., 1995), p. 6.
53   "Training Can Reduce and Defuse."

the "underlying dynamic in this phobia is a loss of control or a fear of such a loss." As a result, he said, "Entering a large, flying aluminum tube and placing one's destiny totally in the hands of others can be extremely anxiety-provoking for these individuals and result in disruptive behavior."[54]

Some components of fear of flying are common to all phobias, while others are unique to fear of flying. When they fly, passengers feel a loss of control under the best of circumstances, and adding intrusive security checks to that experience puts nervous flyers on edge before they board the plane. Pile on the increased chance that their flight will be delayed or cancelled and the lurking fear of terrorism, and even the calmest flyer can become a little anxious, while those who are already scared may progress from fear to panic.

The fear of flying is a fear of many things, not all of which are specific to flight itself. These include:

- Loss of control;
- Heights;
- Enclosed spaces;
- Crowded conditions;
- Turbulence;
- Terrorism;
- Dependence on unknown machines for safety;
- Dependence on an unknown pilot's judgment;
- Sitting in hot, stale air;
- Being required to wait passively;
- Strange actions, sounds, and sensations.

People who suffer fear of flying or aerophobia report both physical and psychological symptoms. The physical reactions to fear include all the manifestations of the fight or flight response: muscle tension and tremors, heavy, labored breathing, heart palpitations, chest pain, abdominal and intestinal discomfort, sweating, weakness, dizziness, prickly sensations, dry mouth, and flushed or pale face.

The psychological symptoms of fear of flying include impaired memory, narrowed perceptions, poor or clouded judgment, negative expectations, and perseveration, which is obsessive, repetitive thinking, often about potential disasters.[55] Flight attendants trying to reason with panicky flyers whose judgment is clouded and perceptions are narrowed have their work cut out for them.

Of course there's little benefit to worrying about the things we can't control— especially since research has shown that panicking over nothing triggers the same destructive stress hormones that would flow if we were in real danger. But telling

---

54   Statement of Captain Stephen Luckey.
55   Lloyd Richmond, "Fear of Flying," *A Guide to Psychology and its Practice* (n.d.), found at http://www.guidetopsychology.com/fearfly.htm.

that to a fearful flyer just gives them one more thing to fret about—the damage worry is doing to their bodies.

Unfortunately, terrified people still have to fly—and the measures they take to get through the ordeal don't make them model passengers. One French woman tried valiantly to cope with her panic, but the results were only marginally successful. Before her flight from Hong Kong to Brisbane in 2005, she drank alcohol and took sleeping tablets to drown her fear of flying. Then midway through the flight, she got up and tried to open an airplane door so that she could step outside for a smoke.[56]

Fear of flying has been exacerbated by the 9/11 attacks. "Whether or not they have reason to be, many people are more spooked than ever by flying, and more prone to respond overtly when further agitated," said pilot Patrick Smith.[57] Angela Dahlberg, author of the book *Air Rage*, agreed, saying that this stress was also taking a toll on crew members. "The stress levels of passengers and crews are higher now," she said. "Triggered by the terrorist attacks, [cabin and cockpit flight crew] response to passenger misconduct induced by heightened stress and perceived service failure has already resulted in over reaction and vigilante-type measures."

"The threat of uncalled-for passenger involvement is real and needs to be controlled," Dahlberg said. "It's very important for everybody to keep a cool, calm head."[58]

Bad Day

Some cases of air rage start long before passengers come to the airport, as they react unhappily to a very bad day. It's doubtful that better customer service would have kept James Joseph Egan from getting drunk on his flight home to Phoenix, Arizona from his mother's funeral in Pittsburgh, or from threatening to beat up the crew and claiming he had a gun in his carry-on bag when they cut off his drinks. His day got worse when his flight landed in Amarillo, Texas and he was removed from the plane.[59]

A father traveling with his wife and children flew into a rage and threatened the flight crew and passengers when a flight attendant refused to serve him more drinks. Later, he said the stress of attending a funeral that day and the antidepressant

---

56   "November 21, 2005—Australia" incident cited in AD Aerospace.

57   Patrick Smith, "Ask the Pilot," *Salon.com*, May 28, 2004, found at http://dir.salon.com/story/tech/col/smith/2004/05/28/askthepilot88/.

58   *"Training Can Reduce and Defuse Disruptive Passenger Incidents."*

59   Associated Press, "Man Accused of Belligerent Behavior on Flight," *Dallas Morning News*, March 15, 2007, found at http://www.dallasnews.com/sharedcontent/dws/dn/latestnews/stories/031607dntexflightdisrupt.164f40b0.html.

he'd taken just before getting on the plane had combined with the alcohol to make him irrational.[60]

Culture Clash

Air rage is happening around the world. It's inevitable that when crowding, fear, or a general tendency towards anger meets bad service, poor air, and alcohol, someone's brain chemistry will produce an explosion. But on many flights, there's one more stressor as passengers from many cultures unwillingly become one enforced community for hours on end.

Air rage can reflect the clash of cultures meeting at jet speed in mid air. People used to live in close proximity with the same group of neighbors their whole lives, and while there might be stresses and feuds, these disputes were localized and limited. The wide range of air travel means a diverse mix of people will find their way onto modern commercial air flights to be jammed close to total strangers and held at the mercy of the airline employees, with no control over their situation for hours at a time. While some cultures might deal with the frustration better than others, this is a new kind of stress, and humanity is developing new ways to cope with these new experiences.

Sensitivity vs. Profiling

Cultural expectations may affect a person's tendency to air rage. A member of an extremely expressive culture may react violently and aggressively to frustration, while someone from a more stoic background calmly accepts or diffuses a potentially explosive situation. Why is this so? The questions of culture and demographics involved in this question are sensitive in the post 9/11 environment. At what point does an assessment of the possible cultural basis of aggressive behavior—for instance, the reaction of a man from a society where women are subservient to being told to do something by a female authority figure—turn from an objective inquiry into "profiling"? It is suspected that profiling is one of the essential tools used by many airlines today for security purposes. However, the airlines should use caution before relying too heavily on profiling, lest they be charged with discrimination under the 1964 Civil Rights Act.[61]

Aggression in Different Cultures

In *A Violent Heart: Understanding Aggressive Individuals*, author Gregory Moffatt remarks on the difference between cultures like those in Asia that value the group first, and those Western cultures that value the individual first. His classic

---

60   Anonymous and Thomas, pp. 85–88.
61   For example, United States v. Sokolow (1989).

comparison is between a Japanese man and an American man losing their jobs. The Japanese man, he says, internalizes the blame, finding the event so shameful he might, at the worst extreme, commit suicide. In the United States, where intense individualism is the norm, the man would externalize blame, tending to blame his former employer, even nursing fantasies of revenge. In the most extreme case, he might buy a gun and head back to work intending to kill his boss and anyone else he blamed for his dismissal.[62]

In discussing road rage, Moffatt says different cultural expectations about rules of the road mean people drive differently in different countries:

> While in Mexico recently, I noticed that traffic signs were largely ignored. Lane markings, speed limits, stop signs, one-way streets, and so forth were routinely ignored. The cultural expectation there appeared to be that the largest vehicle made the rules. When one has become accustomed to driving in one culture (for example, Mexico) and then transitions to the United States, problems are bound to occur.[63]

Cultural differences can mean that even simple disagreements about the appropriate amount of physical space one needs or the degree to which one will recline an airline seat can be fraught with tension. The more people who are on the road or in the air, the wider the range of coping skills, ways of handling conflict and claiming territory, even when the perceived "territory" is a car length on the freeway or a few inches of airplane seat space in coach.

Styles of Expressing Conflict in Different Social Groups

Moffatt says people from different backgrounds, affected by different educational, economic, and environment factors have very different attitudes towards aggression and fighting:

> When I was an undergraduate student I worked for a painting contractor. Our company held contracts with several coal mines in eastern Virginia. Coal miners, construction workers, painters, truck drivers, and all sorts of other workers crossed paths at these sites every day. Conflict was part of our existence. It was not unusual for a man to threaten another man or even to engage in a brawl. . To hear someone say, "I'll beat you to a pulp" to another worker was not unusual. Since we accepted aggression as a part of the world in which we lived, it would have been difficult to distinguish between the individual who would never do anything more than tussle with another worker and the one who had the potential to kill.

---

62 Gregory, A. Moffat, A., *Violent Heart: Understanding Aggressive Individuals* (Westport, CT: Praeger Trade, 2002), p. 22.
63 Ibid, p. 153.

For the past twenty years I have worked in a white-collar profession, a quite different environment. Nearly everyone I work with in all of my interactions is an educated professional. Not once in all of those years have I heard one of my colleagues threaten another. . Those of us in the college arena have the potential to threaten one another and even the potential to act on our aggressive words, just like those on a construction site or a at a coal mine. Yet how long do you think I would keep my job as a professor if I threatened my students, my colleagues, or my bosses? In the blue-collar trades I was a part of, such behavior was not seen as unusual as long as it did not go "too far." As long as one got his work accomplished, it was part of the accepted lifestyle. Therefore the same behavior in one environment is accepted while in another environment it is totally unacceptable.[64]

If individuals from each of Moffatt's former places of employment were forced into very close quarters in the high stress environment of an airliner, they might well react differently to the stress. On the positive side, says Andrew Thomas, because airline travel and service are similar around the world, "the problems confronted during the air travel experience are generally the same worldwide. And because of this reality, we are able to identify a commonality in the kinds of air rage incidents that take place. Further, we can offer informed explanations as to the reasons why" air rage happens. "This ability," he says, makes it possible "to create and implement common solutions."[65]

Unfortunately, violence today has infiltrated the fabric of society. No one is immune from random acts of violence; no safe havens exist. Whether one travels by air, car, bus, or train, individuals can encounter some form of violence, as a victim or, due to one's stress, as a perpetrator. One's own civil and non-confrontational behavior will not necessarily serve as protection.

When the source of air rage lies in the traveler rather than in the experience they're having, airline personnel have three options: Learn the skills needed to identify problem passengers and keep them off the plane; learn the skills needed to negotiate with or soothe mentally ill, enraged or phobic passengers; and get the equipment and training needed to subdue and if necessary restrain the rest. It is hoped that some passengers who might now wrongly appear to be rageaholics or alcoholics or mental patients wouldn't become enraged if the cabin air were healthy and flying conditions were right. The job of airlines is to put the optimal conditions in place to minimize the triggers and incidence of air rage.

The Numbers Game

To some extent the problem of air rage, like that of road rage, may be the unavoidable result of having such large numbers of people flying. A small

---

64   Ibid, p. 3.
65   Anonymous and Thomas, pp. 26–27.

percentage of difficult, demanding people who would normally be diluted in a great mass of humanity have instead been pressured into crowded situations that will stress their already minimal coping skills to the maximum. Based on his 16 years of service dealing with fliers, veteran air steward Hester says:

> Having dealt with these problems for nearly two decades, having ducked punches and calmed nerves and gazed sullenly as yet another passenger whipped out his willy and peed in front of startled frequent flyers, I've come to the conclusion that at least 2 percent of the traveling public is certifiably insane (the percentage is slightly higher for airline crew). With approximately 650 million people traveling annually on U.S. airlines and more than one hundred thousand flight attendants to serve them, many of us at one time or another, will be caught in the grip of plane insanity.[66]

In his droll fashion, Hester reinforces the point that the sheer volume of air traffic increases the odds of encountering people with problems. They are out there, and you may have to sit next to them.

---

66   Elliott Hester, *Plane Insanity*, Introduction.

Chapter 5
Passenger Baggage: Rage Addiction

Hearing a burst of loud swearing, ticket agents working at a US Airways gate at the Charlotte, N.C. airport looked up and saw brawny, red-faced passenger blasting through the concourse spewing every kind of profanity. Without breaking stride, he swung his bags in an arc, using them to knock over a trash bin and strew its contents across the floor, yelling, "You people need to pick up the [expletive] garbage around here." When an agent started to call security, the passenger, William Edwins, took a swing at him, missed, and then slammed him into the podium, bruising two of his ribs. Charges against Edwins were dismissed on the on the condition that he do community service and undergo anger management training.[1]

The "Age of Rage"?

Like the passengers in the previous chapter, William Edwins brought his anger to the airport with him, and no amount of good service was likely to defuse his rage. But unlike those who are rude, addicted, or mentally ill, Edwins showed signs of another problem that is increasing in Western society—rage addiction.

In the twenty-first century, rage in various forms appears with regularity like a haze of emotional pollution that can show up anywhere. Some observers say air rage is growing simply because we live in angry times. According to Leon James, PhD, co-author of *Road Rage and Aggressive Driving: Steering Clear of Highway Warfare*, we are living in "The Age of Rage."[2] In an article in James and Nahl's website, drdriving.org, James says the growing air rage problem is the product of the simple equation: "More of the 'me' generation times the millions of travelers equals explosive situations."[3]

But many observers see an additional reason for the rising tide of anger—a psychological syndrome called rage disorder, also known as Intermittent Explosive Disorder (IED). A study funded by the National Institute of Mental Health (NIMH)

---

1   Barry Estabrook, "A Paycheck Weekly, Insults Daily," *New York Times*, February 15, 2004, found at http://query.nytimes.com/gst/fullpage.html?res=9C0CE3D9173AF936 A25751C0A9629C8B63.

2   Leon James and Diane Nahl, *Road Rage and Aggressive Driving: Steering Clear of Highway Warfare* (Amherst, NY: Prometheus Books, 2000).

3   Annette Santiago, "Air Rage," *AviationNow.com*, August 10, 2001, found at http://www.drdriving.org/rages/.

in the United States found that rage disorder may affect up to 7.3 percent, or 16 million Americans, at some point during their lifetimes. The report finds that Intermittent Explosive Disorder includes "moments of unexpected anger in which the person may attack other people [and] other people's belongings and actually hurt them and damage their property." It occurs in people of all cultural, social, racial, and economic backgrounds, and it can take place anywhere in the world.[4]

In any potential physical confrontation, former pilot Captain Steve Luckey wrote, there are three kinds of people: those who "can fight," those who "may fight," and those who "always look for a fight."[5] In this chapter, we'll be looking at that last group—those who are "cruising for a bruising" and would like to take you with them. To defuse road and air rage, we need to know what rage disorder is and why it happens. We especially need to know what internal forces trigger a rage episode and what's going on inside the mind and body of a rager as he or she is spinning out of control.

The Anatomy of Anger

A rage eruption is sparked by exploding brain chemistry. When we're threatened, our adrenaline shoots up and our bodies automatically snap into the same primitive fight-or-flight mode our prehistoric ancestors did when faced with a saber-toothed tiger. As stress hormones flood our bodies, our hearts pump faster, blood rushes from our brains to our arms and legs to help us run or fight harder, and the logical parts of our minds switch off, leaving us a mindless fighting machine. As a result, the minute our mind screams "Code Blue!" our brain is taken over by the enraged euphoric drive to win whatever battle we're in. If the threat is physical, that fearless drive can save us from fear or uncertainty that could cost us our lives, but in the battles most modern humans face, it just scrambles our ability to think.

Most rage is triggered by an underlying fear—fear of being hurt, overpowered, or simply disrespected, which can feel like the same thing. By filling the mind with blind, euphoric passion, rage blots out that fear. Rageaholics react to any strong emotion—fear, sadness, shame, inadequacy, guilt, or loss—with rage, possibly because being enraged feels more powerful than being scared, sad, ashamed, guilty, or bereft. Author Christina Olvera says angry outbursts happen because rageaholics stuff back their real feelings and emotions until they snap. When they're ready to blow, stress of any kind can trigger the release, and the resulting feeling of power is so seductive that some people become rageaholics. "The rage keeps the adrenaline pumping," Olvera says. "This is a great feeling and we want

---

4   National Institutes of Mental Health, "Intermittent Explosive Disorder Affects up to 16 Million Americans," June 5, 2006, press release relating to a study by Ronald Kessler at Harvard Medical School, found at http://www.nimh.nih.gov/science-news/2006/intermittent-explosive-disorder-affects-up-to-16-million-americans.shtml.

5   Steve Luckey, Captain, "Air Rage," *Air Line Pilot,* September 2000, p. 18.

to keep feeling it so we stay [in] a semi-constant state of rage. We stay on the verge of outrage. It's almost like being drunk." This sets up a neurochemical reaction in the brain that can become addictive.[6]

Addicted to Rage

> The intoxication of anger, like that of the grape, shows us to others, but hides us from ourselves.
>
> —John Dryden[7]

The dirty little secret about rage is that sometimes it feels good. The adrenaline that floods the nervous system when a person becomes angry has an intoxicating quality as the body prepares to fight. "Unfortunately, the arousal side of anger is addictive," says Dr Joanie Connors. "Some people enjoy the rush of anger so much that they constantly seek out reasons to feel it and are predisposed to be outraged as often as possible." When that happens, she says:

> … a negative thinking cycle takes over their lives and they are rarely or never satisfied with the way things are. Anger addicts scan their environments for justifications for more angry outbursts, picking fault with waitresses, coworkers, spouses, their children or the evening news. When they find a target, they anticipate their chance to explode with outrage, and plan how to have the greatest dramatic effect to yield the greatest rush.
>
> Some people have been trapped in a pattern of cyclic angry rages since childhood or since a trauma occurred in their life, and many of them get no pleasure from anger. They know angry rages are harmful, but cannot find a way to stop or escape the cycle. It becomes this way for many long-term addicts.[8]

For rageaholics, expressing anger only triggers the drive for more anger. Like alcoholics who find that the more they drink the more they want to drink, rageaholics find that the more they rage, the more they want to rage. "Anger addiction or 'rageaholism' is the compulsive pursuit of a mood change by repeatedly engaging

---

6   Cristina Olvera, "Anger Management: The Rageaholic's Mind, *Associatedcontent. com*, January 6, 2006, found at http://www.associatedcontent.com/article/16161/anger_ management_the_rageaholics_mind.html?cat=5.

7   John Dryden, in *Wisdom Quotes*, found at http://www.wisdomquotes.com/cat_ anger.html.

8   Joanie Connors, "The Two Parts of Anger: Don't Get Mad, Get Positive Ways to Use Anger," found at http://www.desertexposure.com/200708/200708_bms_anger.php.

in episodes of rage despite adverse consequences," Olvera says. "Rageaholics will continue to rage compulsively without regard to the negative consequences."[9]

Origins: Angry from Birth?

French psychoanalyst Jacque Lacan says our use of rage as a release and a source of power begins at birth. As infants, he says, we learn that things are not always the way we would like them to be and our angry response can increase to the level of rage.[10] Michael Eigen, author of *Rage,* agrees. "A baby screams when beset by trouble," he says. "It lacks a frame of reference for mounting discomfort, pain, hunger, thermal changes, waves of circulatory sensations, irritating wetness, frightening images, sights, sounds, and 'feels.' … Screaming expresses fear and helplessness and makes one feel stronger. It can express a sense of primal might and effort. Mixtures of terror and rage also go beyond what we can articulate."[11] In addition, rage can give one a feeling of power by forcing change, Eigen says. "It can force others to hear that something is wrong, call attention to oneself or one's cause, stimulate the need to help."[12]

Of course that doesn't make it a good strategy for getting one's needs met at 30,000 feet. And when it remains our main coping tool into adulthood, Eigen says, "Rage substitutes for growth, fills holes in self, masks deficiencies. It is allied with a sense of helplessness, disability, frailty."[13]

Profile of a Rager

Psychiatrists' bible of mental illness, the *Diagnostic and Statistical Manual of Mental Disorders,* Fourth Edition (DSM-IV), says that although people suffering from Intermittent Explosive Disorder (IED) overreact to certain situations with uncontrollable rage, experiencing a sense of relief during the angry outburst, they feel remorse about their actions after the outburst is over. And IED is linked to other emotional disorders; 82 percent of those with intermittent explosive disorder were later diagnosed with depression, anxiety, and alcohol or drug abuse disorders, although the symptoms of IED were usually the first to surface.

To be diagnosed with IED, an individual must have had three episodes of impulsive aggressiveness "grossly out of proportion to any precipitating psychosocial stressor," at any time in their life, and have "all of a sudden lost

---

9   Olvera, 2006.

10   Jacques Lacan, "Aggressively in Psychoanalysis" (1948), in *Ecrits: A Selection,* trans. Alan Sheridan (New York and London: W.W. Norton, 1977).

11   Michael Eigen, *Rage* (Middletown, CT: Wesleyan University Press, 2002), p. 192.

12   Ibid.

13   Ibid.

control and broke[n] or smashed something worth more than a few dollars … hit or tried to hurt someone … or threatened to hit or hurt someone."[14]

A study funded by the National Institute of Health (NIH) in the United States found that people with IED are rarely treated for the disorder. Lead author Dr Ronald Kessler, a professor of health-care policy at Harvard Medical School, said that's because "They usually don't think they have a problem. They think somebody else has a problem."[15]

Caught Off Guard By Rage: "But He Seemed So Nice …"

Most cases of road and air rage appear to come out of nowhere, transforming someone who seems perfectly nice into a frothing ogre. Friends may even excuse a road rager, saying, "He is such a good guy, but when he gets behind the wheel, he changes into someone completely different." The implication is that, under stress, we might all behave the same way.

FBI profiler and therapist Dr Gregory K. Moffatt says that's just not true. "These perpetrators are our neighbors, co-workers and friends," he says. Although "their lives overlap ours making us wonder if we, too, are capable of committing such behaviors …that is an unrealistic fear."[16] The truth, Dr Moffatt says, is that great stress, exhaustion, or even being threatened doesn't transform us into different people; it brings out our essential nature, be that heroic or callously selfish.

> A person who would shoot at another driver, or punch a Little League umpire, is a person who will park his car wherever he chooses, regardless of whom he inconveniences. He will do what he wants, follow rules when he chooses or when it is convenient, and deny or rationalize his failure to follow rules when it is convenient. He may seem an unlikely candidate to commit crimes of road rage or air rage because he is not routinely forced to show his true character to those who do not know him well. People like this … will pursue their own personal goals, both personal and recreational, at the expense of their spouses and children. In short, they are self-serving at their core.[17]

---

14   American Psychiatric Association, "Impulse-Control Disorders Not Elsewhere Classified," *Diagnostic and Statistical Manual of Mental Disorders,* Fourth Ed., Text Revision (Washington, DC: American Psychiatric Association, 2000).

15   National Institutes of Mental Health; and Steven Reinberg, "Rage Disorder More Common Than Thought," *HealthDay,* June 5, 2006, found at http://www.healthywomen.org/resources/womenshealthinthenews/dbhealthnews/ragedisordermorecommonthanthought.

16   Gregory A. Moffatt, *A Violent Heart: Understanding Aggressive Individuals* (Westport, CT: Praeger Trade, 2002), p. 141.

17   Ibid., pp. 141–142.

In an earlier book, *Blind-sided: Homicide Where It Is Least Expected,* Moffatt said, "Victims who are blind-sided by this type of violence more often than not had available to them the information that they needed to assess the potential risk."[18]

A study by the Maryland Motor Vehicle Administration seems to confirm Moffatt's theory that people's essential nature remains consistent in all areas of their lives. Researchers examined the driving records of 300 persons who had been ordered by the court to receive treatment for family violence. They found that two-thirds of these people had multiple aggressive violence violations on their driving records.[19] In other words, the violence in the family was mirrored by violence on the road, reflecting a global pattern of poor anger management in all areas of life. Unfortunately, this information, which may be known by family, co-workers, neighbors, and police, is not available to the driver in the next car or the airline passenger sitting next to him in coach.

Rarely Seek Treatment

According to the 2006 Harvard University study at the National Institue of Health (NIH), even though 10 million adult men in the United States are "so angry, they're sick," the disease is not being addressed as a serious condition needing therapy.[20] "Few people see psychiatrists because they can't control their tempers," Kevin Hoffman said. "But if the Harvard researchers are correct, almost 1 out of 10 adult men routinely display aggression and are so angry that they're likely to damage property, or threaten or injure others."[21]

Denial keeps anger addicts trapped as they conclude that their problem isn't their anger—it's "them," those other people who make them angry. "Ignorance of addiction and the inability to examine ourselves, work together to keep rageaholics stuck," one website for rage addicts says. "Knowing no other way to live, we deny that there is anything wrong with us. This system of denial ensures that the process of rage and righteous indignation will continue. Righteous indignation keeps our focus off of ourselves. This is why ragers seldom are able to say, 'I am wrong.'"[22]

The rage spiral is built on blame. The rage addict never stops to reflect on what he or she does to create a difficult situation. No surprise that these aggressively

---

18   Gregory A. Moffat, *Blind-Sided: Homicide Where It Is Least Expected* (Westport, CT: Praeger Publishers, 2000), p. 4.

19   "Anger Free Driving," *Compassion Power* (n.d.), found at http://compassionpower. com/anger%20free%20driving.php.

20   Kevin Hoffman, "Why Are Men So Angry?" Leonard Ingram's blog, posted June 5, 2007, found at http://www.angermgmt.com/blog/entry.asp?ENTRY_IE=35.

21   Ibid., pp. 1–2.

22   "Signs That Rage Has Turned into an Addiction," *RecoveryThroughSupport.com*, January 18, 2005, found at http://www.recoverythroughsupport.com/articles/2005/01/ signs-that-rage-has-turned_110610404539058638.html.

angry people rarely seek out anger management therapy, since from their point of view, it's everyone else who's wrong. They only go into therapy when their behavior has become so disruptive that a judge or an employer orders it.

Like any other addiction, anger addiction has long-term, toxic consequences that are hard to assess for the person who is in the grip of the experience. Anger addicts succumb to the lure of casting themselves as victims set upon by a hostile world. The more they try to blame others for their problems, the worse those problems become. Some recovery programs suggest that addicts need to "hit bottom" before being motivated to seek help. When alcohol and anger combine to set up an air-rage scenario, the low point might be exiting an aircraft in handcuffs.

That's what happened to Tamara Jo Freeman. As her anger revved up before her flight from San Francisco to Denver in July of 2007, she probably didn't imagine the oncoming explosion would cost her her freedom and her children. Before getting on the plane, she began drinking and hitting her son and daughter, aged 2 and 4. During the flight, she kept drinking and "smacking the bejesus out of them," said a reporter from Denver's *Rocky Mountain News*, because they were getting in the way of her watching a movie. As the children cowered in a corner, a flight attendant asked Freeman to stop, to which the out-of-control mother responded by throwing a drink in her direction, backing her into a corner and threatening her. When the plane landed, Freeman was taken into custody, her children were removed from her care, and she faced the possibility of 20 years in jail. That's when she considered entering anger management training.[23]

As human beings, Moffatt says, we are familiar with the nonverbal "language of violence"—tantrums, foul language, sexual harassment, aggressive driving, vandalism, hurled objects, and child and spouse abuse—but like a "Shock and Awe" attack, it catches most of us off guard, leaving us too stunned to respond quickly. "Most of us are not fluent in the language of violence," he says. "Therefore we do not always understand violence." We need to study this nonverbal language like a foreign language, he says, before we can hope to control those who use it to express themselves.[24]

As with substance abusers, rage addicts come to associate with people who share their worldview and rationalize violent behavior. As a result, they become accustomed to that violence over time. "People who live in a world where injury, brutality, murder, hate, and destruction are everyday events eventually fail to even see them," Moffatt says. "'What violence?' they might say."[25]

If a rage addict does go into treatment, they will go into withdrawal like any other addict. "Craving is high during this time," the rage addiction website author says. "Typically, during the first 90 days of abstinence, ragers feel vulnerable and

---

23   "Woman on Frontier Flight Charged with Assault," *Rocky Mountain News*, July 26, 2007, found at http://www.rockymountainnews.com/drmn/local/article/0,1299,DRMN_15_5644588,00.html.

24   Moffatt, *A Violent Heart*, p. viii.

25   Ibid., p. 191.

spend a lot of time thinking and hoping for a situation that will allow us to use violence for some heroic purpose."[26] Pity the poor flight attendant who crosses their path at that point. After 90 days, however, the rager loses the urge to rant and may even be shocked to hear other people behaving as he used to.

Anger alone can cloud the judgment, but if alcohol or other chemicals are added, the combined effects of stress hormones and other mind-altering substances can be far more extreme than those of liquor, drugs, or adrenaline alone, resulting in escalating errors in judgment.

Defusing Rage: The Myth of "Therapeutic Venting"

Unfortunately, in the last 40 years, Western cultures have inadvertently championed the worst possible approach to anger for a rage addict—or anyone else. In an effort to free people from repressed emotion in the 1960s, therapists began advising people to vent their anger to "get it out of their system." However, says University of Arkansas psychologist Jeffrey M. Lohr, his survey of the research showed that "Expressing anger does not reduce aggressive tendencies." In fact, it usually makes them worse.[27] That's why, when a passenger acts out or yells at the airline staff, they don't get the anger out of their system. Instead, by restating and dwelling on all the details that irritate them, passengers who voice their anger become more hostile and aggressive after venting than they were before.[28]

In study after study of venting, Lohr found that among subjects who (a) vented anger against inanimate objects, (b) vented directly against the person who induced their anger, (c) vented hostility by playing football, or (d) vented verbally about an employer—*all* showed more resentment than those who had not vented at all. In some experiments, those who were venting got so revved up they became aggressive with innocent bystanders. Even those who firmly believed in the value of venting ended up more hostile and aggressive after thumping pillows or blowing off steam in other ways than they'd been when they started. "What people fail to realize is that the anger would have dissipated had they not vented," researchers wrote. In fact, "it would have dissipated more quickly had they not vented and tried to control their anger instead."[29]

Newton Hightower, director of the Center for Anger Resolution, Inc. in Houston, Texas, and author of *Anger Busting 101,* agrees that venting is counterproductive. The idea that a rage addict can heal by venting is like thinking an alcoholic can recover by drinking, he says. For example:

---

26   Newton Hightower and David C. Kay, *Anger Busting 101: The New ABC's for Angry Men and the Women who Love Them* (Houston, TX: Bayou Publishing, 2002), p. 35.

27   Jeffrey Lohr, "Angry? Breathing Beats Venting," University of Arkansas *Daily Headlines*, February 28, 2007, found at http://dailyheadlines.uark.edu/10290.htm.

28   Ibid.

29   Ibid.

... let's pretend that we are going to provide treatment for alcoholics. On the way to the treatment center we stop and buy a case of beer. When we get to the meeting, we tell the alcoholics in therapy that they just need to do a lot of drinking to get it out of their system once and for all. This is similar to when therapists tell men with rage problems, "You just need to express yourself and get it out of your system." It is just as absurd. The more alcoholics drink, the more they want. The more ragers rage, the more they want to rage.[30]

"For those who are rageaholics, expressing anger is self-stimulating," he said. "It triggers the compulsion for more anger."[31]

Our level of anger depends on our interpretation of what's happening to us. When people feel they're the victim of one of what I call "the Four I's"—Injustice, Injury, Invasion of their space or privacy, or the Intention to do them harm— they're more likely to get angry. Customers who feel they've just gotten lousy service can easily think they're the victims of all four—and so will the employee who's just gotten an earful from a furious customer.

Defusing Rage in Midair

While venting just ramps up rage, Lohr says, studies show that anger dissipates faster when people take deep breaths, relax, take a time out, or take any action that "makes it impossible to sustain the angry state." In addition, Lohr found, preliminary research showed that "cognitive-behavioral" therapies that involve observing and changing habitual negative thinking were an effective way to reduce anger; and, unlike venting, no one got hurt.[32]

Like Lohr, Hightower believes that abstaining from expressions of anger is the healthy way to go, while the "let me get the rage out of my system and then I will be OK" system just makes the problem worse. If a passenger or airline staff member responds to an explosion of rage by getting quiet, he says, they're modeling the process of abstaining from, dissolving, or containing the anger. Instead of letting the steam escape as angry words and actions, he says, "Leave the lid on the pressure cooker, keep the valve closed, and turn off the fire underneath it."[33] This theory suggests that the best way to cool down is to say very little about the feeling and focus as much as possible on changing the *cause* of the anger— whether that's the angry thoughts or the external situation.

---

30   Hightower and Kay; and Newton Hightower, "Signs That Rage Has Turned Into an Addiction," found at http://ezinearticles.com/?Signs-That-Rage-Has-Turned-Into-An-Addiction&id=19659.

31   Hightower.

32   Lohr, 2007.

33   Hightower and Kay, 2002.

A psychologist tells the story of two furious drivers who slammed their cars over to the side of a highway and leaped out the door, ready to duke it out. Then they looked at each other and realized they were neighbors—and the fight was off.

"There is a deep psychological urge to release aggression against an anonymous other," said Richard Martinez of the National Highway Traffic Safety Administration (NHTSA). "When the other driver is humanized, aggression is less likely."[34]

This reluctance to attack people we know contains within it the kernel of a rage-prevention system. As we'll hear later, airlines are already using techniques to turn planeloads of people into "one big family" that enable aggrieved passengers to deal with stress with better grace. In the case of the clapping passengers trapped for five hours on the tarmac in Baltimore, the planeload of passengers spontaneously formed their own "family" without airline support, so that they could work together instead of turning on each other as the going got rough. Caring about each other instead of feeling alone with their own needs helped passengers deal better with adversity.

Now airlines need to teach more strategies for humanizing and cooling down people who are on the brink of lashing out. And for those times when all else fails and violence has erupted, airline personnel need a specially tailored version of the training that psychiatric aides receive in soothing and subduing mental patients.

The Contagion of Rage

> If you can keep your head when all about you
>
> Are losing theirs and blaming it on you ...
>
> Yours is the Earth and everything that's in it ...[35]
>
> —Rudyard Kipling

Anger can be contagious because humans, as social animals, instinctively take cues from those around them. From infants who learn by imitating their parents to adults who pick up new skills by closely observing those who have mastered them, imitation not only comes naturally, it happens unconsciously. Particularly in an anxiety-producing situation, people can pick up cues on how to react and imitate their companions who are reacting most strongly. In the case of anger, the intoxication of one person's anger can reinforce an angry response in his neighbors. That's how mobs and riots get started.

---

34   Moffatt, *A Violent Heart*, p. 154.
35   Rudyard Kipling, 1895.

According to Dr Eigen, "Rage, more than most states, affords a sense of totality, experiencing one's being with all one's might. A fit of rage provides an illusory sense of obstacles vanishing, euphoric boundlessness, even if one is in pain. For moments, rage that grows from pain obliterates pain."[36]

On an airplane, this physiological high, exacerbated by the sudden need to defend against mortal danger, can combine with a perceived lack of security resources to turn a life-threatening air rage incident into a potentially fatal mob situation. Many who study air rage have observed how dangerous a situation becomes when passengers with no background or training in subduing violence jump into the fray to overpower a raging passenger. As Kipling pointed out in his poem, "If," when your life is on the line, it's hard to think clearly.

Dealing with explosive rage effectively, applying just enough force to control someone violent without hurting them, is skill that comes with training, experience and a measure of maturity. If the airline crew loses control, it's far too easy for passengers to cross the line from overpowering to injuring a threatening person. According to air rage expert Angela Dahlberg, passengers who were already edgy about the threat of terrorist attack and angry about poor service had already overreacted with vigilante-type measures to their fear of fellow passengers when she spoke to an Air Safety Conference in 2002. "The threat of uncalled-for passenger involvement is real and needs to be controlled," she said then.[37] The death of the violent passenger Jonathan Burton at the hands of his fellow passengers on Southwest Flight 1763 in August 2000 is the nightmarish example of what can happen when well-meaning intervention turns into mob violence.

When air rage breaks out, says psychologist Dr Ervin Staub, author of *The Roots of Evil* and an expert on mob violence and other types of group violence, the actions of each witness or bystander can influence other witnesses and make it more or less likely that bystanders take positive action.[38]

The influence people can exert on each other is striking. According to Dr Staub, studies show many people report seeing two lines of clearly different length as equal when a number of other people before them report seeing the lines as equal. He adds that in one of his studies, "when there were sounds of distress and a crash in an adjoining room, what one person in the room said greatly influenced whether the other person remained passive or took helpful actions. The way some people define the meaning of events powerfully influences other bystanders' reactions to emergencies," he says. In other words, if one passenger takes action, yelling

36   Eigen.

37   "Training Can Reduce and Defuse Disruptive Passenger Incidents," *Air Safety Week,* March 11, 2002, found at http://findarticles.com/p/articles/mi_m0UBT/is_10_16/ai_83681236.

38   Ervin Staub, *The Roots of Evil: The Origins of Genocide and Other Group Violence* (Cambridge, U.K.: Cambridge University Press, 1989 and 2002), p. 65 and Ervin Staub, interview by email with the author, October 26, 2008.

something like "We must do something!" others will see that something bad is happening and [see] the need for action.[39]

In an anonymous group situation, no one person feels responsible for what happens. "No one is responsible, or the group is responsible, or the group's leader," Staub says. "But as people speak out, they can jointly define the meaning of events and the kind of action that needs to be taken, and jointly move to action."[40]

The outcome in Burton's case was his death from asphyxiation after being pummeled all over his body with blunt objects, fists, and feet. A Canadian passenger named Dean Harvey told his local newspaper that after Burton passed out, passengers held him down on his back with his arms outstretched while one man jumped off a chair and onto him several times.

"[Burton] was being held with his arms outstretched and he had not a chance," Harvey said.[41] When a burly man jumped repeatedly on Burton's chest, Harvey said he told the man, "'You've got the guy subdued, what more do you want?'"[42]

"The guy was being held with his arms outstretched," he added. "He had no chance to absorb the shock."[43] Perhaps no one could have stopped the men from continuing to wallop Burton, but flight attendants need training to prevent both Burton's original rampage and the passengers' frenzied reaction from getting so far out of control. Unfortunately, says the International Workers' Federation, which represents air crews, only half of airlines have a policy to tackle air rage—and two thirds do not provide any training for cabin crew in how to deal with disruptive passengers.[44]

Getting Out of the Anger Zone

"The key to working with anger," says Leonard Ingram, "is to investigate the nature of the anger."[45] In *Emotional Intelligence: Why It Can Matter More Than IQ*, author Daniel Goleman suggests that a fearful experience is a major anger trigger. "Threats to life, security, and self-esteem trigger a two part limbic surge," Goleman

---

39   Ervin Staub, interview.

40   Ibid.

41   "A Death on Descent," *CBS News*, September 21, 2000, found at http://www.cbsnews.com/stories/2000/09/21/national/printable235154.shtml.

42   Timothy Roche, "Homicide in the Sky," *Time*, Octob er 2, 2000, found in paragraph 8 of http://www.timc.com/time/magazine/article/0,9171,998079,00.html.

43   Michael Janofsky, "U.S. Declines to Prosecute in Case of Man Beaten to Death on Jet" *New York Times*, September 21, 2000 found at http://query.nytimes.com/gst/fullpage.html?res=9406E5DE103BF932A1575AC0A9669C8B63.

44   International Workers' Federation, quoted in "Controlling Cabin Fever," *BBC News*, July 23, 2001, found at http://news.bbc.co.uk/2/hi/in_depth/uk/2001/trouble_in_the_air/1448843.stm.

45   Leonard Ingram, "Anger Management: Theory and Practice." *Angermgmt.com*, p. 2, found at http://www.angermgmt.com/workshops_certification.asp.

says. "First, hormones called catecholamines are released, generating a rush of energy that lasts for minutes. Second, an adrenocortical arousal is created that can put you on edge and keep you there for hours, sometimes days."[46] Understanding that surge might help flight crews deal with the following scenario.

It's late at night and a plane hits unexpected turbulence. After it's over, the flight attendant suddenly has to deal with two unruly passengers who seem to be flying off the handle for no good reason. "Though the two events may be completely unrelated," anger expert Dianne Shilling writes in "How to Cope with Anger," "the anger generated by the second incident builds on the anger left over from the first."[47] If the two irate passengers trigger anger in the flight attendant, an escalating spiral of rage can result. On the other hand, if the flight attendant is well trained, the process of trying to cool down the irate passengers can go into motion. "Research suggests that people [who are angry] need at least 20 minutes to recover from intense psychological arousal," Schilling says.[48] During this time, everyone involved can try these techniques, based on some of Schilling's strategies for defusing anger:

- Try to identify the feelings that preceded the anger—anger often is a secondary emotion erupting in the wake of other feelings like frustration, resentment, humiliation or fear. Try to recognize and express *that feeling* instead of anger. Before exploding, it's good to pay attention to the possibility that anger is triggered by hurt feelings, fear, humiliation or something else.
- Monitor the feelings and bodily sensations experienced while you're *becoming* angry.
- Change the thoughts that trigger the anger, interpreting the situation from a less provocative point of view.
- Flight attendants can speak to passengers in calming, soothing tones.
- Don't sit on your needs, fuming, but don't be aggressive either. Assert your needs calmly, without blaming the other person.
- Respond in a caring and understanding manner.
- Relax. Anger is a physically arousing state, so try to lower your blood pressure by breathing, meditating, visualizing.[49]

What if the crew members themselves are having fits of anger at a time when a passenger needs help soothing their angry feelings? This becomes a lose-lose situation. John Mayer and Peter Salovey first defined emotional intelligence as "a form of social intelligence that involves the ability to monitor one's own anger

---

46 Cited in Dianne Schilling, "How to Cope with Anger," *WomensMedia.com*, found at http://www.womensmedia.com/new/anger-management.shtml.
47 Ibid.
48 Ibid.
49 Ibid.

and emotions, to discriminate among them, and to use this knowledge to guide our actions."[50] This kind of emotional intelligence should be a requirement of all airline industry staff.

Exactly how much does the average airline employee know about anger? Are they aware of the normalcy of anger as an emotion, the level of physical discomfort it causes, and its unpleasant and even destructive consequences if it is not addressed in some way? For example, do they realize that passengers who have an angry outburst often need medication afterwards for the headache, nausea or even back pain that follows? Even if they aren't given an in-depth understanding of the latest theories about anger, they should have a cursory understanding of the best ways to deal with it.

Anger theorists suggest that there are four basic aspects of anger: physical; emotional or feeling; cognitive experience associated with learned behavior; and spiritual beliefs about what is right or wrong. Anger is very often rooted in fear, and angry people generally feel they are being victimized by a person or situation.

Understanding the Irate Customer: Why the "Terrible Twos"?

In *Defusing Hostile Customers*, a workbook for Canadian public servants, Robert Bacal speaks to an issue of great interest to the airline employee: the irate customer confrontation. The first thing to understand, he says, is what is happening to the previously sane customer as he or she panics about needs not being met. Suddenly, before an employee's eyes, the customer regresses to the "Terrible Twos," the time when they could get their way by throwing a tantrum. As the employee watches, Bacal says, "The first thing to remember about angry customers is that while their behaviour is directed at you (and it can be personally insulting), the real source of the anger is elsewhere.[51]

> ... Now that we have explained where and when hostile behavior is learned, we can clearly see that its major purpose is to control, or manipulate the environment. Since we are talking about hostile customers, we can say that the

50   Originally from Peter Salovey, David J. Sluyter (eds) with Contributor Peter Salovey, *Emotional Development and Emotional Intelligence: Educational Implications* (New York, NY: Basic Books, 1997), found in John A. Kaufhold and Lori R. Johnson, "The Analysis of the Emotional Intelligence Skills and Potential Problem Areas of Elementary Educators," Summer 2005, found at http://findarticles.com/p/articles/mi_qa3673/is_200507/ai_n14686573/pg_3.

51   Robert Bacal, "Angry Customers: What Do They Really Want, and How to Give It to Them," 1995, found at http://ezinearticles.com/?Angry-Customers-What-Do-They-Really-Want,-and-How-To-Give-It-To-Them&id=69130. Robert Bacal is a consultant, management trainer and international author on a number of business topics, ranging from customer service through creating more productive workforces.

purpose is to control you, to influence your reactions in the naïve hope that you will do whatever it is the client wants.

… We want to avoid being controlled and that means we must avoid responding to nasty attacks in the ways that the attacker wants.[52]

Bacal emphasizes not engaging in the confrontational game, but recognizing the angry person's needs. Essentially angry people want help, and usually they will become less hostile if they can see someone making a real effort to look for alternatives rather than arguing or shutting them down. Angry people also want choices and alternatives so that they won't feel trapped and helpless. As Bacal puts it:

The analogy I like to use is that of an animal that is cornered. If its only way of escaping is through you, you can be pretty sure that it is going to attack you with great energy. The same is true of your clients. Make them feel they have no options and they will tend to strike out at you, even if they are the authors of their own misfortune.[53]

All airline employees who deal with the public should be taught simple rules and tactics, like those in Anxiety Management Training (AMT) to control rather than escalate these customer tantrums.

Anger's Side Effects: Tearing Down Our Bodies from Inside

"You will not be punished for your anger. You will be punished by your anger," said psychologist and author Vijai P. Sharma, PhD, quoting an ancient Eastern saying. That's physically true, he said:

During an outburst of anger, heart rate goes up to 180 beats per minute or even higher compared to the regular heart rate averaging about 80. The blood pressure too goes up, 220 to 130 or even higher, compared to normal readings of 120 to 80. Other harmful physical and chemical changes take place. [The] body uses up sugar extremely fast creating a sugar deficiency. As a result an angry person shakes in anger.

In the primitive order of the animal world, anger, aggression, and assault are one and the same thing. The body just knows that it is in a "fighting" mode in which it may be injured and bleeding may occur. To safeguard itself in the case of excessive bleeding, the angry person's body releases chemicals to coagulate

---

52   Ibid.
53   Ibid.

(clot) the blood, therefore blood clots form more quickly than usual. Now a truly dangerous situation is at hand, that is, (1) bleeding has not occurred, and (2) a clot is formed which can potentially travel to any organ of the body, including the brain or the heart.

In a fit of uncontrollable anger, in the case of a heart patient, the heart can suddenly stop due to that clot floating up to the heart and getting lodged there. In another case, heart arteries can squeeze off hard enough to choke off the supply of oxygen to the heart which can cause severe chest pains, creating the well known condition of "angina pectoris." A stroke can also occur when a person in an uncontrollable fit of anger bursts an artery in the brain. This is how anger can hurt the subject more than it does the object of the anger.[54]

Knowing the symptoms of anger can help airline staff members recognize it before it explodes in their passengers or themselves. Tristan J. Loo, an experienced negotiator and an expert in conflict resolution, described the physical signs of rage:

1. Unconscious tensing of muscles, especially in the face and neck;
2. Teeth grinding;
3. Breathing rate increases dramatically;
4. Face turns red and veins start to become visible due to an increase in blood pressure;
5. Face turns pale;
6. Sweating;
7. Feeling hot or cold;
8. Shaking in the hands;
9. Goosebumps;
10. Heart rate increases;
11. Adrenaline is released into your system creating a surge of power.[55]

Anger can change people's disposition in the blink of an eye, causing them to act without thinking. Although this hair-trigger readiness for action can keep you alive in a physically threatening situation, it can also prevent you from behaving rationally in a situation that requires a higher order of thought. Not only are you ready to fight or flee, but your body is physically demanding that you take action now, and it doesn't care how wise or foolish that action is. However, Loo says, anger has its uses. Some are not only healthy, they've contributed to the survival of the species for millennia. "Anger is one of our most primitive defense mechanisms," he says. It protects us from "being dominated or manipulated by

---

54   Tristan J. Loo, "What Causes Anger?" August 14, 2005, found at http://www. articleset.com/Self-Improvement_articles_en_What-Causes-Anger.htm.
55   Ibid.

others. It gives us the added strength, courage, and motivation needed to combat injustice done against us or to others that we love." But uncontrolled, it becomes destructive.

According to Loo, the cause of the anger is not what happens to us, but how we perceive it. "Anger is a strong emotion of displeasure caused by some type of grievance that is either real or perceived to be real by a person," he says:

> The cognitive behavior theory attributes anger to several factors such as past experiences, behavior learned from others, genetic predispositions, and a lack of problem-solving ability. To put it more simply, anger is caused by a combination of two factors: an irrational perception of reality ("It has to be done my way") and a low frustration point ("It's my way or no way"). Anger is an internal reaction that is perceived to have an external cause. Angry people almost always blame their reactions on some person or some event, but rarely do they realize that the reason they are angry is because of their irrational perception of the world. Angry people have a certain perception and expectation of the world that they live in and when that reality does not meet their expectation of it, then they become angry.[56]

It's estimated that in America, one in five people has an anger management problem; and as the frustrations of modern life have multiplied, anger management has become a growth industry. Counseling in anger management has joined substance abuse counseling as a management tool to deal with out-of-control workers. Courts are ordering battering spouses and violent parents to take anger management training before they're granted child visitation rights. The fact that this new form of counseling is so widespread gives us an idea of the population that boards airplanes every day, reminding us that more and more passengers are bringing emotional baggage with them when they board the plane.

Many people are totally unaware that they're carrying deep-seated anger into their daily lives. They don't realize that negative feelings influence their perceptions of and responses to everything in the world around them.[57] Because life is unpredictable, every inconvenience may trigger unhealthy coping patterns, including anger that they mistakenly aim at others. A dispute becomes a battle of wills over who is right or wrong and why, with one or both people becoming recalcitrant.

Anger alone is neither good nor bad; anger is merely a feeling. What matters is how it's expressed and used. Unfortunately, too many people see anger as a source of power, using it as a weapon to help them get their way.

---

56 Ibid.

57 "Anger: What Causes Anger?" *Yahoo Geocities*, 1997, found at http://www.geocities.com/Athens/Acropolis/6729/anger2.htm.

The Short Hop from Anger to Rage

Air rage happens when all the aspects of anger mentioned above collide with a loss of impulse control. For some ragers, the rage and lack of impulse control are caused by past trauma, in others by alcohol and/or substance use, coupled with a failure to curb aggressive impulses.[58] A high correlation exists between air rage incidents and drinking, both before takeoff and during a flight. That connection suggests that the same mechanism—lack of impulse control—contributes to both air rage and overuse of alcohol.

As in road rage, ragers blame someone else, the staff or other passengers, for their wrath. If airline employees are seen as disrespectful or insensitive when they respond to passengers' grievances, anger can escalate. This is especially true when grievances include one of "the Four I's"—Injustice, Injury, Invasion of their space or privacy, or the Intention to do them harm. Of course, when passengers are given wrong information or no information about delays or canceled flights, or when luggage is lost or sent to the wrong destination, they may feel that airline personnel are inflicting all of the Four I's on them. If they feel that some of these actions on the part of staff are deliberate, that feeling of being both ill-served and having their concerns dismissed may boil over into rage.

---

58   S.L. McElroy, Recognition and Treatment of DSM-IV Intermittent Explosive Disorder, paper presented at the Closed Symposium Phenomenology and Treatment of Aggression Across Psychiatric Illnesses held in Chicago, Illinois, August 1998, found at http://www.grandrounds.com/supplenet/v60s15.htm.

Chapter 6
The Genesis of Air Rage

The History of Violent Rage

Rage has always been a powerful, untamed and frightening force that human beings have tried to manage and control. For much of history, rage was considered so powerful, it was reserved for God. The bible's Old Testament frequently mentions the wrath of God, and in the Middle Ages, says editor Barbara Rosenwein in her essay collection, *Anger's Past: The Social Uses of an Emotion in the Middle Ages,* "God could express righteous anger, but human anger was conceived as part of a system of vices: it was one of the seven deadly sins."[1]

By the later Middle Ages, royalty had claimed the right to express rage. The king was entitled to get angry when issuing orders, especially as a prelude to military action, as a way of showing he meant business. "The ruler openly displayed anger when he decided to go to war," said author Gerd Althoff in *Anger's Past.*[2] But it was assumed that medieval peasants didn't have the "nature," meaning the intelligence and self-control, or the "capacity," meaning the skills, to express anger, says essayist Paul Freedman. Which is an indirect way of saying they were too lowly and dumb to handle incendiary rage. "To claim the right of deliberate vengeful anger, normally considered the property of nobles," Freedman says, "was to perform an act of defiance."[3]

Curses: "Sky of Brass; Earth of Iron"

Some religious groups tried to harness the power of rage without its dark emotional content. When lords looted property from the churches, monasteries, or villages that supported monks, the monks had no legal or practical method to redress the injustice. In response, some added "organized cursing" to their religious services

---

1   Barbara H. Rosenwein (ed.), "Introduction," *Anger's Past: The Social Uses of an Emotion in the Middle Ages* (paperback), a collection of essays on anger in the Middle Ages (Ithaca, NY: Cornell University Press, 1998), p. 3.

2   Gerd Althoff, "Ira Regis: A History of Royal Anger," in Rosenwein (ed.), *Anger's Past: The Social Uses of an Emotion in the Middle Ages* (Ithaca, NY: Cornell University Press, 1998), p. 62.

3   Paul Freedman, "Peasant Anger in the Late Middle Ages," in Rosenwein (ed.), *Anger's Past: The Social Uses of an Emotion in the Middle Ages* (Ithaca, NY: Cornell University Press, 1998), p. 183.

to ask the Deity to rain trouble on their enemies. The monks were expected to deliver these curses without any angry feelings. Coolly and without malice they focused their attention on reciting a minutely detailed laundry list of every horrible fate they wished upon their enemies. "'May the sky above them be made of brass,' one curse ran, 'and the earth they walk on be made of iron.'"[4] Just as long as they're not mad.

Scribes of the day wrote about these curses—and reported that noblemen died of battle wounds within a year of being cursed. This may be an early example of rage as the first step towards social change. Therapist Michael Eigen points out that rage is a necessary part of the human psyche, and sometimes it is the appropriate reaction to events. Rage against injustice is needed before one can work for change. "Rage against painful facts," he said, "… is a rage that may attach to political causes, rising against perceived unfairness or fueling a tyrant's position."[5]

Using Rage in Battle

The full power of insane rage can best be seen on the battlefield, and warriors have been using this mindless rage to terrify and destroy their enemies since the beginning of time.

In The Iliad, which was written between 2,500 and 3,000 years ago, Homer tells of warriors during the Trojan War being "possessed" by a god or goddess and exhibiting superhuman powers. In fact, the first word of the Iliad is "rage." Homer writes:

> Rage—sing, goddess, the rage of Achilles, the son of Peleus,
>
> the destructive rage that brought countless griefs upon the Achaeans …[6]

Thus one of the most famous poems in history starts by explaining how unbridled rage can fuel mad warfare. Homer's first word is *mēnin*, consuming rage or "wrath," although Achilles shows this wrath by sulking in his tent throughout a great deal of The Iliad. If he were an airline passenger, the cabin crew would have kept an eye on him, but not felt the need to take out the plastic handcuffs.

---

4   Lester K. Little, "Anger in Monastic Curses," in Rosenwein (ed.), *Anger's Past: The Social Uses of an Emotion in the Middle Ages* (Ithaca, NY: Cornell University Press, 1998), p. 10.

5   Michael Eigen, *Rage* (Middletown, CT: Wesleyan University Press, 2002), p. 150.

6   Homer, *The Iliad* (Butler translation, 1903).

The Norse Berserkers

The fighters whose name became synonymous with insane rage were the Norse berserkers whose history spans 2,600 years, from before 1300 B.C.E. in the Bronze Age through the early Middle Ages. Legendary for their deranged aggression and crazed strength in battle, berserkers fought without armor or clothing, heedless of danger. Before a fight, they howled, danced, sang, banged their helmets with their weapons and went into trances to rouse their bloodlust. In Old Norse, says author Michael Speidel, the word berserk meant "a bear-shirt warrior"—an apt name, since along with wearing the skins of bears or wolves into battle to take on the animals' ferocity, berserkers roared, snarled and bit their shields, creating the clacking sound a bear makes just before it attacks.[7]

Under fire, berserkers would throw off their armor, believing themselves immune to pain and weapons as they flew at the enemy in an inhuman frenzy. In a Norse saga in 1220 A.C.E., an Icelandic poet named Snorri Sturlusson said:

> .. Woden's men went without hauberks and raged like dogs or wolves. They bit their shields and were strong like bears or bulls. They killed men, but neither fire nor iron hurt them.[8]

In their rage, berserkers' faces and bodies became contorted and seemed to grow, which may have been the source of the myth of "shape-shifting" werewolves.[9] Their belief that they were invincible made sense—berserkers' racing adrenaline gave them superhuman strength, made them feel no pain and reduced bleeding so they seemed impervious to blows.

They had to be "raging mad" to become fearless killing machines, Speidel says. "Shouting and singing were ways to rouse such rage. Early Greek and Roman warriors screeched like flocks of raucous birds—a mark of manhood."[10] War dances were also used to rouse berserkers' fury. "Rhythmic song and dance bonded the warriors together, entranced them, and aroused their fighting madness," Speidel says.[11]

Linguists have found evidence that this kind of mad fighting was a very old phenomenon that originated as far back as 4000 B.C.E. and spread from India to Iceland to parts of the Middle East, Speidel says:

---

7   Michael Speidel, "Berserk: A History of Indo-European 'Mad Warriors,'" *Journal of World History, 13.2,* 2002, under "The Berserk Mind," found at http://www.heathenharvest.com/article.php?story=20060613085857659.

8   Ibid, under opening paragraphs.

9   Ibid, under *"Berserks and the End of the Bronze Age."*

10   Ibid, under *"The Berserk Mind."*

11   Ibid.

The word for 'mad attack,' eis-, shared by Vedic, Iranian, and Germanic warriors makes it likely that the berserk fighting style comes from the time before the dispersal of the Indo-Europeans.[12]

Berserks thus embody an abiding spirit in unbroken tradition from Vedic and Homeric times to those of the Icelandic sagas. The history of berserk warriors offers rich religious, cultural, and military detail from about 1300 B.C. to A.D. 1300 and links the bronze, iron, and middle ages, three thousand years of history seldom understood as belonging together.[13]

Rome used berserk warriors to help conquer its empire—often hiring northern mercenaries for the job—but by the early Middle Ages it had come to see these fighters as undisciplined barbarians who would attack anything in their path, including their own people. Also, for all their bravado and fury, berserkers began faring badly against larger, more disciplined armies with newer weapons, and by the 1300s, as Christianity transformed Europe's tribal cultures, the berserk fighting tradition was largely dying out.[14] However, as Speidel notes, striking similarities remain between berserkers and mad warriors around the world like Aztec quachics and Malabar amoks raising questions about the origins of the berserk phenomenon.[15]

In the nineteenth century, Zulu warriors went into fierce trance states to achieve battle rage. They considered this ability to summon up a condition of rage their secret weapon and used it to terrify their enemies on the battlefield. We can't know whether Zulus or berserkers had any chemical help heightening their eerie battle trances; that would be in the nature of a trade secret.[16]

However, as Michael Herr observed in his book *Dispatches* and Oliver Stone showed in the film *Platoon*, an overdose of adrenaline, terror and rage can make a modern warrior run wild like a classic berserker.[17]

Civilian Berserkers: Running Amok

There have always been wild outbursts of insane anger that bear a resemblance to air rage. One example of maddened violent behavior that entered the language in the late eighteenth and early nineteenth centuries was the Malaysian phenomenon

---

12   Ibid.

13   Ibid.

14   Ibid, under *"Berserks of the Bronze, Iron, and Middle Ages"* and *"Greece and Rome in Need of Berserks."*

15   Ibid, under "Mad Warriors Worldwide."

16   Michael Speidel, *Ancient Germanic Warriors: Warrior Styles from Trajan's Column to Icelandic Sagas* (Routledge, 2004), p. 228.

17   Therianthropes United, "Berserker History," found at http://www.therianthropes.com/berserker_history.htm.

of "running amok." The word "amok" is derived from the Malay word *mengamuk* that means "to go mad with rage." A man who runs amok suddenly acquires a weapon—usually a sharp dagger called a *kris*—rushes into the street and begins slashing and cutting up everyone he meets until bystanders overpower him. The first outsider to observe this behavior was Captain Cook in 1770. He thought it was a uniquely Malaysian phenomenon, but soon European visitors observed men doing the same thing in the Philippines, Laos, Papua New Guinea, and Puerto Rico.

Until the Western legal system arrived, someone who ran amok would slash an average of ten victims before being subdued by bystanders and beaten to death on the spot. In the 1911 *Encyclopedia Britannica*, author W.W. Skeat wrote, "These frenzies were formerly regarded as due to insanity. It is now, however, certain that the typical amok is the result of circumstance, such as domestic jealousy or gambling losses, which render a Malay weary of his life."[18] In other words, it's an early version of "suicide by cop"—a phrase first used on America's *Fox News* to describe someone who threatens a police officer to compel the use of deadly force.[19]

Running amok is more common outside Asia than we thought. "The truth of the matter is this occurs in every culture," Los Angeles forensic psychiatrist Manuel L. Saint Martin told the *Washington Post*. Saint Martin, who has tracked about 50 cases, said the phenomenon "seems to be occurring more commonly now in Western, industrialized cultures rather than in the Southeast Asian islands where it was first noticed." Saint Martin said this enraged frenzy was "the end product of mental disorder where you get homicidal-suicidal behavior."[20]

Running amok was virtually unknown among women and, as Skeat suggests, may be a means of escape from an intolerable situation in a society where Islamic law forbids suicide. This theory might seem to be confirmed by the steep decline of incidents in Malaysia, now that the punishment for running amok is not instant death, but arrest and a public trial.

Citing a University of Aberdeen in London report, Saint Martin reported that in 1972, "amok behavior existed in all countries, differing only in the methods and weapons used in the attacks," adding, "the number of victims in modern episodes is similar to the number in [traditional] amok despite the fact that handguns and rifles are used in contrast to the Malay swords of two centuries

---

18   "Amok," *NationMaster.com* Encyclopedia, found at http://www.nationmaster.com/encyclopedia/Amok.

19   The phrase "Suicide by cop" was first used in 1998 on *Fox 11 News-KTTV* by former FBI chief negotiator Clinton Van Zandt. The American Dialect Society says it refers to an act where a person threatens a police officer to compel the use of deadly force.

20   Quoted in Shankar Vedantam, "Cho's Case Similar to Other Mass Killings by Loners," *Washington Post*, April 22, 2007, p. A13.

ago."[21] When the behaviors are examined, the Malay amok behavior seems to be a local variation on the sudden, unprovoked multiple homicide cases committed by attackers who have a history of mental illness. "Violent behavior similar to amok has increased dramatically in industrialized countries," Saint Martin wrote, "surpassing its incidence in primitive cultures. This increase may be the result of a better case reporting and heightened public awareness and interest in violence, combined with an increase in the psychopathology responsible for amok."[22] Since it's virtually impossible to stop an ongoing amok attack without risking life and limb, he says, the only way to protect bystanders is to prevent it from starting in the first place.[23]

"Excited Delirium": Diagnosis or Coverup?

Controversy has erupted recently over the increasing number of people dying during an arrest of "Excited Delirium." These suspects—most of whom have drugs in their system and one-third of whom are mentally ill—behave like modern Berserkers, fighting, screaming, kicking, and flailing with superhuman strength until they're subdued—after which they die. Given their symptoms, it's possible some air rage cases are related to this little-understood phenomenon; and by learning from police mistakes, airlines may learn how to subdue a chemically unbalanced human tornado *without* injuring or killing him.

University of Miami neurology professor Deborah Mash said the usual excited delirium victim is "disproportionately large, extremely agitated, threatening violence, talking incoherently, tearing off clothes [because his body temperature is rising], and it takes four or five officers to get the attention of that individual and bring him out of harm's way."[24] He's also impervious to pain, unusually strong, hyperactive, "violent towards objects," and attracted to glass, according to a San Jose, California, police bulletin.[25]

Although the syndrome has been recognized since at least 1849, much about it remains a mystery. Excited delirium is "definitely real," Mash says. "And while we don't know precisely what causes this, we do know it is the result of a neural

---

21   Manuel L. Saint Martin, MD, "Running Amok: A Modern Perspective on a Culture-Bound Syndrome," *Journal of Clinical Psychiatry,* June 1999, *1*(3), pp. 66–70. In his article, Saint Martin attributed this information thus: "Jin-Inn Teoh, a professor of psychiatry at the University of Aberdeen in London, reported in 1972 that ...."

22   Ibid.

23   Ibid.

24   Laura Sullivan, "Death by Excited Delirium: Diagnosis or Cover-up?" in "All Things Considered," *National Public Radio (NPR),* February 26, 2007, Part one of a two-part report, found at http://www.npr.org/templates/story/story.php?storyId=7608386.

25   *Police One.com*, a San Jose, California, Police website, June 11, 2007, found at http://www.policeone.com/edp/articles/1269555-A-look-at-San-Jose-PDs-new-excited-delirium-protocol/.

chemical imbalance in the brain." Mash says the phenomenon came to light in the 1980s, when cocaine burst onto the scene. Mash told National Public Radio (NPR) that most excited delirium victims have drugs in their systems, and all victims "become irrational, their body temperatures rise so fast their organs fail, and then they suddenly die." Death is caused by a chemical imbalance in the brain, Mash said, while Dr Vincent Di Maio, a former chief medical examiner in Texas, said victims were dying of "an overdose of adrenaline."[26] He estimated that there were 600 to 800 excited delirium deaths a year in the United States.[27]

Former policeman William Everett told a conference of law enforcement officers that in his 15 years as a policeman, his encounter with a case of excited delirium was "the closest I ever got to an unarmed life-and-death confrontation." After pounding furiously on the plate glass window of a closed bar that he wanted to go into on a Sunday night, the young man began jumping on the hood of a car.

The difference between this excited delirium sufferer and other suspects, Everett said, was like "the difference between a Tyrannosaurus and a tabby cat. There's no subtlety about the intensity of energy, the physicality. It doesn't seem like you're dealing with anything human."[28]

William Lewinsky, executive director of the Force Science Research Center (FSRC) at Minnesota State University—Mankato, says that while seeming invulnerable, the subject may in fact be experiencing a cluster of life-threatening physiological stresses, including hyperthermia, a change in blood acidity, electrolyte imbalances, a breakdown of muscle cells, and a leaching of cellular contents into the blood stream, all of which put the subject's heart at significant risk.[29]

But Eric Balaban of the American Civil Liberties Union fears that excited delirium is an invented excuse for a suspect's death from excessive force or a Taser blast. In one case, a suspect named Frederick Williams was shown on a grainy video, NPR reporter Laura Sullivan said, "screaming, 'Don't kill me! I have a family to support. I've calmed down!' as several officers carry him into the Gwinnett County Detention Center in a suburb of Atlanta. One officer takes out his Taser and fires it directly onto Williams' chest." As officers held Williams down, he was shot six more times, and died shortly afterwards. The report added,

---

26 Sullivan, "Death by Excited Delirium."

27 Sarah Burge, "Autistic Man's Mother Sues Riverside County, Claiming Deputies Caused His Death," *The Riverside Press-Enterprise (online)*, May 27, 2007, found at http://www.pe.com/localnews/inland/stories/PE_News_Local_B_delirium28.3cd3d33.html.

28 William Lewinski, "10 Training Tips for Handling 'Excited Delirium,'" *PoliceOne. com*, Force Science Research Center, October 14, 2005, found at http://www.policeone. com/writers/columnists/Force-Science/articles/119828-10-training-tips-for-handling-excited-delirium/.

29 Ibid.

"Williams, a deacon in his church and father of four, had no drugs or alcohol in his system."[30]

Cases like this increase the concern of critics like Balaban. "I know of no reputable medical organization—certainly not the AMA [American Medical Association] or the APA [American Psychological Association]—that recognizes excited delirium as a medical or mental-health condition," he says. (He's right; they don't.) Police are using the diagnosis, he said, "as a means of white-washing what may be excessive use of force and inappropriate use of control techniques by officers during an arrest."[31]

Dr Werner Spitz, a well-known forensic pathologist and former chief medical examiner in Michigan, seems to agree. He says it makes no sense that police are a necessary part of the excited delirium equation—that it never happens unless police are present. According to a report in the Riverside, California, *Press-Enterprise*:

> Spitz said the kind of adrenaline-induced cardiac arrest described by proponents of excited delirium exists, but is exceedingly rare. Most of the so-called excited delirium cases with which he is familiar involve someone high on drugs whose breathing was compromised by a police restraint.
>
> "Some people have made a condition out of this," he said, adding that it seems far more likely they were asphyxiated.
>
> "Strep throat is caused by streptococcus," Spitz said. "Excited delirium is caused by police."[32]

The International Association of Chiefs of Police hasn't accepted the diagnosis either, saying more study is needed. But "excited delirium" is showing up as a cause of death in an increasing number of autopsy reports.[33]

The potentially good news for front line employees like flight attendants who may be confronted with this seemingly superhuman insanity is that there is a way to calm them down. According to NPR, several emergency room doctors at Vanderbilt University hospital in Nashville, Tennessee, said they had tranquilized three people who seemed to be in the grip of "excited delirium," and "they woke up fine."

---

30   Laura Sullivan, "Tasers Implicated in Excited Delirium Deaths," in "All Things Considered," *National Public Radio* (*NPR*), Part two of a two-part report, February 27, 2007, found at http://www.npr.org/templates/story/story.php?storyId=7622314.

31   Sullivan, "Death by Excited Delirium."

32   Burge, 2007.

33   Laura Sullivan, "Death by Excited Delirium."

But that was in a hospital, with doctors and intravenous drugs. It's not clear how much first responders like police officers and flight attendants can do medically to tranquilize people this far out of control.[34]

Given people's drinking and partying habits, it's not surprising that most excited delirium (ED) episodes happen in the hot summer months, between Thursday and Sunday, with Sunday being the most common day. Former police officer Everett says ED is most likely to happen to men in their 30s, and least likely to affect people older than 50 or younger than 20, while women succumbing to excited delirium are "extremely rare." The drug most often found in the victim's bloodstream is cocaine, which is involved in more than half the cases, while alcohol is also common. About one-third of all subjects have been diagnosed with mental illness, usually schizophrenia.[35]

Everett, who is now an attorney, says it may not be possible to develop "definitive, scientifically validated 'best practices'" for dealing with dangerous and difficult ED subjects until desperately needed research is done, but based on his review of available data, he says, "the overarching operational objective" must be to bring these suspects under control in a way that does not aggravate them unnecessarily, and to get them immediate medical treatment.[36]

This condition appears to be occurring more often. On the website *PoliceOne.com*, Dr Michael Curtis, an authority on excited delirium, says, "We have been lulled into a sense of security about medication taking care of psychiatric problems. But now we're seeing an increasing number of people who stop taking their meds, along with a rise in methamphetamine and cocaine use." As a result of that dangerous mix, he says, "we're going to see more and more and more ED confrontations. Major cities may see more than rural areas, but it can strike anywhere."[37]

The Road to Road Rage

On a day-to-day basis, the anger explosion we're most likely to encounter in the modern world is road rage. The automobile population explosion clearly demonstrates that increasing numbers lead to increasing friction. As crowding on the roads has increased, so has road rage, until today, when people are whipping out their revolvers on the freeway, proving what Calhoun's mouse study (cited in Chapter 2) showed—that crowding triggers mindless rage.

---

34 Ibid.

35 Lewinski, 2005.

36 Ibid.

37 Charles Remsberg, "Behind the Headlines About Excited Delirium; What Cops and EMS Need to Know," *PoliceOne.com*, December 15, 2006, found at http://www.policeone.com/writers/columnists/Charles-Remsberg/articles/1195879-Behind-the-headlines-about-excited-delirium-what-cops-EMS-need-to-know/.

When the first cars hit the road, crowding was the last problem on anyone's mind. Just as airline travel was once a caviar experience for the elite, automobiles were exotic, adventurous toys for the wealthy few. But even the first horseless carriages had to coexist with other traffic—the pedestrians, horseback riders, and horse-drawn carriages that were already on the roads demanded that the noisy engines obey some laws. In England, the earliest automobiles, which were steam-powered, had to follow strict rules. The Locomotive Act 1865 set a speed limit of four miles per hour in the country, and two miles per hour in town. The act also required that each car be preceded by a then famous "man with a red flag," who walked 60 feet ahead of the car carrying a flag or lantern to warn horse riders and horse drawn traffic that a horseless carriage was coming. His very presence insured that the machines would travel at a walking pace.[38]

In the United States in the early 1900s, automobiles featuring both electric and internal combustion engines became popular, although the high price tag (from $600 to $7,500) put ownership beyond the reach of all but a lucky few. The rich showed off their wealth by racing, parading, and touring their expensive vehicles in public, and the only traffic jams were brief clusters of the cars of the elegantly dressed elite in front of opera houses or elegant parties.[39] However, like the founders of low-fare airlines, Henry Ford realized there was a market for low-priced cars in the workaday world and developed the mass production and assembly line techniques that enabled him to produce the first stripped-down, economy Model T, which sold to working class Americans who were looking for a cheap, reliable, efficient way to get where they needed to go. "By 1923," said author David Gartman, "mass-production efficiencies had lowered the price to a mere $265, and half of the autos in the entire world were Model Ts."[40]

Now drivers had more cars, but few roads in rural areas. In the early years of the twentieth century, people only drove their cars in the summer, when the primitive roads were passable; they had to put them up on blocks all winter long. Still, more traffic demanded better roads, which spread across the countryside, transforming both the landscape and the social fabric. According to David Gartman:

> Mass mobility afforded by the mass-produced car transformed every aspect of Americans' lives, including their culture—their beliefs, desires, and values. The automobile long ago stopped being a vehicle for getting passengers from here to there, and became an embodiment of American dreams and desires—for freedom, progress, individuality. In fact, Americans' investment of cultural meanings and

---

38   "A Brief History Lesson: National Numbers," *NationalNumbers.com* (n.d.), found at http://www.nationalnumbers.co.uk/number-plate-history.htm.

39   David Gartman, "Tough Guys and Pretty Boys: The Cultural Antagonisms of Engineering and Aesthetics in Automotive History," *Automobile in American Life and Society,* found at http://www.autolife.umd.umich.edu/Design/Gartman/D_Casestudy/D_Casestudy1.htm.

40   Ibid.

desires in the automobile has increasingly impeded its development as a safe, efficient tool of transportation. Throughout the history of twentieth-century America, there has been an ongoing conflict between the car as an efficient tool and the car as a carrier of cultural dreams and values. The latter has generally won out.[41]

Roads became highways and then freeways. By the 1950s, automobiles had become so available and integrated into the structure of the society that in many cities, formerly successful mass transit systems simply withered away. As endless roads were being built, we seemed to have entered a golden age of infrastructure, until it collided with the inevitable effects of so many cars on the road. But the unintended consequence of endless drivable roads was endlessly increasing traffic. Having your own car was alluring and empowering, and everyone was driving or planning to, especially since there were few alternatives. As a result, traffic continues to increase exponentially. According to Martin V. Melosi:

> Motor-vehicle use in the United States doubled from one to two trillion miles between 1970 and 1990. Between 1960 and 1990, traffic increased by a factor of five in the Seattle area. In Washington, D.C., traffic almost tripled from 1973 to 1994. In California, vehicle use doubled between 1970 and 1990, growing more than four times faster than population. A 1990 study stated that the average California driver spent 84 hours a year stuck in traffic congestion. This suggests that as much as the introduction of automobiles into cities would come to modify urban space, accommodating them in motion has been a challenging and frustrating problem.[42]

The commuter lifestyle of the early twenty-first century features rush hours that start earlier and earlier, routine fender-benders and grueling daily trips to and from work, often in bumper-to-bumper gridlock. Not surprisingly, road rage has become yet another hazard of the modern car-centered everyday life. According to studies by the American Automobile Association Foundation for Traffic Safety, an average of at least 1,500 men, women, and children in the United States are injured or killed each year as a result of aggressive driving.[43]

In his experiments on crowding and mice cited in Chapter Two, Dr John Calhoun discovered that when mice were overcrowded, their social structure broke down and they began to engage in random aggression. He worried that

---

41   Ibid.

42   Martin V. Melosi, "The Automobile Shapes the City," found at http://www.autolife.umd.umich.edu/Environment/E_Casestudy/E_casestudy5.htm.

43   Louis Mizell, *Aggressive Driving*. A report for the AAA Foundation for Traffic Safety, found at http://www.aaafoundation.org/resources/index.cfm?button=agdrtext.

human beings might well do the same thing.[44] As our roads and planes become more crowded, we need to keep Calhoun's findings in mind as we look for more constructive ways to handle anger and frustration. In the following chapter, we'll examine some possibilities.

---

44   John B. Calhoun, "Death Squared: The Explosive Growth and Demise of a Mouse Population," *Journal of the Royal Society of Medicine,* January 1973, *566*, found at http://www.pubmedcentral.nih.gov/articlerender.fcgi?artid=1644264.

Chapter 7
Reducing Air Rage:
Smiling Customer Service

Flying from Oakland, California, to visit family in Los Angeles, conflict resolution mediator Marvin Schwartz was struck by the flight attendants' buoyant attitude on his Southwest flight. The crew members seemed to be having fun and making sure that the customers had a good time too. Passengers smiled at the funny boarding announcements and laughed when the crew burst into song. By the end of the flight, it was as if everyone in the plane had become part of one big family.

"I finally called a flight attendant over and asked him, 'What does Southwest do to make you guys so much happier than other airline workers?'" Schwartz said. He wasn't surprised to hear that the company had a good payment schedule. But what made them different was their unique hiring procedure that helped them select personnel who were fun-loving, socially adept, and liked working cooperatively. The outcome was the lighthearted feeling that "We're all in this together," that made the flight a pleasure.

Southwest and Jet Blue, both low-cost, low-frills airlines, share this "all in this together" zeitgeist, with the result that the two have the lowest rate of customer complaints of any American airlines. Since 1987, when the Department of Transportation began tracking Customer Satisfaction statistics, Southwest has consistently led the entire airline industry with the lowest ratio of complaints per passengers boarded, with Jet Blue close behind.[1] Having this kind of positive, relaxed atmosphere while traveling would go a long way to reduce air rage.

Three Types of Air Rage

The first step towards preventing air rage is realizing that there are three different kinds of offenders, and we need a different approach for each. First, there's the type of "air rage" that happens most frequently—irascible passengers who explode with rage because they're angry about bad service. Justified or not, their spiraling

---

1 American Customer Satisfaction Index, University of Michigan, found at http://www.theacsi.org/index.php?option=com_content&task=view&id=147&Itemid=155& i=Airlines; Southwest Airlines Fact Sheet, updated 5/25/08, under Southwest Airlines Distinctions, found at http://www.southwest.com/about_swa/press/factsheet.html; and "About SWA," *Southwest.com*, found at http://www.southwest.com/about_swa/airborne. html.

rage can distract and upset a crew, getting in the way of the safe operation of the plane. As my study (below) showed, this is the kind of air rage that Southwest's warm and welcoming culture helps to prevent.

The second type of offender is "disruptive" and "unruly," and definitely fits the FAA definition of someone who "interferes with the flight crew's performance of their duties." They may scream obscenities, make sexual advances, throw a cup of ice cubes at a flight attendant, keep a plane sitting at the gate while they argue about stowing a bag (or, in diva Britney Spears' case, until she could leave because the plane "didn't have leather seats"). Some are explosive and violent; others may be seen as more of a pain in the neck than a threat to life, but by distracting the crew from its duties, they can put a plane at serious risk. As with the first type, improving the flying experience, cabin air, and alcohol policies while establishing strict rules for allowable in-flight behavior might keep most of these folks from flying off the handle. They're obstreperous and difficult, but potentially manageable.

The third, most dangerous, and rarest offenders are the deranged passengers who are incapable of knowing what they're doing because they're blind drunk, on drugs, or psychotic. These include the maniacs who try to strangle a crew member or grab the controls and crash a plane. The only way to prevent the incidents they cause is to keep them off the plane in the first place. However, airlines can reduce the damage they cause by making sure toxic cabin air and freely flowing alcohol don't further scramble their brain chemistry, and by teaching crew members psychological management techniques and ways to restrain offenders once they lash out.

In this chapter we'll look at the ways airlines can reduce all three kinds of air rage, first considering approaches that keep most potential offenders from becoming enraged. Then we'll consider ways to prevent deranged passengers who are beyond the reach of reason from endangering a flight.

Biggest Impact on Passenger Mood? Front Line Employees

As McCrary said, there are two reasons people get angry: frustration; not getting what they want, especially if they were expecting to get it; and the feeling that others do not respect them or care how they feel.[2] Too often, the entire "cattle class" experience, from parking lot to baggage carousel, seems designed to frustrate passengers and make them feel airlines' contempt.

Since front line employees are the human face of the airlines, they create the emotional tone of a flight. The moment when passengers connect with an airline ticket agent or flight attendant can transform their mood for good or ill. When

---

2   Robert John McCrary, Ph.D., "Anger Management: A 'How-To' Guide," G. Werber Bryan Psychiatric Hospital, Columbia, SC, 1998, found at http://www.state.sc.us/dmh/bryan/webanger.htm.

the "tangibles" of flying—bad cabin air, cramped seat, lack of food, or canceled flights—put passengers' stress hormones on red alert, the right word from a caring employee can defuse building anger. On the other hand, a wrong word or disrespectful snarl can send an unexpected jolt of rage through the calmest soul.

Unfortunately, far too many front line airline employees are "shell shocked, depressed, disillusioned and resentful," an unnamed airline professional told ABC News in 2007. That "equates to bad and inattentive service with a 'who cares' attitude. Morale, in other words, is the key, and it's in precious short supply today."[3]

One exception, he said, was Southwest Airlines. Its "brilliance as a company hasn't been in its choice of airplanes or the hedging of fuel expenses, it's been in maintaining a reasonably fun place to work in a harsh environment, and you can see the positive results in the friendliness and helpfulness of Southwest employees."[4] Choosing job candidates who know how to create goodwill, and then keeping these employees happy and training them to deal with all kinds of passengers, are the most cost-effective measures airlines can take to reduce air rage.

Of course airlines need to reduce justifiable anger by improving their tangible service failures—the crowded dirty planes, late arrivals and canceled flights. They should also stop abetting drinkers' rage by serving too much alcohol, and prevent passengers who are raging in the terminal from getting on planes in the first place. But in this cost-cutting era, an airline may get the biggest bang for its buck from building good worker morale and team spirit. Staff appreciation, fun and family feeling, and careful rage-prevention training cost relatively little and can save an airline millions of dollars on air-rage-related flight delays and diversions, lawsuits, and, at worst, accidents, not to mention gaining the goodwill of customers that makes them want to come back.

According to Angela Dahlberg, author of *Air Rage: The Underestimated Safety Risk*, the employees who help defuse rage best are simply those who do their jobs well, keep up to date on changing procedures, and exude a sense that they care. "They understand instinctively the value of first impressions and the halo effect of helping one passenger in need while others are looking on," she said, adding that they're efficient, proactive and genuinely like people. These front line employees also communicate well, listening, asking questions and seeking clarification, providing information and remaining sensitive to people's need to understand what's going on.[5]

As noted earlier, the airline industry may have succeeded too well in making air travel seem routine and easy. By helping passengers forget that they are isolated at 30,000 feet to survive, or not, together, the industry allows some customers to

---

3   "Why Airline Service Suffers," *ABC News online*, April 4, 2006, found at http://abcnews.go.com/print?id=1800726.

4   Ibid.

5   Angela Dahlberg, *Air Rage: The Underestimated Safety Risk* (Aldershot, UK: Ashgate, 2001), p 38.

think it's acceptable to act out on an airplane, when in fact, it's essential that they get along with their fellow passengers and crew. Air rage is an underestimated danger, as Dahlberg says, because one unchecked episode could interfere with the airplane's functioning enough to cause a crash.[6] The industry's success in giving customers a false sense of security may explain the attitudes towards air rage revealed in the following study.

Survey of Passenger Attitudes: How Service Affects Rage

To examine the causes of air rage, I surveyed passengers to see how their feelings about service affected their attitudes towards the phenomenon. Though the FAA divides air rage into three categories ranging from Type I (relatively mild disruptions) to Type III (potentially dangerous threats to flight safety), I focused on how people felt about the most disruptive Type III blowups that could wind up with the raging passenger's being escorted off the plane in handcuffs, or worse.

Surprisingly, though none of the passengers surveyed said they themselves would indulge in air rage, a large percentage of those passengers who arrived at the airport expecting better airline service than they got believed air rage was justifiable in other people. The study found that when the airlines do not provide good service, customers may become more approving of air rage, even though they might not have a great propensity towards air rage themselves.[7]

That raises the possibility that these passengers, who in the cool light of reason say it's fine for "other people" to rage, could, if pressed, blow up themselves. From my years of observation as an airline employee and executive, I suspect several trends may explain society's heightened tolerance of air rage. These include:

- *The Entitlement or "Temper Tantrum" Syndrome:* As instant gratification becomes a way of life, some airline customers feel entitled to certain privileges right now. Whatever they want, be it information or a drink, they consider waiting for it one or two minutes an unacceptable inconvenience. If they don't get the service they expect, or get it fast enough, they become disruptive to get attention.
- *Social Acceptance of Aggressive Behavior:* Society's high tolerance of competitive, assertive and even violent behavior today may have convinced some passengers it's appropriate to react aggressively to a problem when you're on a trip. When demanding behavior is seen as an accepted method of reinforcing higher status and getting your needs met, more people will consider that behavior appropriate and perhaps indulge in it themselves.

---

6   Ibid., pp. 5–6.

7   Joyce A. Hunter, D.B.A., *"An Empirical Study of the Effects of Airline Customer Service and Consumer Perception of the Air Rage Phenomenon,"* Argosy University, Orange County, California, 2004, p. 120.

Clamoring loudly for service is becoming more fashionable as society as a whole becomes less polite.

- *Anonymity: Hit-and-Run Rage:* The anonymity of travel may also raise passengers' approval of air rage. When we think no one knows us, we generally feel fewer inhibitions and less fear of retaliation for bad behavior. Like hit-and-run drivers, hostile travelers expect to be long gone before they can pay any consequences for what they consider justifiable demands for service.
- *Zero Sum Game:* Passengers' sense of anonymity is compounded by the "get it while supplies last" mentality that stems from the fear one is competing with strangers for a limited amount of service. Aggressive travelers may think they need to get their demands in first and loudest before an anonymous competitor snatches the last of little bit of what they want from their grasp.

Finally, on airplanes like anywhere else, some people are simply looking for a fight, regardless of the service they get.[8]

Though my survey results showed that customers' bad attitudes might open the door to air rage, several additional findings pointed towards solutions to the problem. First, the survey implied that if the service customers received was better than, or as good as, the service they expected, they would be less tolerant of air rage. In other words, if airlines stop promising more than they can deliver and improve the service they do give, the approval of air rage will start to decline.[9]

Second, passengers said the single factor that made them madder than late flights, tight seating and bad cabin air was rude treatment by employees. But the reverse was also true—kindness and courtesy were actually more important to them than on-time performance.[10] It should be good news for financially strapped airlines that one well-placed act of kindness by an employee can go far to counteract the effects of a long, bad flight.

The implications are clear. To reduce the most common forms of air rage, airlines need to (a) create a happier atmosphere on board by improving the "tangibles" of the flying experience like crowding and lateness; (b) reduce the sense of cynicism and anonymity among passengers; (c) give passengers realistic expectations of their flight quality and a clear picture of the good behavior that is expected of them on board; (d) prevent intractable ragers from boarding planes in the first place, and (e) hire, train and support high quality front line employees so they can prevent problems, foster a positive customer experience, defuse rage, and, if all else fails, subdue offenders.

---

8   Ibid.
9   Ibid.
10   Ibid.

Compassionate Crowd Management: Creating Community

Behind the carefree antics of the Southwest flight attendants, whether by accident or design, is a measure of positive crowd control. The fun reduces passengers' sense of alienation and anonymity, and according to several air rage experts, this is exactly what's needed to keep peace on a crowded, uncomfortable airplane. Expert Angela Dahlberg puts it in stark terms. "Each time the aircraft doors close, it opens the curtain for a high-risk experiment in group dynamics," she says. "The aircraft contains an instant global village, or more accurately, a global prison camp." Picture this, she says:

> ... the chances are that cabin crews face a group of people of which between 50 and 60 percent share a fear of flying. All of them experienced a degree of stress prior to getting on the aircraft. Some of them have a personal history of violence. Some of them are on medication for a variety of reasons, including anxiety and depression, medications that magnify the effects of alcohol. Some harbor strong discriminatory views against authority figures, women, gays, people from minority groups, people who drink, people who smoke, people with poor personal hygiene and the list continues ....[11]

Passengers may be traveling for sad or stressful reasons, Dahlberg says. When they climb on the plane and rub up against people different from themselves, "the seeds of stress and hostility have been sown." Social biologists tell us that the invasion of our personal space in cattle class triggers stress and anger. All in all, plane travel "is, for many, reminiscent of torture, and wears down the thin veneer of civility. The potential for tempers to flare is ever present."[12]

Even worse, say road rage and air rage experts Leon James, PhD, and Diane Nahl, PhD, air rage is closer to the surface for all of us than we think. It "is just part of the background feeling that goes along with the stress of travel and transportation. This background below-the-surface simmering feeling of anger explodes into rage at unpredictable moments."[13]

The solution, they say, is using "community-building" exercises to turn that flying prison camp into a supportive group. James and Nahl do this with "Compassionate Crowd Management Techniques" that keep the group focused on collective activities that help them get to know each other and release some frustration. In a sadly apt comparison, they compare stranded passengers' response

---

11   Dahlberg, p. 25.
12   Ibid.
13   Leon James and Diane Nahl, "The Psychology of Air Rage Prevention," "Psychology" section of *www.SelfGrowth.com*, June 6, 2008, found at http://www.selfgrowth.com/artman2/publish/psychology_articles/The_Psychology_of_Air_Rage_Prevention_printer.html.

to crowd management techniques to the camaraderie volunteers feel working together to clean up after a natural disaster.

The point of community building is to reduce isolation and anonymity, say James and Nahl. When people feel alone and isolated, they become "trapped in their suspicions, standardized imaginings, and attribution errors," imagining dire scenarios that include the airline "taking advantage of me." And when they feel anonymous, they feel free to react with rage.[14]

Southwest projects an image of community at all times. In the Thanksgiving, 2007 edition of "*Spirit*" magazine, President Colleen Barrett wrote a letter listing the company's blessings. After a hymn to her employees, she said, "You, my dear Customers, are another of my fondest blessings ... you are much more than Customers: You are ardent supporters, loyal advocates, and most importantly, trusted Friends. Thank you!"[15] Of course that's public relations, but it's meant to make customers feel like a bonded group. On Thanksgiving, Southwest held a "Customer Appreciation Day" at key airports "to thank you for your patronage." Again, a corny move that costs little money, but reinforces the idea that the customer is a family member who will come back soon, and counteracts the kind of anonymity that allows people to act out.

Sometimes passengers themselves form impromptu communities that keep rage from boiling over in spite of the airlines. A community spontaneously formed by passengers stranded on the tarmac in Baltimore for five hours (see p. 31) found a benign and creative way to express their unhappiness—clapping and drumming on the overhead bins until they were taken off the plane. Afterwards, they worked together to find constructive solutions to problems, drumming up wheelchairs for the sick and supporting each other as they tried to get flights out of town.

The same thing happened, a Mrs Logan told the New York Times, when her daughter was stranded overnight in Chicago at Christmas. It was "horrible, horrible," she said, but the stranded passengers pulled together. "One girl said, 'I have goodies for Christmas in my bag,' and opened it up and shared with everybody." For a young man who had less than $20 in his pocket, everybody chipped in so he could get a hotel room.[16]

There's huge power in a sense of community. As the following story shows, it can even save lives:

---

14   Ibid.

15   Colleen Barrett, "Colleen's Corner," *Spirit Magazine* (for Southwest Airlines), November 2007.

16   Laura Mansnerus, "Turbulent Manners Unsettle Flyers," *New York Times*, February 15, 2004, found at http://query.nytimes.com/gst/fullpage.html?res=9805E2D9173AF936A 25751C0A9629C8B63.

Maui, Hawaii
April 28, 1988

Aloha Airlines Flight 243

The flight climbed without incident to a flight level of two four zero (twenty-four thousand feet), with the first officer at the controls, while the captain was attending to non-flying pilot duties. As the flight reached its flight level, both pilots heard a loud "clap" and a "whoosh" sound followed by rushing air behind them. The first officer felt her head jerk back. Debris flew in the cockpit. The door was gone. There was "blue sky" where the first class cabin's ceiling was meant to be. Due to metal fatigue and corrosion, the entire upper fuselage of the aircraft tore off, from the cockpit door to the back of first class, leaving those passengers essentially riding in the open air. The captain started an emergency descent, extended the speed brakes on the wings and dropped airspeed. The first officer tried to declare an emergency over the radio but because of the loud level of noise she did not know whether her declaration was heard. The pilots communicated back and forth with hand signals.

Female, Seat 4A

… I reached up to lock my tray into the table … and then there was this thunderous explosion, and I was startled, because there was a great big jolt, and I looked up. My hair was flowing up into the sky and just above me were clouds. I thought we had lost the whole front end of the airplane.… My arm was outside, and I thought I looked out and saw clouds ….

I had no feeling in my arm and pulled it back in, and looked down, and realized I was going [out of the plane] … because my seat had tilted into what looked like on a [single] rail, and my seat was stuck in that rail, but it was jostled from where it should have been … because I was sitting at an angle, I could not reach [for my life vest], and I told [the man beside me] I had no [life vest], so [the gentlemen beside me] both reached over and hung on to me. And then I put my arms around the fellow next to me, because he let go of me and tried to find me a life vest under my seat, and then said [the life vest was gone]. So he leaned forward while I clamped myself into his vest, and the fellow on the aisle reached over behind him and just clung to me for dear life. And by their very reaction [alone] I did not go out that window.

We hung together, and I don't know how long it took us, but we were down on the ground and [we made] the most beautiful landing. I have to say, I thought we had no pilot, no front of the plane, no nothing. … In that long period when I was holding on to those gentlemen I could hear the plane's engines still running. … The whole time we were up there [in the air] I could hear this rushing of winds, like a wind tunnel. I have never experienced anything like this. I have no words for it.

The arm of my chair was ripped off. ... When I looked down all I could see was the [chair] rail that the chairs are supposed to be inside of.... That is all that I could see there. And, of course ... way down there all of that beautiful mass of ocean. I am very appreciative of the fact that [the gentleman who held on to me preventing me from flying out of the aircraft] said, "You know, we thought you were going over the side, and we decided that we had better hang on, because if you have to go, we are all going to go together." And so, it was because of their actions that I am still here.[17]

Anything airlines can do to create that sense of community will go a long way to prevent passengers from turning on each other or their crew members when they're feeling stressed.

There are also many steps airlines can take to prevent rage before passengers even walk into the airport.

Rage Reduction Step One: Start Before Take-Off

Eliminate False Advertising

In a 2000 marketing study, Rust and Oliver speculated that customers whose expectations were raised and then dashed might be more dissatisfied than if high quality service was never promised in the first place.[18] As my study showed, passengers' approval of rage was higher when they expected better service than they got. If airlines lower expectations by creating more realistic airline ads that stress practicality and price over luxury, passengers may feel less outrage at actual airline conditions.

Jet Blue and Southwest Airline's "fun, not food" approach to marketing and service are the best known of these strategies. Since Southwest was the most profitable of the U.S. airlines in 2001, it is evident that, from a marketing standpoint at least, this strategy works for many passengers.[19] Both airlines continue to attract large numbers of customers, and Southwest had the lowest rate of complaints overall

---

17   Malcom MacPherson (ed.), *On a Wing and a Prayer: Interviews with Airline Disaster Survivors* (New York, NY: HarperCollins Publishers, 2002), pp. 181–182, p. 187 and p. 190.

18   Roland T. Rust and Richard L. Oliver, "Should We Delight the Customer?" *Journal of the Academy of Marketing Science*, 2000, 28(1), pp. 91–92.

19   W. Zellner, "Southwest: After Kelleher, More Blue Skies," *Business Week Online*, News: Analysis and Commentary, April 2, 2001, found at http://www.businessweek.com:/print/magazine/content/01_14/b3726061.html

in 2002, with only 0.4 for every 100,000 air travelers.[20] It's reasonable to assume that this low complaint rate could be translated into a low incidence of air rage.

"Some passengers seem to feel that the airlines should just acknowledge that the flying experience is no longer a glamorous or, at times, even a tolerable one—especially back in coach—and that it's something passengers are going to have to accept," says *New York Times* reporter Michelle Higgins.[21]

"I actually have more respect for Southwest Airlines in this area," an executive assistant from Los Angeles named Julie Hurwitz told Higgins in a 2007 *New York Times* article. "They've never pretended to have more than they do."[22]

Rage Starts in the Terminal

In her book *Air Rage*, Angela Dahlberg suggests that the seeds of a midair outburst are often planted in the airline terminal. The passenger's frustration about delayed or canceled flights, rude service, seat assignment mix-ups, lack of information, or arguments about carry-on luggage begin to pile up before the passenger even sets foot on the plane.

According to Dahlberg, this can result in overt conflict after the plane takes off. For example, passengers who are already angry about bad service in the terminal can climb on the plane and immediately start making demands of the flight crew, not realizing they are busy with mandatory safety procedures. When passengers start out angry, they're more likely to seethe about being "ignored," not realizing that safety procedures must take priority over passenger service during critical phases of the operation. On the other hand, travelers who get good service in the terminal, Dahlberg says, are more likely to assume the flight attendant has their best interests at heart and less likely to pick a fight. The less stress passengers experience before boarding, the better able they'll be to keep bad behavior in check.[23]

After they've created the happiest, best-trained front line employees possible, airlines can take a number of other relatively inexpensive steps to improve passengers' airport experience and send them onto their flight in a better mood. Air and road rage experts Leon James and Diane Nahl list a few of the most important:

1. Provide non-stop, accurate information, both in person and through announcements and signs.
2. "Elevate the importance of the travelers' comfort. Show that you care about it. Apologize if you can't provide decent seating. Make up for it by giving

---

20   David Ho, "Air Travel Complaints Rise," *ABCNews.com*, February 3, 2003, found at http://abcnews.go.com/sections/travel/DailyNews/aircomplaints000203.html.

21   Michelle Higgins, "Aboard Planes, Class Conflict," *New York Times*, November 25, 2007, found at http://travel.nytimes.com/2007/11/25/travel/25conflict.html?pagewanted=print.

22   Ibid.

23   Dahlberg, p. 38.

something else in return so the traveler doesn't feel cheated or neglected."

3. Manage lines better, making it possible for people to sit and wait rather than stand in line as much as possible. Make sure customers don't have to physically compete for a seat near the place they're expected to stand. Only have people form a line when you're actually ready for them to board the plane.

4. Use community-building techniques to knit waiting passengers into a social group, so they no longer feel anonymous. Encourage discussion and help them form a support group.

5. Establish better security in waiting rooms so travelers can take a nap without worrying their bags are going to be stolen.[24]

Screen Disruptive Passengers

Perhaps the most important way airline employees can prevent air rage is to keep the most violent and irrational passengers off the plane. The most dangerous air rage incidents can happen after harried gate agents, rushing to process passengers and get the flight off on time, fail to flag signs of trouble in potentially disruptive passengers. For example, one captain said, in a hearing:

> While boarding, the #1 Flight Attendant advised that we had a drunk passenger. … In a very short time the #2 Flight Attendant advised me that he was a problem and that she wanted him off the plane. I called the ramp tower and asked for police and the proper people. He left the airplane peacefully. The agent working the flight was very helpful. All in all, this was no big deal except for one major problem. I later found out that the guy was so drunk that he had to be helped on the plane by the passenger assistance people.[25]

Airplane flight crews want ground personnel trained to prevent this kind of incident. According to a Gulf Air official, after Gulf Air added a one-day training course for its ground staff, the number of air rage cases declined by 50 percent in one year.[26]

Gate agents are expected to meet on-time performance standards. To reduce the resulting pressure to board passengers of doubtful conduct, KLM airline is now using a special reporting code to cover cases of drunken, agitated passengers

---

24   Leon James and Diane Nahl, quoted in Annette Santiago, "Air Rage," *AviationNow. com*, August 10, 2001, found at http://www.drdriving.org/rages/.

25   National Aeronautic and Space Administration (NASA), Aviation Safety Reporting System (ASRS), April 2000, 250, p. 1, found at http://asrs.arc.nasa.gov/callback_issues/cb_250.htm.

26   "Training Can Reduce and Defuse Disruptive Passenger Incidents," *Air Safety Week,* March 11, 2002, found at http://findarticles.com/p/articles/mi_m0UBT/is_10_16/ai_83681236.

who delay boarding, said Ben van Ernich. "We may refuse up to 10 people per day from boarding," he added.[27]

Working with security specialists, the airline industry may need to create a better behavioral screening system. Step one may be developing a profile listing behaviors typical of passengers who go on to become disruptive. Front line employees could use these profiles to identify customers who are likely to create an air rage incident in the terminal and keep them off the plane.

In many countries, officials monitor customers who exhibit erratic behavior that indicates they may have a behavioral disorder, and they prevent them from boarding airplanes. The staff of the Aviation Safety Reporting System (ASRS), a voluntary system for reporting airline safety issues sponsored by the National Aeronautic and Space Administration (NASA) in the United States, said America's airlines should establish a similar monitoring system. In addition, all airlines could use a central reporting system to gather, consolidate, and track data on disruptive customers. Such a system is sorely needed. Finally, airline professionals should also be trained in proper procedures for denying boarding to disruptive customers. This combination of careful screening, closer cooperation between security and boarding gate personnel, and the development and study of profiles of disruptive travelers can help to keep many "bad news" passengers from getting on planes in the first place.

Simple common sense would dictate that certain passengers should, at the very least, be examined more closely before boarding. These include:

- Passengers who show signs of heavy inebriation, drugs, or mental instability. As it stands now, agents and offenders often find ways to suppress outbursts just long enough to roll the troublesome passenger onto the plane, literally "kicking the problem upstairs." Safety would seem to require dealing with the disruptive person while he is still on the ground.
- People who are explosively hostile, particularly if they are verbally or physically abusive to airline personnel. Those who are already abusive on the ground are a major risk in the air. Many ground personnel tell stories of passengers who screamed threats and grabbed, hit and threw things at them—and then walked on a plane without any consequences. If such disorderly passengers are allowed to board, the flight crew should at the very least, be warned that they're coming.
- Offenders who have been involved in previous air rage incidents; a shared database combining information compiled by all airlines would help keep these troublemakers off of planes.

---

27   Ibid.

Backup from Security Guards

When airline employees who aren't hired for their law enforcement skills decide to stop agitated, blind drunk, or potentially violent customers from boarding a plane, they need security guards nearby to back them up. These would-be passengers can't be allowed to fly, but given their condition they may become even wilder when told they aren't going anywhere, and gate agents should have trained and physically imposing security staff available to help them deal with the resulting explosion.

Warn Potential Offenders

Because it's hard to punish passengers for behavior they thought was acceptable, the general public should be informed of the consequences of disruptive behavior before they get to the airport, or at least before they climb on a plane. Airlines should prominently post signs warning that existing Federal Aviation Administration (FAA) rules prohibiting disruptive behavior will be strictly enforced. These warnings should give passengers a clear list of the infractions that could get them kicked off their flights. Airlines should also make public service announcements in airports and during flights to inform passengers of the dangers caused by air rage.

Printed warnings should also be: posted at all airport facilities, ticket counters, lounge areas and boarding gate areas; included in frequent flyer announcements and bulletins; printed on airplane boarding passes and ticket jackets, and circulated to travel agencies, trade associations, chambers of commerce, and convention centers.

Advertising campaigns could also be developed to increase public awareness of the consequences of disruptive customer behavior. Ideally such ads would present a more reasonable view of the flying experience while emphasizing the benefits of cooperation between passengers and crew.

When the flight attendant steps up to the front of the plane and starts reading the federal regulations warning that "federal law prevents you from tampering with smoke detectors, carrying a gun onboard" and so on, many passengers tune out. To ensure passengers hear and pay attention to air rage warnings, crew members should make them at a separate time from the boilerplate safety briefings. A federal law might be needed mandating this separate announcement of the risks and consequences of air rage.

"Everybody is a Suspect": Prevention Overkill

While it's wise to let passengers know the limits of tolerable behavior up front, airline consultant Mike Boyd says there's a right and a wrong way to do it. Boyd invites readers of his newsletter *Hot Flash* to imagine this scenario: They've just finished buying an expensive suit at the upscale department store, Nordstrom, when:

> ... The sales person hands you back your credit card, along with the carefully-wrapped $800 designer clothing you just purchased. But instead of expressing any appreciation for the sale, the clerk looks you sternly in the eye and orders, "We have a shoplifting problem. It will not be tolerated in this store! It's illegal and if you do it we'll have you arrested. Do you understand?"
>
> A heck of a way to end a business transaction. Accusing every customer of being a potential shoplifter would be an egregious breach of good customer service. Such behavior on the part of a high-quality merchant would be unthinkable.
>
> But think again. One such merchant, United Airlines, is doing this sort of thing right now, today, to passengers checking-in at its hubsite airports. If there were any doubts that management at some airlines are totally out of touch with their customers, they were eliminated this past week, when United decided to give out leaflets warning every one of its passengers not to get "unruly." The intention— to reduce inflight incidents—may be laudable. But the execution is like using a depth charge to unclog the sink.[28]

The yellow notices he's describing have written, in large, jagged letters like a sign at a circus Haunted House, "UNRULY BEHAVIOR WILL NOT BE TOLERATED." Boyd's point is that they're insulting. "Sure, Nordstrom's does probably have a shoplifting problem," he says. "But they don't address it by accusing every customer of being a potential petty thief."[29] Beyond the insult factor, the notice puts an image in passengers' heads that wasn't there before—that of themselves as unruly, or as having to hold themselves back from being unruly. It's not only insulting, it plants an image in our heads of ourselves as hooligans that makes the travel experience that much darker.

A New Kind of "Offender": Air Rage vs. Justified Anger

As we've seen, airlines report several kinds of offenders. The most dangerous and deranged usually aren't capable of grasping what they're doing. The second type is "disruptive" and "unruly," and definitely fits the FAA definition of someone who "interferes with the flight crew's performance of their duties."

But, says Michael Boyd, in recent years, a new type of "unruly passenger" has started to emerge. The FAA definition of air rage as "anything that interferes with a flight crew's duties" is pretty loose, and some airline employees stretch that definition to apply to anyone who complains vigorously. That could become dangerous, Boyd says. United Airline's flyer "signals that any passenger, cornered

---

28   Michael Boyd, "Enlightened Customer Service: Everybody is a Suspect," *Hot Flash*, August 6, 2001, found at http://www.aviationplanning.com/airline1.htm#Hot%20Fl ash%20%20August%206,%202001.

29   Ibid.

and abused, better not raise his voice or get demanding" or "The retribution could be swift, with the employee simply declaring the passenger as 'unruly.'"

"What's 'interference,' for example?" Boyd asks. "What constitutes 'intimidation'? Let's run the possibilities:"

> A gun? A verbal assault? A raised voice? A loud complaint? Hitting the call button too many times? Referring to the in-flight food as Alpo? Or simply expressing to the flight attendant that he or she is nasty and rude?

Where does "intimidation" stop and the free-speech right of a consumer to express himself begin? It may sound simple, but there are incidents of passengers—justifiably—raising their voices, only to be threatened.

For example, while the vast majority of flight attendants are professional, doubtless there is a small percentage that may decide that a passenger who raises his or her voice to a rude, uncaring employee is being "intimidating" and should be arrested. The message is that the passenger is at the mercy of the opinion of the employee.[30]

This already seems to be happening, as the Denver passenger described earlier found out when his ticket agent told an airport police officer that she had been "threatened and assaulted" when he and his wife tried to get her to sell them a ticket. As he complained in a *Denver Post* blog, the agent "tried to have my wife and I arrested for the crime of complaining to her and not just leaving her alone and using the automated check-in machines. Anyone who actually does assault an airline employee needs to be dealt with appropriately by law enforcement," he wrote, "but creating a blacklist of fliers looks ripe for abuse."[31]

While it's clear that many fulminating passengers are simply rage addicts getting their fix, the question remains: What is true "air rage," and what is the natural reaction of passengers who have been pushed beyond their limits by wretched airline service? At what point along the spectrum of anger does "air rage" intersect with righteous indignation? According to Boyd, the airlines who want to stay in business need to pay more respectful attention to these so-called ragers—the angry passengers who snap in less disruptive ways, writing angry letters and refusing to fly their airline again.[32]

Disposable Customers = False Economy

Unfortunately, said *New York Times* reporter Michelle Higgins, "Airlines, flying so close to full capacity today have realized that they really don't have to cater

---

30 Ibid.

31 Gryphon99, blog post on "Article Discussion: 'Air Rage' Upsets United," *Denverpost.com,* posted September 17, 2007, found at http://neighbors.denverpost.com/viewtopic.php?t=6913089.

32 Ibid.

to economy passengers—most of whom are booking on price alone, and who increasingly have no real airline loyalty—because the cost of doing so would never be worth it in pure bottom line terms." This belief is confirmed by Spirit Airline President B. Ben Baldanza's in-house reaction to a customer request for compensation that seems to reflect many airlines' sense of the customer as an anonymous, interchangeable cog in the company machine. "Please respond Pasquale," Baldanza wrote, "but we owe him nothing. Let him tell the world how bad we are. He's never flown us before anyway, and will be back when we save him a penny."[33]

That sounds hard-headed and practical, but research has shown it's a false economy. As the findings in my study demonstrated, passengers' perceptions of airline service do have a profound effect on their attitude towards air rage. To change their perceptions, airlines will have to make serious improvements in their service. Given their current budget problems, this may seem like a lot to ask, and it would require some shifting of priorities and investment of time and resources. However, saving money by ignoring service problems is a mistake, since the current atmosphere of widespread low-level air rage is bad for business. Even if it doesn't erupt in full-blown outbursts, simmering anger among customers will cause travelers to gravitate toward other airlines. Budget problems are real, but the safety problems and liabilities that come with air rage are also real and costly. It would behoove the airline industry to focus on improving the service in ways that provide the most "bang for the buck." To quote the old British military adage of the "Six P's, "Proper planning prevents piss poor performance."

Rage Reduction Step Two: Fix the Tangibles, from Sardine Seating to Canceled Flights

Changing the concrete physical horrors of flying would force the airline industry to break open its collective wallet, but it's key to the passengers' travel experience. The behind-the-scenes improvement that might go farthest to prevent the worst and most unexpected air rage disasters could be providing clean, fresh, oxygenated air to passengers and crew. The potential for toxic, under-oxygenated air and low air pressure to boost the effects of alcohol and scramble brain chemistry are unknown, but it's assumed they are drastic.

Springing for bigger seats and larger planes would also reduce hostility caused by crowding, claustrophobia, and competition for space. "There is no question the cattle-class experience has contributed to the rise and intensity of air rage incidents all over the world," said Andrew Thomas. "More people in a smaller space experiencing a naturally stressful environment will trigger different reactions in some folks, and a number will be violent," he told the *New York Times*. "With

---

33   Higgins, 2007.

the cutbacks continuing and the number of air travelers projected to triple in the next 20 years, air rage will be a problem for the foreseeable future."[34]

The lack of cleanliness in a plane is a visible mark of disrespect for the passenger that says, "We don't care; we don't have to," loud and clear. Like the graffiti on New York subways, it tells riders, "here you can be rowdy, because here no one cares." Stories of used diapers in seat pockets and years-old grime in carpets were topped by the saga of this flight from hell: Passengers on one direct flight from Amsterdam to New Jersey were forced to stop a night in Shannon, Ireland, so workers could fix a toilet that had sent human excrement running down the aisle next to passengers' feet. Unfortunately, when passengers climbed back on the plane the next morning, the mess was still there (but riper) and only one bathroom was half working for the seven-hour flight that followed. As a final insult, flight attendants serving meals in the mess and stench advised passengers not to eat much (lest they would need to use the lavatory).[35] A little rage in this situation might be justified.

Carolyn Andre of Berkeley, California, who flies 100,000 miles a year in business class, said banning liquor on planes would be a mistake. "When I fly, I like to drink myself into oblivion and then I go to sleep," she said. "It helps. I don't feel so good when I land, though."[36] Experts say airlines need to improve the flying experience so passengers won't need to drink themselves into a coma to get through it. Calls are coming for them to restrict the number of flights, hire more pilots, and better compensate people whose flights are delayed or canceled.

Deregulation and Air Rage

Many of the horrors of flying are the result of airline deregulation that started in the United States in 1978. "The architect of that change —Cornell economics professor Alfred Kahn, who possessed no apparent understanding of how the airline business really worked—helped sell Congress on the incredible illusion that the airline industry was not a vital public utility," said an unnamed airline professional who wrote for *ABC News*.[37] "Worse," he said, Kahn

> ... sold both Republicans and Democrats on the concept that the United States
> would be better served by inducing vicious, predatory competition in the industry
> that helped foster a field of new airlines doing things on the cheap.

34　Higgins, 2007.

35　"Sewage-Spewing Plane Disgusts Passengers: Continental Flight Soars Across Atlantic Despite Overflowed Toilets," *MSNBC News Services,* last updated June 20, 2007, found at: http://www.msnbc.msn.com/id/19332724/.

36　Steve Rubenstein, "Flight Attendants Fight 'Air Rage,'" *San Francisco Chronicle* (online), July 7, 2007, found at http://www.sfgate.com/cgi-bin/article.cgi?file=/chronicle/archive/2000/07/07/MN99774.DTL.

37　"Why Airline Service Suffers."

Such instant airlines such as Air Florida (of crash-into-the-14th-Street-bridge-in-D.C. infamy) and People's Express, by their very low-cost existence and sponsorship by government, were in essence a rebuke to the established legacy carriers for being stupid enough to pay for such frills and extras as established, professional maintenance bases and established, professional flight-training academies.[38]

The ultimate result is a flying experience that is survived rather than enjoyed, and, when things go wrong, experiences like this: A first class passenger flying from Istanbul to Los Angeles was bumped in New York City in the dead of winter without either warm clothes or his suitcase. Having had his credit card "chewed up" in the airport in Istanbul, he was left without money for food, and put up for the night in a frightening filthy flophouse until he could be sent home "cattle class" the next day with no compensation for his first class ticket.[39] Another passenger who'd paid $600 to fly to Hawaii discovered his seat wouldn't sit upright for the whole flight and the food for sale had run out.[40] These offenses are relatively routine in today's airline industry.

The long flights caused by hub and spoke routing also cause stress and ultimately contribute to rage. Southwest does not use the more traditional "hub and spoke" flight routing system of most other major airlines, preferring instead the "Point to Point" system. If more airlines followed suit, rage might diminish.

"We have seen an increase in (air rage) incidents throughout the industry," said Sara Nelson, a spokeswoman for the Association of Flight Attendants at United. "The biggest frustration is delays and cancellations, and that has the added problem of people sitting at airports and going to a bar and drinking alcohol. Alcohol is a leading cause of air-rage incidents."[41] More passengers with fewer airline employees tending to passengers, the frustrations of traveling, fewer amenities, and packed planes also increase "the opportunity for passengers to show their unreasonable side," Nelson said.[42]

The suggested changes do cost money. But they can be made. Again, Southwest seems to prove that. In one small example, Southwest continues to have the best rate of baggage delivery of all airlines surveyed. For all the leanness in comforts that helped it pass through the post-9/11 travel slump as one of the few profitable major American airlines, Southwest manages to maintain excellent customer satisfaction ratings.

---

38   Ibid.

39   Turboturk, blog post on a site sponsored by *IndependentTraveler.com*, posted March 25, 2006, found at http://gonomad.independenttraveler.com/archive/index.php?t-1081.html.

40   Higgins, 2007.

41   Kelly Yamanouchi, "United's New Committee Targets 'Air Rage,'" *Denver Post*, September 17, 2007, found at http://www.unitedafa.org/news/pdetails.asp?ID=281.

42   Ibid.

Flying Blind Drunk

For passengers like the woman who decides to start drinking before she hits the airport to gird her loins for the flight ahead, or the sober alcoholic who falls off the wagon because he dreads flying so much, a better flying experience might reduce the chance of getting drunk and making a scene. Since between 40 and 90 percent of all air rage incidents involve someone who's had too much to drink, it would seem to be a simple decision to stop serving alcohol on planes. However, alcohol may soothe as many nerves as it inflames. And like the candy and popcorn sold at the movies, the drinks sold on low-cost flight can be where the real money is made. If airlines can pay for flights with the profits from pushing drinks, they won't be abandoning in-flight liquor any time soon.

The real solution may lie in training flight attendants to recognize the signs that a passenger is getting drunk and at least refrain from offering that person another drink. An analysis of alcohol-related incidents on one airline revealed a "lack of crew coordination and communication" contributed to the majority of the alcohol abuse problems, Dahlberg said.[43] Drinkers on planes play one of the first parent-manipulation tricks children learn—when Mom says no, ask Dad. In other words, when one crew member won't give them a drink, they simply ask someone else. If crew members don't come to an agreement on how many drinks to serve, the passengers can suffer the consequences.

In 2001, in response to a flood of complaints about passenger inebriation, Senator Dianne Feinstein, Democrat of California, considered sponsoring a bill that would impose a two-drink limit on airline passengers. According to her spokesman, Howard Gantman, "Flight attendants told her horrible stories" about drunken passengers. Gantman said the senator still favored the limit, but had not proceeded with legislation because other issues of airline security had taken priority since the terrorist attacks on the World Trade Center and Pentagon.[44]

In a 2003 British House of Commons debate on a bill to limit or ban alcohol from airplanes, one member said, "When I first considered this Bill—for the record, I am teetotal, but I am not against drink—I asked myself whether taking alcohol off flights was the answer to some of the drunken and destructive behaviour. That would not be right either, however, as people enjoy a drink, many find it relaxing, and I have been told by the industry that it defuses the situation for many, as a glass of wine offers an escape valve. It is not the alcohol that causes the problem but the people who drink it and how it affects them."[45]

---

43   Dahlberg, p. 46.

44   Barry Estabrook, "A Paycheck Weekly, Insults Daily," *New York Times*, February 15, 2004, found at http://query.nytimes.com/gst/fullpage.html?res=9C0CE3D9173AF936 A25751C0A9629C8B63.

45   Parliamentary Publications and Records for 7 Feb 2003: Column 584, comment of Mr Roy, found at http://www.publications.parliament.uk/pa/cm200203/cmhansrd/vo030207/debtext/30207-14.htm.

Knowledge is Power ...or at Least Comfort

When stranded travelers wait hours for delayed or cancelled flights, they get angry when airlines don't tell them what's happening and why. Many feel airlines are holding them hostage to an unknown timetable while refusing to give them the facts they need to plan their next move.

On the other hand, when an airline gives customers information it gives them a sense of power and participation that makes them feel good about the company. Federal Express package service has based its strategy on that principle. Although only tangentially connected to commercial airlines, Fed Ex does transport objects from point A to point B, and its legendary reputation for customer satisfaction is built largely on its policy of including customers in the information loop. The company pioneered its package scanning and tracking system partly so they'd be able to tell customers where their packages were at any moment. The theory was that though customers would prefer their package to be delivered on time, if there should be a delay, they'd be happier simply knowing where it was. That knowledge gave them an invaluable sense of power and control.[46]

Federal Express also empowers customers and employees by listening to their ideas. "More important than our achievements," a company statement says:

> ... is our outside-in approach. That means we discover our customers' wants and needs and focus our innovation in those areas. By allowing innovation to be customer driven, FedEx has developed the most sophisticated technologies in our industry.
>
> This philosophy of innovation is enhanced by our commitment to foster a culture where people are empowered to create and present new ideas. In the FedEx work environment, more than 7,000 professionals ... are charged with improving existing products, services and technologies.[47]

Federal Express's success gives weight to the theory that airlines can make employees and passengers feel like stakeholders in their success by soliciting, valuing, and responding to their ideas.

The first thing airlines can do to reduce air rage, say experts James and Nahl, is "Provide a continuous stream of accurate updated information. No five minutes should go by without an update. This should be provided in a variety of formats and media: electric board, signs, announcements, and face to face telling."[48]

The airlines seem to be doing the opposite, even withholding the information employees need to do their jobs. When problems arise, like an airline strike or a

---

46   FedEx.com (Federal Express website), 2007, found at http://commitment.fedex.designcdt.com/innovation.

47   Ibid.

48   James and Nahl, quoted in Santiago.

cascade of plane delays or strandings triggered by one closed airport, employees often can't give angry passengers the information they need because they don't have it themselves. When management decides to stonewall about problems, it's the front line employees who take the heat. Management's "no comment" policy makes life hard for the workers who get blamed for the information blackout. Caught between passenger rage and management decisions, employees live with growing apprehension and frustration over airline policies as they try to maintain a working relationship with the traveling public.

In one notable case, the pilot of a plane stranded on the tarmac for ten hours who could neither reach his superiors to tell them his situation nor get any information back from them, finally snapped. He sent an electronic message to Northwest officials: "Would U pass on that the next problem they will have to deal with is blown slides." In other words, he was ready to release the emergency slides and let his passengers slide out of the plane at a cargo carrier's ramp if they weren't released soon.[49]

Step Up and Take Responsibility

Obviously, front line employees should be given the information they need to help their customers make connections and plan their time. When problems arise, airlines need to step up and focus on fixing the situation instead of scrambling to protect their image. Pitching in to clean up a mess is not the same thing as admitting misconduct, and even if a situation can't be reversed, just acknowledging that the customer is suffering and trying to make it better can earn an airline invaluable goodwill.

A blogger named Betty Lou painted a clear picture of how that principle would work if applied to airlines' worst recent public relations failures—the stranding of thousands of passengers on airport runways. "Given that these things will occur, there needs to be protocol and training," she said, "so act like it matters and BE PREPARED."

> ... Consider being trapped on a plane a high profile event. Have food available to zip out to a stranded plane. Have movies available free. Games for stranded kids. Be like the Boy Scouts—prepared. Each airport could even have a delayed plan SWAT team in place, ready to bring creature comforts, all the things necessary to manage the situation. Have staff medical personnel available to respond. Develop a passenger rotation [system determining] who will walk the aisles, rotating who walks, to avoid thrombophlebitis. Give the crew basic training in what to say. Basics, like we understand this is unacceptable, and we will still do all we can to help. PROVIDE INFORMATION. Airlines are famous for treating us like mushrooms. Provide people with as much control and

---

49   Anonymous and Andrew R. Thomas, *Air Rage: Crisis in the Skies* (Amherst, NY: Prometheus Books, 2001), p. 82.

respect as possible. Give free tickets as compensation. Most importantly, treat the situation as abhorrent. Agree with the passengers that it is over the top. They will respond. Be clear about any extra measures being taken to help. People are more cooperative when they feel they are heard and cared about, even if nothing concrete can be done.[50]

Rage Reduction Step Three: Value Front Line Employees; Train and Treasure This Key Asset

Hire the Right People

Since just 10 percent of employees are involved in 90 percent of air rage incidents, airlines need to review their hiring policies, Dahlberg said, filtering out potential employees who are still looking for glamour instead of a chance to do service work. "The flight attendant job, attracting a large number of applicants for life style reasons rather than professional skills and management, is now on the verge of becoming a true profession," she said. "Airlines need to rethink their service product design and aircraft cabin environment. This includes a new profile of flight attendants to meet the changed reality of air travel."[51]

Since flight attendant jobs are still in high demand and frequent layoffs mean there are always more applicants than jobs, airlines can be particular about who they hire. With this in mind, they should demand higher levels of competence and superior performance from existing staff by rewarding those who perform well and replacing those who do not.

After choosing the best candidates for the job, airlines need to maintain their workers' morale and pride in their work. There are many low-cost ways to do that. Southwest's Colleen Barrett opened her Thanksgiving letter by saying, "As a Company, we are blessed to have 33,000-plus employees who continually amaze me with their ability to Live the Southwest Way. ... Their Warrior Spirit, Servant's Heart, and Fun-LUVing attitude are part of my Thanksgiving blessings."[52] (LUV is Southwest's stock market symbol.) Though this is obviously a public relations effort, illustrated as it is with a picture of Ms Barrett looking like a sensible but loving grandma, it does reflect a culture in which employees are taught to see themselves as noble workers with a warrior spirit, instead of underpaid security guards. Reminding workers that the company values the "heart and fun" possible

---

50   Bunny Lou, blog comment posted August 15, 2007, in reaction to Rick Seaney, "Airline Passengers Boston Tea Party?" August 14, 2007, on airline service blog, *FareCompare.com,* found at http://rickseaney.com/2007/08/14/airline-passengers-boston-tea-party/.

51   "Training Can Reduce and Defuse Disruptive Passenger Incidents."

52   Barrett, 2007.

in giving service would improve employee morale and, with it, the customer's experience.

Some of the legacy airlines had this spirit 40 years ago. When I started working for Delta in 1966, they had the lowest customer service complaints, and the philosophy was, "We are the Delta family!" They had an open-door policy that welcomed employees to walk in and talk to anyone in the company at any time. Now that culture is found at Southwest and Jet Blue. Southwest is also the most heavily unionized airline, which may be reflected in salaries and pension benefits that add to employee contentment.

"You go into some airlines headquarters and you'll see pictures of happy employees on the wall," said airline consultant Mike Boyd on *PBS News Hour* in November 2001. "You do the same thing at Southwest. The only difference is at Southwest they're not actors; they're real employees. Employees like working there. When you like working at the place you work, you do better..You do a better job for the customer."[53]

"Statistics back up the assertion that Southwest has a happy workforce," said moderator Tom Bearden. "The employee retention rate is 92.3 percent, and each of its 32,000 employees recently agreed to give back some of their pay this month. Some believe the September 11 attacks have triggered a fundamental restructuring of the industry. In August, Daryll Jenkins predicted that Southwest would be carrying more domestic passengers than any other airline within five years. Now he thinks it'll take just three years."[54]

Little PR touches over the years have reinforced Southwest's sense of fun. Shortly after Southwest started using the "Just Plane Smart" motto, Stevens Aviation, which had been using "Plane Smart" for their motto, threatened a trademark lawsuit. In an inspired bit of public relations, the CEOs for both companies decided to stage an arm wrestling match instead of filing a lawsuit. They held it at the Dallas "Sportatorium," a then-famous wrestling center. To keep the motto, the CEO had to win two out of three rounds, with the loser of each round paying $5,000 to the charity of their choice. A promotional video showing the CEOs "training" for the bout featured Southwest CEO Herb Kelleher being helped to complete a sit-up, after which he had a cigarette and glass of Wild Turkey whiskey waiting. The mock training video and a video of the match were distributed to employees and the press. When Herb Kelleher lost the match for Southwest, Kurt Herwald, CEO of Stevens Aviation, immediately granted the use of "Just Plane Smart" to Southwest Airlines. As a result both companies had use

---

53   Michael Boyd, interview in "High Flyer," *Online NewsHour (from PBS News Hour)*, November 28, 2001, found at: http://www.pbs.org/newshour/bb/transportation/july-dec01/southwest_11-28.html.

54   Tom Beardon, interview in "High Flyer," *Online NewsHour (from PBS News Hour)*, November 28, 2001, found at: http://www.pbs.org/newshour/bb/transportation/july-dec01/southwest_11-28.html.

of the trademark, $15,000 went to charity, and everyone garnered a healthy dose of goodwill.[55]

Invest in Human Assets: "Disposable" Employees Aren't Cost-Effective

Airline employees caught between passenger abuse and management demands can become so stressed or feel so abused that their own exhaustion or rage keeps them from concentrating well enough to do their jobs effectively. Rude employees are usually overstressed and frustrated employees.

As one disgruntled former customer put it in a *Denver Post* blog, "United Airlines is so badly run that the cops could spend all day arresting unruly passengers." As a result, he said, "I avoid flying United as much as possible. The way they screw over their rank and file [sic] is outrageous and low morale is very contagious."[56]

His conclusion—"Don't fly the unfriendly 'skies' of United"—has serious implications for airline managers.[57] While airline management may think it's cheaper to hire "disposable" workers and fire them when they burn out, the price in rudeness, poor quality work, and time wasted reinventing the wheel while training new staff is high in the long run. More important, to run safely, an airline depends on competent, well-trained, long-term employees, and although it seems to take a back seat to the bottom line lately, safety must be the first priority of the airline industry.

Properly motivated employees can offer service with a smile and perform miracles for the customer, and they're proud to do so. Just as anger is contagious, so is professionalism. That's why it's cost-effective to recognize, support, and encourage high quality service by giving employees incentives to perform better, and service upgrades and other rewards for ongoing excellence in service.

The High Value of Kindness

Kindness cannot be demanded or taught. Airline management can no more force employees to be kind than it can force them to be happy, but airlines can inspire employees to be kind by offering kindness to them. They can begin by ensuring that employees are treated with respect and consideration. Employees who are treated kindly are more likely to pass along the favor. In a concrete example, when management kindly gives employees the information they need to help passengers, the workers are happier and better able to please passengers, and their behavior to

---

55   Timothy R.V. Foster, "How to Protect Your Slogan: Malice in Dallas," *AdSlogans. com*, 2000, found at http://www.adslogans.co.uk/ww/prvwis09.html.

56   Gwats, blog post on *Denverpost.com*, in response to "'Air Rage' Upsets United," posted September 17, 2007, found at http://neighbors.denverpost.com/viewtopic. php?t=6913089.

57   Ibid.

the passenger will show it. This one gift of honest information helps workers by making their day more pleasant, helps passengers by getting them on their way, and helps the airline by generating goodwill.

Airlines also need to invest in employee training. Some employees haven't been taught how to behave when dealing with the public. They need to be given the emotional tools to avoid arguments and defuse difficult situations. Many also need counseling or other resources to deal with the anger, stress, and stress-related illness resulting from customer abuse. If not addressed, this stress can cost the company sick pay while eroding workers' ability to get along with passengers. An Employee Assistance Program to address these problems should be established for all airline employees. While airlines have some personnel assistance systems, employees who deal with both customers and management are in particular need of back-up personally as well as professionally. No one-size-fits-all solution exists to help personnel cope with day-to-day interactions with others; having a staff member on site to provide resources and answer questions would help airline personnel develop better skills for coping with the general public while meeting the demands of management.

Finally, airlines show they value their employees when they give them the air rage training courses they need to defuse anger, prevent incidents from spiraling out of control, and, if the worst happens, subdue an explosive passenger. After evaluating the available courses, management can either provide air rage training courses as part of in-service training, or provide a list of acceptable courses staff members can take at the airlines' expense.

In the past, some airlines have offered staff members the chance to take air rage management courses at their own expense—a cruelly ironic gesture, given how little many of the employees who are on the front lines get paid to deal with potentially violent customers. By refusing to finance these classes, the airlines send a message that they don't think their workers' safety and training are worth paying for. To inspire excellent performance, they must send the opposite message by giving employees the tools they need to keep themselves and their passengers happy and safe.

Rage Reduction Step Four: Provide Specific Air Rage Training

Why Training is Lacking

Airline employees aren't getting the training they need to prevent air rage, in part because airlines are sweeping the problem under the rug. The major airlines avoid reporting air rage incidents because they're afraid bad publicity will tarnish the industry's image—which raises the question: Just what pristine area of their reputation is left to *be* tarnished when airlines are ranked as one of the bottom three service industries? Instead of spending energy protecting their sullied image, airlines might do better to clean up their act, polishing their service so it can stand up to scrutiny.

Airlines are also reluctant to admit fault for problems that contribute to rage because they're afraid of lawsuits. Sadly, in the current sue-happy business world, the willingness to step up and say "we're responsible" can be admitted as evidence in court to win a judgment that costs a company millions. Industry executives are also inhibited by the bad publicity that comes with admitting mistakes. If the industry could take this heat, stand behind its front line employees, and change the conditions that trigger air rage, they would reap the rewards of more effective employees, customer loyalty, and positive press coverage.

Enhance Courtesy with Competence: Verbal Judo

Along with choosing good front line employees, keeping them happy, and training them to work well with customers and use "Compassionate Crowd Management" to knit passengers into a coherent group, airlines need to train both ground personnel and flight crews to defuse a raging passenger's anger when it threatens to erupt. While there are all kinds of mechanical fixes and databases to minimize air rage, disruptive passengers are human beings, and human intervention is the primary means of coping with them. Front line employees, and particularly cabin crew, need training in welcoming passengers while firmly conveying that zero tolerance of disruptions will be allowed. They need courses in dealing with disruptive passengers by taking charge with their "command voice" and verbal judo.

In September 2007, Sara Nelson, a spokesperson for the Association of Flight Attendants at United Air Lines, said the flight attendants union would like to see additional training for flight attendants to "de-escalate" conflicts.[58] Retired pilot Captain Stephen Luckey said Cathay Pacific Airways had produced a booklet and training video for training crew members on how to deal with passengers who are out of control, something he'd like to see America's airlines do. "Most [American flight attendants] are not trained on how to prevent passenger disruptions or how to de-escalate confrontations before they become violent," he said. Flight and cabin crews need to know how to work together to handle such passengers, including how to use restraint devices if necessary.[59] In the United Kingdom, planes have been provided with a kind of straightjacket or harness for out-of-control passengers that is not available on airlines in the United States.

Midwest Airlines is providing flight attendants, pilots, and ticket and gate agents extra training on how to better communicate with customers, deal with their

---

58   Yamanouchi, 2007.

59   Statement of Captain Stephen Luckey, Chairman, National Security Committee, Air Line Pilots Association, Before the Subcommittee on Aviation, Committee on Transportation and Infrastructure, U.S. House of Representatives, Passenger Interference with Flight Crews and the Carry-on Baggage Reduction Act of 1997, June 11, 1998, found at http://cf.alpa.org/Internet/TM/tm061198.htm.

problems and defuse their anger when things go wrong. The first step to defusing a rage situation is to recognize the subtle signs of trouble so they can be addressed before the tipsy person becomes roaring drunk or the irritable one irate—or before the mental patient who's in deep trouble can climb on the plane.

When passengers get angry, a front line employee's first impulse may be to try to slap a lid on a difficult situation by telling them what they can't do. But saying a quick no is what psychologists call "negative reinforcement." For some people, that "no," that negative attention, is still attention or "reinforcement," and they will keep repeating the unwanted behavior as long as it draws your notice. More important, "You can't do that!" plants the picture of the thing they can't do in their head. It's like the old joke: "Don't think about an elephant!" As soon as they're told they can't do something, that's all they can think of, so that image of "doing that" becomes the focus of their attention. Crew members need the image in passengers' head to be what they can do, what crew members want them to do.

Persuasion Trick: Positive Reinforcement

The best approach to defusing anger is to tell people about the appealing option they *do* have, and explain why it would be helpful. This restores the passenger's feeling of control and agency in the situation. Telling difficult passengers that they are breaking the rules just makes things worse. The more you stress obedience, the angrier the offender gets, Dr August Dragt, PhD, a social psychologist at KLM told a seminar on dealing with unruly behavior in 2002. "People are frustrated about rules and regulations."[60]

At the seminar, which took place at the 19th annual International Aircraft Cabin Safety Symposium in 2002 in Los Angeles, a United Airlines crew member recounted the case of an irate woman who plunked herself into the flight attendants' crew rest seats and refused to return to her assigned seat:

> The woman complained loudly that she's been promised added legroom, didn't have it, and was availing herself of the greater legroom provided by the crew rest seats. In a way, she was taking control of her situation. The airplane had not yet been retrofitted to provide passengers with the greater legroom hyped in the airlines' marketing campaign.

> Told that she was prohibited from sitting in those seats by regulation, she refused to leave and was escorted by police off the aircraft upon landing, biting the officer as she was hauled off.[61]

It might have worked better to reason with her in a way that gave her the choice to leave rather than telling her she had no power and would be forced to. Dragt

---

60   "Training Can Reduce and Defuse Disruptive Passenger Incidents."
61   Ibid.

suggested that, instead of citing regulations, a crew member explain that the crew rest seats also are there for in-flight turbulence, and that flight attendants must be able to quickly move to these seats and belt themselves in. "You have to show understanding, give rational arguments and lead the passenger's attention to the desired behavior," Dragt said.[62]

He suggested telling a smoker, "Please, sir, you're standing and smoking next to a fire extinguisher that contains oxygen." He added, "It's totally illogical [a fire extinguisher containing oxygen] and often works."[63]

James and Nahl said that negative crowd control—the external imposition of enforced regulations—doesn't eliminate rebellion when people feel cynical and alienated. They say in our society, thanks to cultural influences like violent television programs and movies, we feel entitled to be violent in public, which is a form of cynicism. When people in such a society find themselves in lines that are unusually long or their plane is stuck on the tarmac when it should be moving, their expectations are violated—they feel robbed of what they were promised—so they feel alienation on top of the societal cynicism. Add external "thou shalt nots" to that brew and you get rebellious behavior. "People whose social inhibition against violence has been weakened," say Nahl and James, "experience this combination of cynicism and disentitlement as a legitimate opportunity for suspending the rules of civility."[64]

"Social peace in the aircraft passenger cabin is important for reasons of safety, economics and competitive advantage," says Angela Dahlberg. "The astute airline will take on the challenge with a broad-based strategy and specific goals. One aspect is linked to educating airline workers on how human factors impact on passenger performance on-board."[65]

"It's Not About You": Learning Not to Take Anger Personally

Front line workers need to learn that "passengers' rudeness and non-compliance to safety rules is not necessarily a deliberate affront to cabin crew members' personal dignity and authority," Dahlberg says. "Hostility is a symptom of a host of emotions. Fear of flying, the threat of losing control, fatigue, and personal and environmental stress are common experiences associated with air travel."[66]

Alcohol and drug abuse or withdrawal lowers inhibitions and can lead to real rage, Dahlberg said, and on-board smoking prohibitions may produce similar effects. "Self-protection, including from fear of flying, may be expressed in a number of ways: 'Why can't I drink as much as I want, have the seat I want, move my seat back, sit with my friend, smoke?'" Because passengers' apparent, defensive

---

62   Ibid.
63   Ibid.
64   James and Nahl, quoted in Santiago.
65   Dahlberg, pp. 43–44.
66   Ibid., p. 43.

emotion often masks a hidden vulnerability, she said, front line employees need to remember:

- Defensiveness covers embarrassment. Cabin crew members' reading the rules to customers risks escalation of hostility to aggression.
- A sense of helplessness relates to one's inability to change conditions or one's environment.
- A resentment of authority may be triggered by the image of someone with more power, influence or information to the point of hostility and anger.
- A person experiencing isolation is someone who is the only one who feels differently from the other people. Sometimes, a feeling of extreme isolation may cause overreaction and anger.[67]

When airline employees remember that these fears and tensions are prompting their customers to lash out, Dahlberg said, they may react less angrily to bad behavior. In the interest of safety, the crew can use the design and delivery of service as tools to "safeguard passenger performance," she said. "Exceptional cabin crews understand service as a strategy to calm the nerves of stressed air travelers."[68]

Dahlberg concluded that the passengers see the recitation of safety rules, which is the most visible part of the flight attendants' jobs, as rote jargon that's either boring or scary. It's the workers' personal ability to connect with each passenger and show that they work as a happy team that will calm passengers down.[69] Repeating pat phrases, like the rote "Buhbye Now! Buhbye Now!" at the cabin door that was mocked so effectively by comedian Ellen Degeneris, just alienates passengers.

"CARP" Negotiating with Verbal Judo

Airline workers need training to defuse building rage using the kind of "verbal judo" contained in Canadian Robert Bacal's CARP system for dealing with difficult customers or in fact any negotiations. CARP—which stands for Control, Acknowledge, Refocus, Problem-solve—was developed to help people in civil service and customer service jobs deal effectively with angry or abusive customers. Thinking about the acronym CARP, Bacal says, is "a way to remind yourself about the four major pieces of defusing hostility ... what we call an umbrella strategy":

1. *Control*—the key in reasserting control is to behave in ways that send the subtle message "your techniques (attempts to cause you [the worker] to

---

67 Ibid.
68 Ibid., p. 44.
69 Ibid., p. 45.

become defensive, angry, or off-balance) are not going to work on me."

2. *Acknowledge*—It is important the angry person see that you understand his/her emotional state and the situations. Two major techniques to apply here are empathy and active listening.

3. *Refocus*—Refocusing involves making the transition from dealing with the emotions to dealing with the actual problem.

4. *Problem-solve*—Problem-solving involves actions like getting and giving information, suggesting possibilities, and appearing helpful, offering choices.... and following through.[70]

When Persuasion Won't Work: Subduing Deranged Offenders

Captain Stephen Luckey said that in every one of the most serious attempts to break into a cockpit, "passengers have ultimately saved the day!" When the incoherent 250-pound, 6′ 2″ passenger took over the Alaska Airlines jet screaming "I'm going to kill you!" the captain had the good sense to call for help from passengers over the PA system. "We have an important resource in the passengers on every flight," Luckey said. "Unfortunately, most crew members remain unaware of this valuable tool because of lack of adequate flight-crew training to control air rage. We need to fix that."[71]

However, if they call on passengers, crew members need to prevent "reverse air rage," in which the unruly passenger is injured or killed by in-flight vigilantes. Crew members need to know how to work as a team to subdue a violent passenger—and when and how to ask passengers to help, without losing control of the situation or allowing their "helpers" to turn into vindictive vigilantes. Finally they need the ability to judge whether a passenger is dangerously unstable and needs to be restrained, and to know simple restraint techniques such as those learned by psychiatric aides. Without that training, an air rage incident can end up with a crew member, a passenger, or the offender himself injured or killed, or even worse, with the plane crashing. Unfortunately, most airlines aren't providing this kind of training.

Psychological Blocks to Self-Defense Courses

There's a simple human reason airline management resists the idea of training flight attendants in self-defense techniques, says Simon Squires, who teaches a course in dealing with disruptive passengers at a British company called Global Air Training. "It's absolutely unacceptable to be thinking of stewards or stewardesses

---

70   Robert Bacal, "Customer Service Knowledgebase," Web-page copyright 2004–2007, found at http://customerservicezone.com/faq/angercarp.htm.

71   Stephen Luckey, "Air Rage," *Air Line Pilot*, September 2000, p. 18 found at http://cf.alpa.org/internet/alp/2000/sept00p18.htm.

on a plane punching or kicking a member of the public."[72] Airline employees are programmed to think the customer is always right; even when enduring appalling treatment, they are encouraged to maintain a calm, pleasant demeanor because that's generally the wisest way to keep passenger anger from escalating. At first glance, self-defense courses would seem to fly in the face of that practice, setting up an adversarial relationship between flight attendants and passengers and bringing the mean streets into the airline cabin. That's the last thing airlines or flight attendants want to imagine (except maybe with the very worst passengers with whom even the mildest-mannered flight attendant might be excused for having Clint Eastwood fantasies).

However, as valuable as it is to maintain a pleasant atmosphere, airline workers need to regard self-defense the way they do cardiopulmonary resuscitation—it's something you never want to use, but want to know if you need it. Crew members all hope their passengers will stay healthy, but they still learn first aid and CPR just in case. And though everyone wants to rely on cordial, positive interactions to keep the flight safe, crew members face a growing number of passengers who are too far gone to be reached with gentle courtesy. If airlines can't offer a full-blown course in managing disruptive behavior, they should at least give cabin crews training like that given to psychiatric aides on how to subdue violent patients.

It's significant that psychiatric staff members at psychiatric facilities meet as often as once a week to evaluate their clients and figure out how they'll handle those who get out of control. Obviously flight crews can't do that, given how frequently crews reassemble and the changing passenger population. However, after receiving in-depth security training, supervisory staff members like pursers could briefly outline a security strategy at the beginning of each flight, pointing out the location of security equipment like handcuffs, lap belts, and other restraint devices. After air rage incidents, employees could hold security debriefings that would enable them to compile information and give gate agents and ground crew an opportunity to suggest better ways to handle incidents and to learn from strategies that did work.

Self-Defense and Physical Restraint

When persuasion and "verbal judo" don't work, the second phase of the two-pronged approach to air rage control is nonviolent physical restraint of violently raging passengers. Global Air Training, tucked away in the village of Llay on the outskirts of Wrexham in England, offers training in restraint techniques. Although it is 50 miles from the nearest international airport in Manchester, says the company website, it still draws "some of the biggest names in the air industry asking the company to help train their staff to deal with the rapid rise in air rage

---

72   "Air Rage Training for Cabin Crew," *BBC News*, February 28, 2004, found at http://news.bbc.co.uk/2/hi/uk_news/wales/north_east/3487282.stm.

incidents."[73] In their course, "Managing Disruptive Passenger Behaviour," airline staff members learn how to subdue aggressive travelers "in a non-confrontational manner." The techniques are designed to be very short, not particularly violent, but designed to "break contact between two people." Global Air Training does not train people to use unacceptable force when dealing with a fraught situation, Defense trainer Simon Squires told the BBC. "Our course is aimed at controlling the situation and diffusing it at all costs."[74]

In the United States, the Gracie Jiu-Jitsu Academy offers a similar safety training program called G.A.R.D.® (Gracie Air Rage Defense) for pilots and air marshals and another course for flight attendants. As it stands now, their website says, airline employees have relatively few techniques available to subdue disruptive passengers, including:

- Primary Restraint Techniques (PRT), a passive holding method;
- Basic flight attendant training that does not include suitable training in air rage situations;
- Plastic handcuffs on board planes; and
- "Yellow Card" warning notices that are handed out to disruptive passengers.[75]

"Obviously," the G.A.R.D. founders say, the "methods currently provided by the airlines are not solving the problem, because air rage is constantly on the rise." Because the problem is the same in every airline, they call for a standard, industry-wide program to deal with the issue. "It's a common problem," they say. "It requires a common solution."[76]

They developed G.A.R.D. to teach workers to identify potential threats and take preventive measures to protect themselves and their passengers. The program provides "non-lethal methods to effectively stop and subdue potentially dangerous individuals before situations escalate." It's unique, they say, because:

> … It addresses not only the physical and technical aspects of the situation, but also instills in the participants confidence that they will be able to execute the moves when required. This is crucial in situations where it is common that a flight attendant will be a woman facing a larger, stronger male passenger.

> Unfortunately, there are no guarantees that this or any other Self-Defense program will prevent a flight attendant from being attacked or, if attacked, will always enable her/him to subdue the unruly passenger without being harmed. The G.A.R.D.® program does, however, address the most common situations

---

73   Ibid.
74   Ibid.
75   The Gracie Jiu-Jitsu Academy, Web page copyrights 2005-2006, found at http://www.gracieacademy.com/gard_fattendants.html.
76   Ibid.

that occur when a flight attendant is involved in a confrontation with an abusive passenger. It also empowers flight attendants with the confidence that they CAN execute the techniques.[77]

One way airlines can ensure that employees get the most effective training to avert air rage is to evaluate the available courses and either integrate the instruction into the cabin crew training and/or offer tuition or expenses for employees to take the courses. Many such courses offer group rates to organizations. This is a comparatively minimal investment that can have immediate results in terms of better security.

Rage Reduction Step Five: Stand Behind the Employees; Enforce Air Rage Rules Consistently

Airline flight crews have been calling on airlines to stand behind them consistently. In September 2007, United Airlines created a "passenger incident review committee" to formally review air rage incidents where passengers physically abuse or threaten employees and are an "ongoing safety risk." The Association of Flight attendants pressed United to create the program, under which a committee will (a) decide how the passenger will be punished and whether they'll be able to travel again with United, (b) provide legal and emotional support for the employee, and (c) create a system to track the incidents.

Even with the enlightened, non-confrontational approach to conflict that Dragt recommends, he stresses that it's important to uphold policies more consistently. "If you enforce policies more uniformly, we've seen a decrease in incidents," he said, adding that he's aware of many cases "where the pursers did not support the flight attendants."[78]

Police sergeant Donald "Ward" Gagner of Bangor, Maine in the United States said that Great Britain is more forceful than the United States when it comes to prosecutions of unruly passengers. "The Brits try to make an example out of them," Gagner said. "They'll give them a year [behind bars]."[79]

When passengers who verbally and physically attack airline personnel walk away with no consequences, it sends the message that behavior that is intolerable in society as a whole is fine when taken against airline workers. Also, even nonviolent disruptive acts can affect everyone on a flight. For example, if an incident involves an individual who smokes in the lavatory, starts a small fire in the trash bin, which sets off the smoke detectors and causes a panic onboard the aircraft, there is no

---

77   Ibid.

78   "Training Can Reduce and Defuse Disruptive Passenger Incidents."

79   Sara Kehaulani Goo, "Bangor Is Used to Surprise Landings," *Washington Post,* October 17, 2004, p. A03, found at http://www.washingtonpost.com/wp-dyn/articles/A38685-2004Oct16.html.

legal basis for criminal action from local law enforcement agencies. While the sheer volume of air rage incidents continues to escalate, unfortunately the lives of innocent passengers will be put at risk again and again if the individuals are allowed to go free without any consequences.[80]

Air rage assaults should be treated as the criminal behavior that they are, and prosecuted to the fullest extent of the law. Management should provide employees who are victims of air rage with mentors to help them file complaints, testify, and pursue their cases to prevent the perception that flight attendants who complain about air rage are "troublemakers" and to ensure that their careers aren't damaged by their pursuit of air rage complaints. When cases go to court, airlines must support workers by providing legal counsel and guaranteeing the company's support.

Airlines can pay an immediate high price for an air rage incident. Lawrence Hoareau, a 28-year-old plumber from London traveling with his parents, allegedly began drinking from a bottle of vodka that he smuggled on board a Zoom airlines flight to Ottawa in 2006. According to court testimony, Hoareau "began to shout and swear, claiming someone had stolen a CD. He soon began to act aggressively," as his parents looked on, "horrified." The pilots made a quick decision to turn back to the closest airport, which was in Glasgow, and passengers cheered as officers dragged Hoareau off the plane. His mortified parents went on to Canada without him. In court, the airline claimed the diversion cost £100,000—or about $188,000—in airport landing fees and re-fueling charges. Hoareau was sentenced to 240 hours of community service.[81]

But airlines also pay a larger long-term price for air rage. When ticket prices have finally reached a floor, all airlines will have left to compete with is their reputation. No airline will want to be known as the one with the lunatic ragers, or the one who inspires rage in sane people.

Public Accountability

Too often, the last words flight attendants and gate agents hear from irate customers are, "I'll never fly your airline again!" Customers will certainly avoid any company that puts them through a horrible experience. Most airline service leaves a great deal of room for improvement, but it's hard to shoot for a goal when the industry has set no clear service standards and each airline does things differently. Experts say a few changes in airline policies and modest investments in employee training can yield a dramatic reduction in the incidence of air rage. The industry needs to develop service standards so airlines will have a yardstick against which to measure their performance. In addition, when customers can expect the same

---

80   Anonymous and Thomas, pp. 110–111.
81   "Air Rage Incident Costs Airline $188,000," *USA Today* (online), September 14, 2006, found at http://blogs.usatoday.com/sky/unruly_passengers/index.html.

service from all airlines, their expectations will be met more often and they'll be less likely to engage in air rage.

MSNBC columnist Ed Hewitt says the airlines need to clean up their acts because the sky belongs to the people. "This is no abstract notion," he says. "We pay for it every time we buy an airline ticket laden with taxes; we pay for it every time we bail out mismanaged airlines with public money. The airlines know they will be bailed out because air travel is essential to the business of America, but that status comes with responsibility too. ... it's time that, at least when it comes to routine and humane treatment of customers, the airlines understand it is our world they fly in—and if it takes laws to do this, so be it. They certainly have not been able to police themselves."[82]

While observers like consultant Michael Boyd want to see the airlines solve their own problems voluntarily, Hewitt says, "Let's give the public air space back to the public that flies—and owns—the friendly skies. That would really be something special in the air."[83]

Whatever is done about regulation, ignoring air rage won't make it go away. The only way to solve the problem is to face it, take steps towards eliminating the causes, and learn more about the cures, while giving the flying public the kind of service that can turn each planeload of passengers into a united mini-community. With the right training, airline employees can learn the psychological techniques they need to defuse anger along with the self-defense skills needed to subdue out-of-control passengers. By giving better service and restoring airline accountability, airlines can regain the trust of customers and employees. If airlines show that they value their employees and their passengers by listening carefully to their suggestions and addressing their concerns, they can bring about the dawn of a new era of flight, serving happier more contented passengers.

---

82 Ed Hewitt, "The Airline Passenger's Bill of Rights," *MSNBC.com*, February 16, 2007, p. 3, found at http://www.msnbc.msn.com/id/17173370/.
83 Ibid.

Afterword

Lessons Learned

In the "Age of Rage," as the threat of air rage and terrorism loom over the flying public, airline employees are looking for the simplest, most efficient, and cost-effective ways to prevent air rage. More than anything, they'd like to short-circuit air rage before it erupts. Two important ways to achieve this are to keep passengers who are destined to rage off the plane and reduce the stressful flying conditions that inflame rage. At this point, if these two approaches fail and air rage breaks out, the only solution grows from the grace under fire of inspired passengers and flight crews. But we should not be dependent on that grace to guarantee the survival of planeloads of fliers.

The Road from Low Fares to Rage: Why Unhappy Workers = Unhappy Passengers

Air rage has increased as airfares have dropped. Fighting for financial survival when there's no limit to how low fares can go, airlines have cut every corner, slashing every expense to the bone and then cutting into the marrow. Operating under the fear of imminent bankruptcy, many airlines send employees the message they should count themselves lucky to have a job at all.

The result is a demoralized work force. Flight attendants stagger under heavy workloads and physical hardships, including exposure to toxic fumes and long workdays without food. They may spend 10 or 20 hours serving meals to others, knowing they themselves have nothing to eat—their airline doesn't provide food for them and regulations prevent them from bringing their own lunches. Often their reward for enduring these hardships has been cuts in their pension plans and benefits. As a result, their "customer is always right" ethos has given way to mutinous thoughts, like "What kind of service do Cattle Class passengers expect for their low fares? At these prices they should shut up and not complain."

Passengers in turn, no longer expect comfort or even convenience when they board a plane. They figure it's a near miracle if they make their flight, arrive more or less when expected, and don't lose their luggage. Given this mutual disrespect and apprehension, passengers and crew are on edge even when flights run smoothly, and the number of things that can go wrong during a trip seems to grow every year.

In addition, airlines set customer service employees up to fail when they barely train them to deal with difficult situations, limit their authority to make decisions, and fail to support them under fire. When employees complain of mistreatment or even physical assault by passengers, they may find that they, not their attackers, are the ones being disciplined. Watching offenders walk away scot-free, even if they themselves have been injured, these employees understandably conclude that they are considered unimportant and expendable.

In spite of all this, gate personnel and cabin crews are told to smile and "behave professionally" while being prevented from giving angry customers much information and trying to control rude, unruly, or downright violent passengers. Powerless and devalued, they can only vent their emotions covertly on hapless fliers. When passive aggression is the only way to strike back, it isn't surprising that a gate agent might send a passenger's bags on a northbound flight as the passenger heads west, or a flight attendant might simply ignore a demanding passenger's requests. Empty slogans promising "teamwork" and "valuing employees" will not solve this problem. Flight attendants in particular need a status upgrade from "flying waitress" to professionals given an appropriate level of training, recognition, and authority. At any moment during a flight, the cabin crew may be forced to make life-and-death decisions to ensure the safety of the plane and its passengers. Travelers will all benefit if airline employees are valued according to their real importance.

Keeping Problems Off the Plane: Warning Signs of Rage

Given that an estimated one in ten adult males in America is a rage addict, it's unavoidable that at least some passengers with toxic anger problems will be climbing on airplanes. Contrary to popular myth, these rage addicts don't suddenly blow a fuse without warning. They're angry in their everyday lives, and it's likely that their relatives, friends and co-workers know they have an anger problem. Unfortunately, there's no way for airline personnel to know that.

But forewarned is forearmed, and rage addicts do give warning signs when they're starting to spiral into rage. Alert ground personnel and flight crews can spot the signs that passengers are "looking for a fight" in time to create a plan to deal with the problem. From pre-boarding onward, it pays to keep an eye on individuals who make "me first" demands with a sense of entitlement. Other clear warning signs include overtly ignoring airline rules; confronting crew or other passengers with hostility, rudeness, and abusive language, including cursing and swearing; and verbal or sexual harassment of crew members. When front line employees see this behavior, they need to tell ground employees and flight crews, so they can have a defensive strategy ready when the potential serious troublemaker boards their flight.

Although they have a physical and emotional addiction to rage, rage addicts may still be pushed over the edge by bad flying conditions—and by implication, some might be kept from erupting by a pleasant experience. Like most addictions, toxic rage is accompanied by physical changes that are exacerbated by the lack of control, high frustration, close confinement, and low oxygen levels on an airliner. When the brain's usable oxygen is reduced, other addictive substances, such as nicotine, alcohol, or drugs, make these physical symptoms worse; and withdrawal from drugs or nicotine increases this agitation.

Once anger has erupted, the flight crew has a delicate dance to perform. Rage addiction thrives on righteous indignation, and rage-filled people blame everyone for their anger but themselves. Confronting them when they're angry just pours fuel on the flames. The most effective technique for defusing the rage is to engage the raging individual in working with the airline employees to solve the problem.

Mass Transit = Mass Problems with No Exit

When deregulation set the stage for fare wars, airlines began to compete for a larger customer base. They didn't plan for the consequences of reinventing air travel as a mass transit option—including the problems of dealing with a broader spectrum of society. Cramming this newly expanded flying population into ever-smaller seats placed an increased number of people from all walks of life at very close quarters where no escape was possible.

On the ground, mass transit operators like bus drivers and railroad conductors can stop and eject an offensive passenger. In extreme emergencies they can have police on the scene relatively quickly. Even on a ship there is enough space to isolate someone who's out of control. By contrast, potentially unruly airline passengers are crowded into a densely populated, stress-filled environment with only a small crew to keep order and no way to isolate or remove them. In rare situations a pilot can divert the flight to make an emergency landing, but this option is not always available and has its own dangers. This crowd control problem is one reason airplanes are such attractive targets to terrorists. Maintaining safety with a limited number of crew members at 30,000 feet requires thoughtful planning that is only beginning to take place.

The Expanding "Right to Rage"

Rage has been with us as long as humanity. However, in the beginning rage was seen as such an awesome and uncontrollable power, its expression was reserved for the gods. As time passed, the right to express rage was extended to legendary heroes, and then to kings and some religious leaders. But through medieval times, the right to express rage went hand in hand with the power (and by implication, the ability) to manage it. In medieval histories, warriors induced rage to rev up the adrenaline-induced powers that flowed from the fight-or-flight response. However, while rulers and elite soldiers might use anger to force enemies to submit, even righteous indignation was not tolerated among those of lower rank. Imploded rage did explode among everyday people in some cultures, as when Malaysians and others committed suicide by running amok, killing everyone in their path until they were killed themselves. But this rage was still punished by death.

In modern times, the loosening of social inhibitions has contributed to a situation in which large masses of people feel perfectly entitled to feel and express rage in public. Once the province of gods, rage is now paraded by more and more ordinary people who crave the illusion of power that arises with the adrenaline-fueled fight-or-flight response. The consequences when this happens on an airplane can be disastrous.

Real Versus Ideal

In a perfect world, flying would be such a lovely experience that it wouldn't provoke anger. Ideally, each flight would be on time, cabins would be roomy and filled with clean air, and airlines would support their employees in learning the most effective techniques to short-circuit air rage and protect the safety of everyone on each flight. Cabin crews would build teamwork and reward skillful crisis avoidance among flight attendants, and passengers would bring patience and common sense to a potentially difficult flying experience.

But what should happen and what does happen are two different things, and these changes may be a long time in coming. What is often missing and deeply missed during a flight is the simple yet heroic act of rising above the swamp of tension and often-real danger created by running low-fare airlines on the razor's edge between discomfort and torture. When airlines throw their flight crews into the front lines with minimal training and little support, when no one cooperates during difficult situations, and when passengers rage out of control, the only answer is for thoughtful individuals to rise above their feelings and act with restraint and tact.

Airline employees and passengers can make a choice to use forbearance and good humor, not because it is required of them—no law can force grace on anyone—but for their own good. Calm, level-headed behavior is essential because air travel is more dangerous than passengers realize when they're cradled in the padded illusion created by muffled engine noise and a soothing décor. While traveling together at 30,000 feet in a fast-moving metal cylinder with no escape, one person's violent and irrational behavior can be fatal to everyone. When tension threatens to erupt into rage, quiet heroism, calm endurance, and sensible action can save everyone's lives. Flight crews and passengers alike want to reach their destination unharmed, and this enlightened self-interest is a strong motivator.

First Steps: What We Can Do Now

The first tactic that airline employees have to combat air rage is to control who gets on the plane to begin with. Both gate agents and cabin crew need clear guidelines to screen out real troublemakers and prevent them from boarding, as well as to defuse a hostile situation that manifests itself before takeoff. Front-line employees need the authority to prevent any passenger who is seriously impaired by alcohol or rage from boarding, or to remove the passenger from a plane before it takes off. When they do so, they should have trained security staff on call to back them up.

Once the plane is in the air, flight attendants must rely on their people skills. Airline cabin crew will benefit by learning strategies to "turn down the heat" on angry passengers. Frustration leads to aggression, and many flyers become hostile because they feel no one is listening when they ask for help. Ignoring the passengers, arguing with them, or shutting them down can pour fuel on that fire. The first step in trying to calm a passenger should always be to listen and try to work through the problem together. A frustrated passenger can become less hostile when the cabin crew make it clear that they are aware of the passenger's situation and trying to find possible solutions. Many irate passengers are acting out because of a fear of flying, which includes the fear of loss of control. When a flight attendant can offer these passengers realistic choices, it gives them a sense of power that can soothe their anxiety and reduce their sense of being trapped and helpless. Tools the flight attendant can learn to use effectively to defuse tense situations include speaking in calm tones, smiling, and using soothing body language. Of course only when all else fails should the crew member consider restraining out-of-control passengers.

Rage Prevention Can Be Fun: Southwest and Jet Blue

Cultivating a warm, humane airline culture goes a long way towards decreasing confrontational situations. Two airlines, Southwest and Jet Blue, have had notable success fostering a people-friendly, "fun, not frills" atmosphere that has garnered top ratings in customer relations and profitability for many years now. Southwest in particular makes a point of listening to, respecting, and rewarding its employees. Happier employees treat passengers better because they enjoy their jobs. Southwest employees have fun, joking with and even singing to customers. When employees present this kind of friendly face to passengers, they create a warmer atmosphere that goes a long way toward short-circuiting the feeling of being anonymous and ignored that can lead to angry outbursts. Good humor in difficult situations can be contagious. Author Maya Angelou puts it well: "I've learned that people will forget what you said, people will forget what you did, but people will never forget how you made them feel." Excellent customer service builds customer loyalty, fosters profits, and increases safety. It pays to study what works, and when it comes to reducing air rage, what works is good service.

References

"2007: The Year of Mishandled Luggage." *CBS 4* online service, October 1, 2007. Found at http://www.topix.com/content/cbs/2007/10/2007-the-year-of-mishandled-luggage-6 and also found at the CBS News site, http://cbs11tv.com/consumer/airports.airlines.travel.2.507448.html.

"About SWA." *Southwest.com*. Found at http://www.southwest.com/about_swa/airborne.html.

Acohido, Byron. "Verdict Expected Soon on Toxic Air Aboard Jets." *USA Today,* May 9, 2002. Found at http://www.usatoday.com/travel/news/2002/2002-05-09-cabin-air.htm.

AD Aerospace. "Is FlightVu the Answer?" August 1, 2006. Found at http://www.ad-aero.com/products_witness_news.php.

"Air Rage Crackdown Backed." *BBC News*, May 16, 2003. Found at http://news.bbc.co.uk/2/hi/uk_news/politics/3034889.stm.

"Air Rage Death Clarified." *Las Vegas Review-Journal*, September 17, 2000. Found at http://www.reviewjournal.com/lvrj_home/2000/Sep-17-Sun-2000/news/14407481.html.

"Air Rage Incident Costs Airline $188,000." *USA Today* (online), September 14, 2006. Found at http://blogs.usatoday.com/sky/unruly_passengers/index.html.

"Air-Rage Incidents Double in Two Years." *Daily Telegraph*, November 25, 2006. Found at http://www.telegraph.co.uk/travel/737102/Air-rage-incidents-double-in-two-years.html.

"Air Rage Increasing, Expert Says." *Akron Beacon Journal*, September 28, 2007. Found in Securityinfowatch.com, at http://www.securityinfowatch.com/article/printer.jsp?id=12650.

"Air Rage Passenger Faces Prison." *BBC News*, September 5, 2007. Found at http://news.bbc.co.uk/2/hi/uk_news/england/6980172.stm; and "Air Rage." *AD-Aero.com*, published by FlightVu, found at http://www.ad-aero.com/products_witness_news.php.

"Air Rage Stops 1173 UK Deportations." *Scotsman.com*, May 16, 2007, originally found on Scotsman site but more recently found at http://frontexwatch.wordpress.com/2007/05/16/air-rage-stops-1173-uk-deportations/.

"Air Rage Training for Cabin Crew." *BBC News*, February 28, 2004. Found at http://news.bbc.co.uk/2/hi/uk_news/wales/north_east/3487282.stm.

"Airlines Reject AFA Attacks on Air Rage, Alcohol Policies." *World Airline News*, July 13, 2001. Found at http://findarticles.com/p/articles/mi_m0ZCK/is_28_11/ai_76547444.

"Airlines Tolerate Air Rage." *USA Today*, March 21, 2001. Found at http://archives.californiaaviation.org/airport/msg13957.html.

"Airplane Rage Costs Fla. Man $12,000." *CBC News*, March 28, 2007. Found at http://www.cbc.ca/canada/newfoundland-labrador/story/2007/03/28/airplane-rage.html.

Airsafe.com, 2002. Found at http://airsafe.com.

Alexander, Keith L. "Knee Defender Keeps Passengers Upright, Uptight." *Washington Post*, October 28, 2003, E01. Found at http://www.washingtonpost.com/wp-dyn/content/article/2003/10/28/AR2005033109087_pf.html.

Althoff, Gerd. "Ira Regis: A History of Royal Anger." pp. 59–74 in Rosenwein (ed.), *Anger's Past: The Social Uses of an Emotion in the Middle Ages* (Ithaca, NY: Cornell University Press, 1998).

American Customer Satisfaction Index. University of Michigan. Found at http://www.theacsi.org/index.php?option=com_content&task=view&id=147&Itemid=155&i=Airlines.

American Psychiatric Association. "Impulse-Control Disorders Not Elsewhere Classified." *Diagnostic and Statistical Manual of Mental Disorders*, Fourth Ed., Text Revision (Washington, DC: American Psychiatric Association, 2000).

"Amok." *NationMaster.com Encyclopedia*. Found at http://www.nationmaster.com/encyclopedia/Amok.

"Anger Free Driving." *Compassion Power* (n.d.). Found at http://compassionpower.com/anger%20free%20driving.php.

"Anger: What Causes Anger?" *Yahoo Geocities*, 1997. Found at http://www.geocities.com/Athens/Acropolis/6729/anger2.htm.

Anglin, Lisa, Neves, Paula, Giesbrecht, Norman, and Kobus-Matthews, Marianne. "Alcohol-Related Air Rage: From Damage Control to Primary Prevention." *Journal of Primary Prevention*, March 2003, 23(3). Found at http://www.springerlink.com/content/u1338427v01282h1/.

Anonymous. Blog comment about "Flight Attendants Advocate for Legislation and Join Coalition in Passenger Rights Fight!" *Coalition for Airlines Bill of Rights Hotline*, posted June 22, 2007. Found at http://strandedpassengers.blogspot.com/2007/06/flight-attendants-advocate-for.html.

Anonymous and Thomas, Andrew R. *Air Rage: Crisis in the Skies* (Amherst, NY: Prometheus Books, 2001).

Associated Press. "Hawaii-Bound Flight Diverted after Unruly Passenger Strikes Pilot." *USA Today*, April 3, 2007. Found at http://www.usatoday.com/travel/flights/2007-04-03-passenger-strikes-pilot_N.htm.

Associated Press. "Florida Man Charged with Punching Out Airplane Window in Flight." *USA Today*, October 14, 2005. Found at http://www.usatoday.com/travel/news/2005-10-14-window-punch_x.htm.

Associated Press. "Man Accused of Belligerent Behavior on Flight." *Dallas Morning News*, March 15, 2007. Found at http://www.dallasnews.com/sharedcontent/dws/dn/latestnews/stories/031607dntexflightdisrupt.164f40b0.html.

Association of Flight Attendants, AFL-CIO. "Oil Switch on the B737 Fleet." *Safety and Health Alert*, November 2002. Found at http://ashsd.afacwa.org/docs/291to254.pdf.

Association of Flight Attendants–CWA. *Flight Attendant Certification*, posted November 11, 2004. Found at http://ashsd.afacwa.org/print_article.cfm?homeID=10814.

"Australian Flight Crews Overcome by Toxic Fumes." *Sydney Morning Herald*, October 22, 2007. Found at http://www.smh.com.au/articles/2007/10/22/1192940945399.html.

Australian Services Union. "Qantas to Act on Rage at Airports." *ASU National Net*, May 13, 2004. Found at http://www.asu.asn.au/media/airlines_general/20040513_airrage.html.

Australian Services Union National Office, "'Zero Air Rage' Survey, Preliminary Survey Results." October 20, 2003. Found at http://www.aph.gov.au/house/committee/jpaa/aviation_security/submissions/sub62a.pdf.

"BA Jet Plunges in Cockpit Struggle." *BBC News*, December 29, 2000. Found at http://news.bbc.co.uk/2/hi/uk_news/1092164.stm.

Bacal, Robert. "Angry Customers: What Do They Really Want, and How to Give It to Them." 1995. Found at http://ezinearticles.com/?Angry-Customers-What-Do-They-Really-Want,-and-How-To-Give-It-To-Them&id=69130.

Bacal, Robert. "Customer Service Knowledgebase." Web-page copyright 2004–2007. Found at http://customerservicezone.com/faq/angercarp.htm.

Bailey, Jeff. "Bumped Fliers and No Plan B." *New York Times*, May 30, 2007. Found at www.nytimes.com/2007/05/30/business/30bump.html?pagewanted=print.

Bailey, Jeff. "Rough Summer is on the way for Air Travel." *New York Times*, May 21, 2006. Found at http://www.nytimes.com/2006/05/21/business/21AIRTRAVEL.htm.

Barach, Alvan L., and Kagan, Julia. "Disorders of Mental Functioning Produced by Varying the Oxygen Tension of the Atmosphere." *Psychosomatic Medicine*, 2(1), January, 1940, p. 54 and pp. 64–66. Found at http://www.psychosomaticmedicine.org/cgi/reprint/2/1/53.pdf.

"Barbarians Apologize." ABC, *Channel 7 in Denver* online, August 23, 2005. Found at http://www.thedenverchannel.com/news/4885984/detail.html.

Barrett, Colleen. "Colleen's Corner." *Spirit Magazine* (for Southwest Airlines), November 2007.

Barron, Paul E. "Air Rage: An Emerging Challenge for the Airline Industry." *Asia Pacific Journal of Transport*, Summer 2006, 4, pp. 39–44.

Baskas, Helen. "Flying with Children Doesn't Have to Get Ugly." *USA Today*, April 20, 2004. Found at http://www.usatoday.com/travel/columnist/baskas/2004-04-20-baskas_x.htm.

Beardon, Tom. Interview in "High Flyer." *Online NewsHour* (from PBS News Hour), November 28, 2001. Found at: http://www.pbs.org/newshour/bb/transportation/july-dec01/southwest_11-28.html.

BNET Business Network. "Airlines Reject AFA Attacks on Air Rage, Alcohol Policies." *World Airline News*, July 31, 2001. May be found through Google.com or at http://findarticles.com/p/articles/mi_m0ZCK/is_28_11/ai_76547444.

Bonvie, Linda, and Bonvie, Bill. "Airline's Insecticide May be Affecting More than Bugs, Australia and New Zealand Demand That All Incoming Planes (and People) be Sprayed with Pesticides Before Debarking." *safe2use*, March 4, 2001. Found at http://www.safe2use.com/ca-ipm/01-03-04.htm.

Bor, Robert. Proceedings of the 10th International Symposium on Aviation Psychology. Columbus, OH, May 3–6, 1999, pp. 1161–1166.

Bor, Robert, Russell, Morris, Parker, Justin, and Papadopoulos, Linda. Managing Disruptive Passengers: A Survey of the World's Airlines, 1999. Found as a 2000 reprint at http://www.skyrage.org/pdf/academic/rbor.pdf.

Boyd, Malcolm. "The Airline CEO Challenge: Experience What You Put Your Passengers Through." *Hot Flash*, July 23, 2001. Found at http://www.aviationplanning.com/airline1.htm#Abuse.

Boyd, Michael. "Abusive" Passengers. Ever Wonder How Some Get That Way?" *Hot Flash*, 2001. Found at http://www.aviationplanning.com/airline1.htm#Abuse.

Boyd, Michael. "Air Rage: Battle Lines Are Drawn." *Hot Flash*, August 2, 1999. Found at http://www.aviationplanning.com/airline1.htm#Abuse.

Boyd, Michael. "Enlightened Customer Service: Everybody is a Suspect." *Hot Flash*, August 6, 2001. Found at http://www.aviationplanning.com/airline1.htm#Hot%20Flash%20%20August%206,%202001.

Boyd, Michael. "The Airline CEO Challenge: Experience What You Put Your Passengers Through." *Hot Flash*, July 23, 2001. Found at http://www.aviationplanning.com/airline1.htm#CEO.

Boyd, Michael. Interview in "High Flyer." *Online NewsHour* (from PBS News Hour), November 28, 2001. Found at: http://www.pbs.org/newshour/bb/transportation/july-dec01/southwest_11-28.html.

Brady, M.K., and Cronin, Jr., J. "Customer Orientation: Effects on Customer Service Perceptions and Outcome Behaviors." *Journal of Service Research*, 3(3), pp. 241–251.

"A Brief History Lesson: National Numbers." *NationalNumbers.com* (n.d.). Found at http://www.nationalnumbers.co.uk/number-plate-history.htm.

"Britney Demands to Leave Plane Minutes Before Takeoff." *Celebitchy*, May 21, 2007. Found at http://www.cclebitchy.com/3935/britney_demands_to_leave_plane_minutes_before_takeoff/.

Brower, Katherine, Shannon, Ellyn, and Berger, Karyl. Permanent Citizens Advisory Committee to the MTA. "Best Foot Forward: Training Front Line Personnel to Provide Quality Customer Service." November 2003. Found at http://pcac.org/reports/pdf/Best%20Foot%20ExecSumm.pdf.

Bunny Lou (online identity). Blog comment posted August 15, 2007, in reaction to Rick Seaney, "Airline Passengers Boston Tea Party?" On airline service blog, *FareCompare.com*, August 14, 2007. Found at http://rickseaney.com /2007/08/14/airline-passengers-boston-tea-party/.

Burge, Sarah. "Autistic Man's Mother Sues Riverside County, Claiming Deputies Caused His Death." *The Riverside Press-Enterprise* (online), May 27, 2007. Found at http://www.pe.com/localnews/inland/stories/PE_News_Local_B_ delirium28.3cd3d33.html.

Calhoun, John B. "Death Squared: The Explosive Growth and Demise of a Mouse Population." *Journal of the Royal Society of Medicine*, January 1973, 566. Found at http://www.pubmedcentral.nih.gov/articlerender.fcgi?artid=1644264.

Clemmer, Jim. "Blame Management for Poor Service." *Expert Magazine*, January 9, 2006, p. 1. Found at http://www.expertmagizine.com/artman/publish /article_818.shtml.

Clothier, Julie. "When Cabin Fever Turns to Air Rage." *CNN.com*, August 8, 2006. Found at http://www.cnn.com/2006/TRAVEL/08/08/air.rage/index.html.

Cockburn, Alexander. "In Transports of Horror and Delight." *The Nation*, December 3, 2007, p. 9.

"Comfort for Smokers." GlobeLife Travel section of *Globeandmail.com*, November 8, 2000. Found at http://www.theglobeandmail.com/servlet/Page/ document/v5/templates/hub?hub=Travel&subhub=activities&activity=smoking.

Connors, Joanie. "The Two Parts of Anger: Don't Get Mad, Get Positive Ways to Use Anger." Found at http://www.desertexposure.com/200708/200708_bms_ anger.php.

"Corsair Selects FlightVu CDMS for Aircraft." August 24, 2004. Found at http:// www.ad-aero.com/news_nr_details.php?news_id=33.

Cummings, Claire. "Passengers Stuck on Plane Over 8 Hours." *Dallas Morning News*, December 30, 2006. Found at http://www.dallasnews.com/sharedcontent/ dws/bus/industries/airlines/stories/123006dntswstranded.331dc32.html.

D'Amato, Erik. "Mystery of Disgust." *Psychology Today*, January/Februry 1998. Found at http://www.psychologytoday.com/articles/pto-19980201-000032. html.

Dahlberg, Angela. *Air Rage: The Underestimated Safety Risk* (Aldershot, UK: Ashgate, 2001).

De Lollis, Barbara. "Job Stress Beginning to Take Toll on Some Airline Workers." *USA Today*, November 19, 2004. Found at http://www.usatoday.com/travel/ news/2004-11-29-unhappyair_x.htm

"A Death on Descent." *CBS News*, September 21, 2000. Found at http://www. cbsnews.com/stories/2000/09/21/national/printable235154.shtml.

DeMary, Richard (Interview). In "Sudden Impact—A Flight Attendant's Story of Courage and Survival." *Cabin Crew Safety*, March/April and May/June 1995. Found at http://www.flightsafety.aero/ccs/ccs_mar_june95.pdf.

Diane (online identifier, St. Paul, MN). "Frustrations on a Plane." Blog comment posted August 21, 2007, in response to "Peeved Passengers Want Answers from Airlines." summary by Kathleen Schalch for Blog of the Nation, *National Public Radio*, August 21, 2007. Found at http://www.npr.org/templates/story/story.php?storyId=13831847.

Drummond, M. "Customer Service Woes: At a Time When Companies Should be Doing Everything in Their Power to Keep Customers and Keep Them Happy, Many Aren't." *Business 2.0.*, June 4, 2001. Found at http://www.business2.com/articles/web/0,1653,15896,FF.html.

"The Drunken Defecator." *That's Plane Funny* (online; no date). Found at http://www.thatsplanefunny.com/cornecopia.html.

Dryden, John, cited in Wisdom Quotes, found at http://www.wisdomquotes.com/cat_anger.html.

Early, Jay. "Letter Written in Response to an Editorial Supporting Southwest Airlines 'Two Seats for Fat People' Policy." 2003. Found at http://www.maadwomen.com/lynnemurray/essays/southwest.html.

Eigen, Michael. *Rage* (Middletown, CT: Wesleyan University Press, 2002).

Elliott, Christopher. "Revenge of the Ticket Agents." *MSNBC.com*, October 1, 2007. Found at http://www.msnbc.msn.com/id/21080989/.

Estabrook, Barry. "A Paycheck Weekly, Insults Daily." *New York Times*, February 15, 2004. Found at http://query.nytimes.com/gst/fullpage.html?sec=travel&res=9C0CE3D9173AF936A25751C0A9629C8B63&fta=y.

FedEx.com (Federal Express website), 2007. Found at http://commitment.fedex.designcdt.com/innovation.

Fine, E.W. "Air Rage Behavior: Implications for Forensic Psychiatry." Paper presented at the 2001 symposium conducted at the meeting of American College of Forensic Psychiatry, April 2001, p. 3. Found at http://www.forensicpsychonline.com/psychiatry2001.html.

FlightStat News. 2007 Performance Reports, January 12, 2008. Found at http://www.flightstats.com/go/Home/spotlight.do?newsItemId=41.

"Flying the Unfriendly Skies." *Power of Attorneys Online Newsletter* (no date given). Found at http://www.power-of-attorneys.com/unfriendly_skies.htm.

Foster, Timothy R.V. "How to Protect Your Slogan: Malice in Dallas." *AdSlogans.com*, 2000. Found at http://www.adslogans.co.uk/ww/prvwis09.html.

Franken, H. "The Friendly Skies Falling Victim to 'Air Rage.'" *Central Ohio Source*, March 1999. Found at http://centralohio.thesource.net/Franken/99/Mar11/tag.html.

Freedman, Paul. "Peasant Anger in the Late Middle Ages." pp. 171–190 in Rosenwein, Barbara H. (ed.), *Anger's Past: The Social Uses of an Emotion in the Middle Ages*. Ithaca, NY: Cornell University Press, 1998.

Freeman, Simon, and Jenkins, Russell Jenkins. "Air-Rage Passenger Dumped on Paradise Island." *Times Online*, December 29, 2005. Found at http://www.timesonline.co.uk/tol/news/uk/article783301.ece.

Gartman, David. "Tough Guys and Pretty Boys: The Cultural Antagonisms of Engineering and Aesthetics in Automotive History." *Automobile in American Life and Society*. Found at http://www.autolife.umd.umich.edu/Design/ Gartman/D_Casestudy/D_Casestudy1.htm.

Gershaw, David A. "A Line on Life: Road Rage." February 21, 1999. Found at http://www.members.cox.net/dagershaw/index.html.

Gillespie, Mark. "Public Confident in Security of Airline Travel." February 15, 2002. Found at http://www.gallup.com/poll/5335/Public-Confident-Security-Airline-Travel.aspx.

"The Girls Who Painted the Planes: Introducing the Air Strip." *Fortune Magazine*, August 1966, p. 146. Found at http://www.ciadvertising.org/studies/student/ 96_fall/lawrence/braniff.html.

Goo, Sara Kehaulani. "Bangor is Used to Surprise Landings." *Washington Post*, October 17, 2004, p. A-3. Found at: http://www.washingtonpost.com/ wp-dyn/articles/A38685-2004Oct16.html.

Glaser, Susan. "Be Sure to Pack Some Patience for Your Journey." *Cleveland Plain Dealer*, November 16, 2007. Found and available for sale at http://pqasb. pqarchiver.com/plaindealer/search.html.

The Gracie Jiu-Jitsu Academy, Web page copyrights 2005-2006. Found at http://www.gracieacademy.com/gard_fattendants.html.

Graham, Ross Lee. "Environmental Anemia, A Basis for Sky-Rage." Linkoping University, Sweden. Found at http://www.rosslg.com/works/WebNotes/ Systems/skyrage01.html.

gryphon99 (online identifier). Blog post on "Article Discussion: 'Air Rage' Upsets United." *Denverpost.com*, posted September 17, 2007. Found at http:// neighbors.denverpost.com/viewtopic.php?t=6913089.

Gwats (online identifier). Blog post on *Denverpost.com*, in response to "'Air Rage' Upsets United." posted September 17, 2007. Found at http://neighbors. denverpost.com/viewtopic.php?t=6913089.

Harrison, T., and Kleinsasser, J. Airline Quality Rating, Press Release, 1999. Found at http://www.unomaha.edu/~unoai/aqr/aqr99press.html.

Hester, Elliott. *Plane Insanity: A Flight Attendant's Tales of Sex, Rage, and Queasiness* (New York, NY: MacMillan, 2003).

Hester, Elliott Neal. "Bad Passenger, Bad!" Out of the Blue, *Salon.com*, April 13, 1999. Found at http://archive.salon.com/travel/diary/hest/1999/04/ 13/passenger/index.html.

Hester, Elliott Neal. "Cockpit Assault." *Salon.com*, April 8, 2000. Found at http://archive.salon.com/travel/diary/hest/2000/04/08/cockpits/index.html.

Hester, Elliott Neal. "Eating on the Fly." *Salon.com*, May 16, 2000. Found at http://archive.salon.com/travel/diary/hest/2000/05/16/eating/print.html.

Hester, Elliott Neal. "Flying in the Age of Air Rage." Travel and Food section, *Salon.com*, September 7, 1999. Found at http://www.salon.com/travel/diary/ hest/1999/09/07/rage/index.html.

Hester, Elliott Neal. "Out of the Blue: Lies in the Sky—An Inside Look at United Airlines' Abysmal Service." *Salon.com*, July 28, 2000. Found at http://dir.salon.com/story/business/col/hest/2000/07/28/united/.

Hester, Elliott Neal. "The Passenger from Hell." *Salon.com*, August 17, 1999. Found at http://dir.salon.com/story/travel/diary/hest/1999/08/17/passenger/.

Hester, Elliott Neal. "The Sky's the Limit." *Salon.com*, 2002. Found at http://archive.salon.com/travel/diary/hest/2000/03/21/flyfree/index1.html.

Hester, Elliott Neal. "When Passengers Rage." *Salon.com*, October 20, 2000. Found at http://dir.salon.com/story/business/col/hest/2000/10/20/rage/.

Hewitt, Ed. "Air Rage: Readers Speak Out." *IndependentTraveler.com*. Found at http://www.independenttraveler.com/resources/article.cfm?AID=165&category=13.

Hewitt, Ed. "Air Rage: Why the Caged Bird Sings." *MSNBC.com*, October 30, 2007. Found at http://www.msnbc.msn.com/id/21384567/.

Hewitt, Ed. "The Airline Passenger's Bill of Rights." *MSNBC.com*, February 16, 2007. Found at http://www.msnbc.msn.com/id/17173370/.

Hewitt, Ed. "The Shrinking Airline Seat." *IndependentTraveler.com*. Found at http://www.independenttraveler.com/resources/article_print.cfm?AID=161&category=13.

Higgins, Michelle. "Aboard Planes, Class Conflict." *New York Times*, November 25, 2007. Found at http://travel.nytimes.com/2007/11/25/travel/25conflict.html?pagewanted=print.

Hightower, Newton. "Signs That Rage Has Turned into an Addiction." Found at http://ezinearticles.com/?Signs-That-Rage-Has-Turned-Into-An-Addiction&id=19659.

Hightower, Newton, and Kay, David C. *Anger Busting 101: The New ABC's for Angry Men and the Women Who Love Them* (Houston, TX: Bayou Publishing, 2002).

"Hijacker Wanted to Crash Plane." *Fairfax Digital*, July 12, 2004. Found at http://www.smh.com.au/articles/2004/07/12/1089484298190.html?oneclick=true.

Ho, David. "Air Travel Complaints Rise." *ABCNews.com*, February 3, 2003. Found at http://abcnews.go.com/sections/travel/DailyNews/aircomplaints000203.html.

Hobica, George. "How to Upgrade Your Seat Cheaply." Posted April 17, 2008, on *Airfarewatchdog.com*. Found at http://www.aviation.com/travel/080418-upgrade-your-seat-cheaply.html.

Hobica, George (of Aviation.com). "10 Most Obnoxious Airline Fees." *MSNBC.com*, December 2, 2007. Found at http://www.msnbc.msn.com/id/22041918/.

Hobica, George, and Tan, Kim Liang. *Daily Herald* correspondence, 2007. Found at http://www.scribd.com/doc/2116568/tag1210047pagenews1tExamining-those-annoying-hidden-airline-feesd25.

Hoffman, Kevin. "Why Are Men So Angry?" Leonard Ingram's blog, posted June 5, 2007. Found at http://www.angermgmt.com/blog/entry.asp?ENTRY_IE=35.

Holding, Reynolds. "Tall Folks Say Plane Seating Doesn't Fly." *SF Gate*, March 5, 2000. Found at http://www.sfgate.com/cgi-bin/article.cgi?file=/chronicle/archive/2000/03/05/SC67249.DTL.

Homer. *The Iliad* (Butler translation, 1903).

Hume, Mark, and Dhillon, Sunny. "Questions Hang Over Taser Death." *Globe and Mail*, October 26, 2007. Found at http://www.theglobeandmail.com/servlet/story/RTGAM.20071025.wtaser1026/BNStory/National/.

Hunter, D.B.A., Joyce A. "An Empirical Study of the Effects of Airline Customer Service and Consumer Perception of the Air Rage Phenomenon." Argosy University, Orange County, California, 2004.

Ingram, Leonard. "Anger Management: Theory and Practice." *Angermgmt.com*, p. 2. Found at http://www.angermgmt.com/workshops_certification.asp.

International Workers' Federation. Quoted in "Controlling Cabin Fever." *BBC News*, July 23, 2001. Found at http://news.bbc.co.uk/2/hi/in_depth/uk/2001/trouble_in_the_air/1448843.stm.

Isidore, Chris. "Your Vacation at Risk." *CNNMoney.com*, July 12, 2007. Found at http://money.cnn.com/2007/07/12/news/companies/canceled_flights/index.htm?postversion=2007071211.

James, Leon, and Nahl, Diane. "The Psychology of Air Rage Prevention." *www.SelfGrowth.com*, June 6, 2008. Found at http://www.selfgrowth.com/artman2/publish/psychology_articles/The_Psychology_of_Air_Rage_Prevention_printer.html.

James, Leon, and Nahl, Diane. *Road Rage and Aggressive Driving: Steering Clear of Highway Warfare* (Amherst, NY: Prometheus Books, 2000).

Jamison, Kay Redfield. *An Unquiet Mind* (New York, NY: Alfred A. Knopf, div. of Random House, Inc., 1995).

Janofsky, Michael. "U.S. Declines to Prosecute in Case of Man Beaten to Death on Jet." *New York Times*, September 21, 2000. Found at http://query.nytimes.com/gst/fullpage.html?res=9406E5DE103BF932A1575AC0A9669C8B63.

J.D. Power. "Airline Customers Dissatisfied." June 17, 2008. Found at http://www.btnmag.com/businesstravelnews/headlines/article_display.jsp?vnu_content_id=1003817456&imw=Y.

"Jet Passenger Jailed Over Air Rage." *Sky News*, September 28, 2007. Found at http://news.sky.com/skynews/article/0,70131-1286214,00.html?f=rss.

"Jet set" definition. Found at http://www.allwords.com, 2003.

"Jetstar: Low Cost but at What Cost?" Australian Services Union Zero Air Rage Survey, on ASU net, the ASU Website, February 21, 2005. Found at http://www.asu.asn.au/media/airlines_general/20050221_airrage.html.

Joe Pilot (online identifier). "How Does Alcohol and Smoking Contribute to Hypoxia for Pilots Flying Aircraft?" *Yahoo Answers*. Found at http://answers.yahoo.com/question/index?qid=20070720230014AAGxaB1.

Kaufhold, John A., and Johnson, Lori R. "The Analysis of the Emotional Intelligence Skills and Potential Problem Areas of Elementary Educators." Summer 2005. Found at http://findarticles.com/p/articles/mi_qa3673/is_200507/ai_n14686573/pg_3.

Kelley, J.K. "Review of JoAnn Kuzma Deveny's 99 Ways to Make a Flight Attendant Fly off the Handle (2003)" *Amazon.com*, November 8, 2007. Found at http://www.amazon.com/review/R3RSDAYGEEV6AE/ref=cm_cr_pr_viewpnt#R3RSDAYGEEV6AE.

Kern, Harry A. "The Faces of Air Rage." The FBI Law Enforcement Bulletin, August 1, 2003. Found at http://www.encyclopedia.com/doc/1G1-107930060.html.

Knee Defender website. Found at http://www.kneedefender.com/html2/buy2.htm

Lacan, Jacques. "*Aggressively in Psychoanalysis*" (1948). In Ecrits: A Selection, trans. Alan Sheridan (New York and London: W.W. Norton, 1977), pp. 8–29.

Leanna621 (online identifier). Posting on *IndependentTraveler.com*, August 2, 2007. Found at http://boards.independenttraveler.com/showthread.php?t=10863.

Lester K. Little, Lester K. "Anger in Monastic Curses." pp. 9–35 in Rosenwein (ed.), *Anger's Past: The Social Uses of an Emotion in the Middle Ages* (Ithaca, NY: Cornell University Press, 1998).

Levere, Jane L. "Flying in a Snit." *New York Times*, January 2, 2006. Found at http://www.nytimes.com/2006/01/24/business/24rude.html?_r=1&oref=slogin.

Lewinski, William. "10 Training Tips for Handling 'Excited Delirium.'" *PoliceOne.com*, Force Science Research Center, October 14, 2005. Found at http://www.policeone.com/writers/columnists/Force-Science/articles/119828-10-training-tips-for-handling-excited-delirium/.

Little, Lester K. "Anger in Monastic Curses." pp. 9–35 in Rosenwein, Barbara H. (ed.), *Anger's Past: The Social Uses of an Emotion in the Middle Ages* (Ithaca, NY: Cornell University Press, 1998).

Lohr, Jeffrey. "Angry? Breathing Beats Venting." *University of Arkansas Daily Headlines*, February 28, 2007. Found at http://dailyheadlines.uark.edu/10290.htm.

Loo, Tristan J. "What Causes Anger?" August 14, 2005, found at http://www.articleset.com/Self-Improvement_articles_en_What-Causes-Anger.htm.

Loraine, Tristan. "Toxic Airlines: Is Your Plane Trip Poisoning You?" *Daily Mail*, February 8, 2008. Found at http://www.dailymail.co.uk/news/article-513209/Toxic-airlines-Is-plane-trip-poisoning-you.html.

Luckey, Steve (Capt., Northwest, Ret.). "Air Rage." *Air Line Pilot*, September 2000. Found at http://cf.alpa.org/internet/alp/2000/sept00p18.htm.

MacPherson, Malcom (ed.). *On a Wing and a Prayer: Interviews with Airline Disaster Survivors* (New York, NY: HarperCollins Publishers, 2002), pp. 181–190.

"Man Bites Passenger, Jumps from Moving Jetliner onto Tarmac." *USA Today*, January 24, 2006. Found at http://blogs.usatoday.com/sky/unruly_passengers/index.html.

"Man Who Jumped Aircraft in Fort Lauderdale Suffers Heart Attack." *Airline Industry Information*, January 30, 2006. Found at http://www.allbusiness.com/operations/shipping-air-freight/859245-1.html.

Mansnerus, Laura. "Turbulent Manners Unsettle Fliers." *New York Times*, February 15, 2004. Found at http://query.nytimes.com/gst/fullpage.html?res=9805E2D9173AF936A25751C0A9629C8B63.

Marra, William. "'Bye-Bye' Baby: Mother, Son Booted from Plane." *ABC News*, July 13, 2007. Found at http://abcnews.go.com/GMA/story?id=3371901.

Martin, Gary. "Road Rage." *The Phrase Finder*, found at http://www.phrases.org.uk/meanings/303700.html.

McConnell, Michael. "Air Rage Takes Back Seat in Our Post-9-11 World." *Detroit Metro Connections*, September 19–October 2, 2002. Found at http://metro.heritage.com/dtw100202/story3.htm.

McCrary, Robert John. "Anger Management: A 'How-To' Guide." G. Werber Bryan Psychiatric Hospital, Columbia, SC, 1998. Found at http://www.state.sc.us/dmh/bryan/webanger.htm.

McCuen, Barbara. "Are Airlines to Blame for Passenger 'Air Rage?'" *SpeakOut.com*, June 15, 2000, p. 2. Found at http://www.speakout.com/activism/issue_briefs/1340b-1.html.

McGee, Bill. "Readers Weigh in on Airline Passenger Rights." *USA Today*, March 27, 2007. Found at http://www.usatoday.com/travel/columnist/mcgee/2007-03-27-passenger-rights_N.htm.

McElroy, S. L. Recognition and Treatment of DSM-IV Intermittent Explosive Disorder. Paper presented at the Closed Symposium Phenomenology and Treatment of Aggression Across Psychiatric Illnesses held in Chicago, Illinois, August 1998. Found at http://www.grandrounds.com/supplenet/v60s15.htm.

McVeigh, Karen. "Branson All Kisses But No Love Lost for Crew." *Scotsman.com*, February 7, 2003. Found at http://www.scotsman.com/uk/Branson-all-kisses-but-no.2400125.jp.

Melosi, Martin V. "The Automobile Shapes the City." Found at http://www.autolife.umd.umich.edu/Environment/E_Casestudy/E_casestudy5.htm.

Mendick, Robert. "Drink Does it. Sex Does it. But the Real Reason Air Rage is Rising is 11 Sept." *Independent*, January 13, 2002. Found at http://www.independent.co.uk.

Michael, R. "Anthropometry and Ergonomics in Airline Seating." *Ergonomics Today* (online magazine), November 6, 2001. Found at http://www.ergoweb.com/news/detail.cfm?id=432.

Michael, R. "Passenger Wins Suit Over Airplane Seating Space." June 10, 2002. Found at *http://www.ergoweb.com/news/detail.cfm?id=541*.

Milgram, Stanley. *Obedience to Authority: An Experimental View* (New York, NY: HarperPerennial, div. of Harper Collins Publisher, 1974).

Miller, Marilyn, "Air Rage Taking Off, Expert Says." *Akron Beacon Journal*, September 28, 2007, quoting Andrew Thomas. Found at: http://www.ohio.com/business/10099131.html.

Mizell, Louis. "Aggressive Driving." A Report for the AAA Foundation for Traffic Safety. Found at http://www.aaafoundation.org/resources/index.cfm?button=agdrtext.

Moffat, Gregory A. *Blind-Sided: Homicide Where it is Least Expected* (Westport, CT: Praeger Publishers, 2000).

Moffat, Gregory A. *A Violent Heart: Understanding Aggressive Individuals* (Westport, CT: Praeger Trade, 2002).

Morrison, Blake. "FAA Seldom Punished Violence." *USA Today*, December 5, 2001. Found at http://www.usatoday.com/news/sept11/2001/12/05/air-violence.htm.

Moses, Terry. Blog comment posted August 21, 2007, in response to "Peeved Passengers Want Answers from Airlines." summary by Kathleen Schalch for Blog of the Nation, *National Public Radio*, August 21, 2007. Found at http://www.npr.org/templates/story/story.php?storyId=13831847.

Myhill, Sarah. "Aerotoxic Syndrome: The Poisoning of Airline Pilots, Cabin Crew, and Passengers that is Possible in Any Air Flight." Found at http://www.aerotoxic.org (in right margin, click on "Dr Sarah Myhill's briefing sheet") or http://www.aerotoxic.org/articles/20071118_3.

Nassar, Sal, Pharm.D. Pharmaca Pharmacy (Solano Ave., Berkeley, California). Interview by email on February 1, 2008.

National Aeronautic and Space Administration (NASA), Aviation Safety Reporting System (ASRS). "Passenger Misconduct: Effects on Flight Crews." Callback, April 2000, 250, pp. 1–2. Found at http://asrs.arc.nasa.gov/callback_issues/cb_250.htm.

National Institutes of Mental Health. "Intermittent Explosive Disorder Affects up to 16 Million Americans." June 5, 2006. Press release relating to a study by Ronald Kessler at Harvard Medical School. Found at http://www.nimh.nih.gov/science-news/2006/intermittent-explosive-disorder-affects-up-to-16-million-americans.shtml.

The News Hour, PBS, November 15, 2007.

Newell, L. Anne. "Crew 'Antagonized' Agitated Air Passenger, Police Report Indicates." *Seattle Times*, September 29, 2000. Found at http://community.seattletimes.nwsource.com/archive/?date=20000929&slug=TTN11O26L.

Newell, L. Anne. "Was Killed Air Rage Passenger Provoked?" *ABC News.com*, September 29, 2000. Found at http://abcnews.go.com/Travel/story?id=118734&page=1.

Olvera, Cristina. "Anger Management: The Rageaholic's Mind." *Associatedcontent.com*, January 6, 2006. Found at http://www.associatedcontent.com/article/16161/anger_management_the_rageaholics_mind.html?cat=5.

Parliamentary Publications and Records for 7 Feb 2003: Column 584. Comment of Mr Roy, found at http://www.publications.parliament.uk/pa/cm200203/cmhansrd/vo030207/debtext/30207-14.htm.

Parsons, Dana. "Heresy! Pulling for Flight Attendant Over Rev. Schuller." *Los Angeles Times*, Orange County edition, July 4, 1994. Found at http://pqasb. pqarchiver.com/latimes/access/12801059.html?dids=12801059:12801059&F MT=CITE&FMTS=CITE:FT&date=Jul+04%2C+1997&author=DANA+PA RSONS&pub=Los+Angeles+Times&desc=Heresy!+Pulling+for+Flight+Att endant+Over+Rev.+Schuller&pqatl=google.

"Passenger Detained After Trying to Break into Delta Cockpit." *USA Today*, July 7, 2006. Found at http://blogs.usatoday.com/sky/unruly_passengers/index. html.

Paul, Gordon. Interview by email with the author, October 6, 2008.

PoliceOne.com. A San Jose, California, Police website, June 11, 2007. Found at http://www.policeone.com/edp/articles/1269555-A-look-at-San-Jose-PDs-new-excited-delirium-protocol/.

"The Politics of Airline Travel." *CBSNews.com*, September 27, 2007. Found at www.cbsnews.com/stories/2007/09/27/travel/printable3303567.shtml.

Proverbs 15:1, King James version.

Putman, Gene. "Coalition for an Airline Passengers' Bill of Rights." August 17, 2007. Found at http:// strandedpassengers.blogspot.com/2007/06/flight-attendants-advocate-for.html.

Redfern, Paul (in London), and Mugonyi, David (in Nairobi), "Air Drama Man Was a Student." *Daily Nation on the Web*, December 21, 2000. Found in paragraph 31 of http://www.nationaudio.com/News/DailyNation/31122000/News/News72.html.

Reed, Dan. "Are Extra Fees in Southwest Airlines' Future?" *USA Today*, March 26, 2007. Found at http://www.usatoday.com/travel/flights/2007-03-25-southwest-fees_N.htm.

Reiley, Catherine. "Air Rage? Try This Nicotine Gel, Sir." *Times Online*, November 11, 2006. Found at http://travel.timesonline.co.uk/tol/life_and_style/travel/news/article1086958.ece.

Reinberg, Steven. "Rage Disorder More Common Than Thought." *HealthDay*, June 5, 2006. Found at http://www.healthywomen.org/resources/womenshealth inthenews/dbhealthnews/ragedisordermorecommonthanthought.

Remsberg, Charles. "Behind the Headlines About Excited Delirium; What Cops and EMS Need to Know." *PoliceOne.com*, December 15, 2006. Found at http:// www.policeone.com/writers/columnists/Charles-Remsberg/articles/1195879-Behind-the-headlines-about-excited-delirium-what-cops-EMS-need-to-know/.

Reynolds, Dave. "No Clear Answers Yet on Inmate's Death." *Inclusion Daily Express*, June 26, 2006. Found at http://www.inclusiondaily.com/archives/06/06/26/062606flrigby.htm.

Rich Street (online identifier). Blog post from Denverstreetcar, Zip Code 32828, on *Denver Post* "Neighbors" website, September 17, 2007. Found at http:// neighbors.denverpost.com/viewtopic.php?t=6913089.

Richmond, Lloyd. "Fear of Flying." *A Guide to Psychology and its Practice*, n.d. Found at http://www.guidetopsychology.com/fearfly.htm.

Riley, Terry. Interview by email with the author on September 24, 2008.

"Robert Schuller." Notable Names Database (NNDB), Soylent Communications, 2008, found at http://www.nndb.com/people/603/000022537/.

Roche, Timothy. "Homicide in the Sky." *Time*, October 2, 2000. Found at http://www.time.com/time/magazine/article/0,9171,998079,00.html.

Rosato, Donna. "Airlines Pile on the Fees." *CNNMoney.com*, April 30, 2007. Found at http://money.cnn.com/2007/04/30/pf/airline_fees.moneymag/index.htm.

Rosenwein, Barbara H. (ed.). "Introduction." pp. 1–7 in *Anger's Past: The Social Uses of an Emotion in the Middle Ages* (paperback). A collection of essays on anger in the Middle Ages (Ithaca, NY: Cornell University Press, 1998).

Rubenstein, Steve. "Flight Attendants Fight 'Air Rage.'" *San Francisco Chronicle*, July 7, 2007. Found at http://www.sfgate.com/cgi-bin/article.cgi?file=/chronicle/archive/2000/07/07/MN99774.DTL.

Rust, Roland T., and Oliver, Richard L. "Should We Delight the Customer?" *Journal of the Academy of Marketing Science*, 2000, 28(1), pp. 86–94.

Saint Martin, Manuel L., MD. "Running Amok: A Modern Perspective on a Culture-Bound Syndrome." *Journal of Clinical Psychiatry*, June 1999, 1(3), pp. 66–70.

Salovey, Peter, and Sluyter, David J. (eds), with Contributor Salovey, Peter. *Emotional Development and Emotional Intelligence: Educational Implications* (New York, NY: Basic Books, 1997).

Santiago, Annette. "Air Rage." *AviationNow.com*, August 10, 2001. Found at http://www.drdriving.org/rages/.

Schilling, Dianne. "How to Cope with Anger." *WomensMedia.com*. Found at http://www.womensmedia.com/new/anger-management.shtml.

Scott, David Meerman. "US Airways Flight Attendants Paid $50 Commission to Interrupt Us in Flight." *Weblink*, September 2007. Found at http://www.webinknow.com/2007/09/us-airways-flig.html.

Scott, K. Michelle. "The Phenomenon of Road Rage: Complexities, Discrepancies and Opportunities for CR Analysis." *The Online Journal of Peace and Conflict Resolution*, Fall 2000. Found at http://www.trinstitute.org/ojpcr/3_3scott.htm.

Scotty (online identifier). Blog post from gryphon99 on *Denver Post* "Neighbors" website, September 17, 2007. Found at http://neighbors.denverpost.com/viewtopic.php?t=6913089.

"Seat Pitch, Kneecaps and Passengers Behaving Badly." *ABC.com*, July 1, 2005 (Copyright ABC Ventures). Found at http://abcnews.go.com/Business/FlyingHigh/Story?id=888873&page=1.

"Sewage-Spewing Plane Disgusts Passengers: Continental Flight Soars Across Atlantic Despite Overflowed Toilets." *MSNBC News Services*, last updated June 20, 2007. Found at: http://www.msnbc.msn.com/id/19332724/.

Shoenfeld, B. "We're Fed Up!" *Cigar Aficionado*, July/August 2002. Found at http://www.cigaraficionado.com/Cigar/Aficionado/Archies/200208/fa802. html.

Sharkey, Joe. "Right There on the Tarmac, the Inmates Revolt." *New York Times*, August 14, 2007. Found at www.nytimes.com/2007/08/14/business/14road. html.

Sheffer, Michael P. "The Problem Passenger: A History of Airline Disruption; 1947 to Present." 2000. Found at http://www.skyrage.org/PDF/SKYRAGE/scsi.pdf.

Siddiqui,Tahir. "Schedule of Many Flights Disrupted." October 18, 2007. Found at http://www.dawn.com/2007/10/18/local2.htm.

"Signs That Rage Has Turned into an Addiction." *RecoveryThroughSupport. com*, January 18, 2005, found at http://www.recoverythroughsupport.com/ articles/2005/01/signs-that-rage-has-turned_110610404539058638.html.

Smith, Patrick. "Ask the Pilot." *Salon.com*, December 6, 2002. Found at http:// archive.salon.com/tech/col/smith/2002/12/06/askthepilot21/index.html.

Smith, Patrick. "Ask the Pilot." *Salon.com*, May 28, 2004. Found at http://dir. salon.com/story/tech/col/smith/2004/05/28/askthepilot88/.

Smith, Patrick. "Ask the Pilot." *Salon.com*, June 11, 2004. Found at http://dir. salon.com/story/tech/col/smith/2004/06/11/askthepilot89/index.html.

Smith, Patrick. "Ask the Pilot." *Salon.com*, November 9, 2007. Found at http:// www.salon.com/tech/col/smith/2007/11/02/askthepilot252/ or http://www. salon.com/tech/col/smith/2007/11/09/askthepilot253/.

Spector, R., and McCarthy, P.D. *The Nordstrom Way: The Inside Story of America's #1 Customer Service Company* (New York, NY: John Wiley & Sons, Inc., 1995).

Speidel, Michael. *Ancient Germanic Warriors: Warrior Styles from Trajan's Column to Icelandic Sagas* (New York, NY: Routledge, 2004).

Speidel, Michael. "Berserk: A History of Indo-European 'Mad Warriors.'" *Journal of World History*, 13.2, 2002, pp. 253–290.

Sperry, Paul. "INS to Deport Arab Aliens on Airliners." *Worldnetdaily.com*, August 1, 2002. Found at http://www.worldnetdaily.com/news/article.asp?ARTICLE_ ID=28474.

Starmer-Smith, Charles. "Is Cabin Air Making Us Sick?" *Telegraph.co.uk*, Travel section, first appeared February 23, 2008, (last updated May 29, 2008), paragraph 15. Found at http://www.telegraph.co.uk/travel/759562/Is-cabin-air-making-us-sick.html#continue.

Statement of Captain Stephen Luckey, Chairman, National Security Committee, Air Line Pilots Association, Before the Subcommittee on Aviation, Committee on Transportation and Infrastructure, U.S. House of Representatives, Passenger Interference with Flight Crews and the Carry-on Baggage Reduction Act of 1997, June 11, 1998. Found at http://cf.alpa.org/Internet/TM/tm061198.htm.

Staub, Ervin. Interview by email with the author on October 26, 2008.

Staub, Ervin. *The Roots of Evil: The Origins of Genocide and Other Group Violence* (Cambridge, U.K.: Cambridge University Press, 1989 and 2002).

Staudt, Bill. Blog post from billstaudt, Zip Code 19425, on *Denver Post* "Neighbors" website, September 17, 2007. Found at http://neighbors.denverpost.com/viewtopic.php?t=6913089.

Stoller, Gary. "Flight Attendants Feel the Wrath of Fliers." *USA Today*, June 10, 2007. Found at http://www.usatoday.com/travel/flights/2007-06-10-air-abuse-usat_N.htm.

Streshinsky, Shirley. "Airline Seat Space, Cruel or Unusual Punishment." *Via Magazine*, AAA Traveler's Companion. Found at http://www.viamagazine.com/top_stories/articles/airline_seat_space00.asp.

Sullivan, Laura. "Death by Excited Delirium: Diagnosis or Cover-up?" In "All Things Considered." *National Public Radio*, February 26, 2007, Part I of a two-part report. Found at http://www.npr.org/templates/story/story.php?storyId=7608386.

Sullivan, Laura. "Tasers Implicated in Excited Delirium Deaths." In "All Things Considered." *National Public Radio*, February 27, 2007, Part II of a two-part report, found at http://www.npr.org/templates/story/story.php?storyId=7622314.

"Tall Passengers May Be More Prone to Deep Vein Thrombosis." *Tall Houston* website, July 24, 2004. Found at http://tall-houston.com/old-news/tall-airline-deep-vein-thrombosis.html.

Testimony by Dr. Leon James, Professor of Traffic Psychology, University of Hawaii, Honolulu, Before the Subcommittee on Surface Transportation and Infrastructure, U.S. House of Representatives, July 17, 1997. Found at http://www.drdriving.org/articles/testimony.htm.

Therianthropes United. "Berserker History." Found at http://www.therianthropes.com/berserker_history.htm.

"These Small Cracks in Your World View: Derrie Air Charging Fliers by Weight." *Johnson Lab*, June 11, 2008. Found at http://johnsonlab.wordpress.com/2008/06/11/cracks-in-your-world-view-1-derrie-air-charging-fliers-by-weight/.

Thomas, Andrew. "The Continuing Scourge of Air Rage." *Jagua Forbes Group and Security Technologies International*, August 2007. Found at http://www.jagwaforbes.com.au/continuing-scourge-air-rage.

Thomas, Andrew (Interview). *Court TV*, April 3, 2002. Found at http://www.courttv.com/talk/chat_transcripts/2002/0403safety-airrage.html.

"Today in the Sky." Blog posted on February 12, 2007, *USA Today*, found at http://blogs.usatoday.com/sky/2007/02/manila.html.

"Today in the Sky." Blog posted on April 19, 2007, *USA Today*, found at http://blogs.usatoday.com/sky/unruly_passengers/index.html.

"Tourists Rampage on Holiday Plane." *BBC News*, May 23, 2007. Found at http://news.bbc.co.uk/2/hi/uk_news/scotland/glasgow_and_west/6685197.stm.

"Travel: Lose Your Cares, Luggage, Sanity." *CBS News* online, October 1, 2007. Found at http://www.cbsnews.com/stories/2007/10/01/travel/main3314904.shtml.

Traveler (online identifier). "So You Are Tall." *Airlinecrew.net Bulletin Board*, April 7, 2005. Found at http://www.airlinecrew.net/vbulletin/showthread. php?t=179321.

"Training Can Reduce and Defuse Disruptive Passenger Incidents." *Air Safety Week*, March 11, 2002. Found at http://findarticles.com/p/articles/mi_m0UBT/ is_10_16/ai_83681236.

Turboturk (online identifier). Blog post on a site sponsored by *IndependentTraveler. com*, posted March 25, 2006. Found at http://gonomad.independenttraveler.com/ archive/index.php?t-1081.html.

Tyler, K. "Afraid to Fly and it Shows. Air Rage is an Escalating Problem. So, Why Don't Airlines Adequately Train Their Employees for This?" *HR Magazine*, 2001, 46(9). Found at http://www.shrm.org/hrmagazine/articles/0901.

United States vs. Sokolow, 490 U.S. 1 (1989).

University of Nebraska at Omaha. "Organization Theory and Behavior" (PA 8090). Air Rage, 2002, p. 2. Found May 16, 2003, at http://www.unomaha.edu/ ~wwwpa/pa8090/ryberg/airrage.htm.

"Unruly Passenger: 'I'm Homeless.'" *USA Today*, November 28, 2005. Found at http://blogs.usatoday.com/sky/unruly_passengers/index.html.

U.S. Department of Transportation. Air Travel Consumer Report (Washington, DC: Office of Aviation Enforcement and Proceedings, 2001). Found at http:// www.dot.gov/airconsumer.ost.gov/report.htm.

U.S. Department of Transportation, Office of the Inspector General. Final Report on Airline Customer Service Commitment (Report AV-2001-020), February 12, 2001, pp. 10–11. Found at http://www.house.gov/transportation/aviation/ issues/service.pdf.

U.S. Department of Transportation, Research and Innovative Technology Administration (RITA), Bureau of Transportation Statistics. "Airline On-Time Performance Slips, Cancellations, Mishandled Bags Up in June." August 6, 2007. Found at http://www.bts.gov/press_releases/2007/dot077_07/html/ dot077_07.html.

Usborne, David. "Murder debate on air-rage killing." *The Independent*, September 24, 2000. Found at http://findarticles.com/p/articles/mi_qn4158/is_20000924/ ai_n14324057.

Vedantam, Shankar. "Cho's Case Similar to Other Mass Killings by Loners." *Washington Post*, April 22, 2007, p. A13.

Wang, Y. Annotated Bibliography on the Age of Rage: Rage Topics on Air Rage, Media Rage, Message Rage, and Office Rage, February 7, 2001. Found at http://www.soc.hawaii.edu/leonj/409bs2001/wang/report_1.html.

Ward, Terry. "Confessions of an Airline Pilot: Captain 'No Name' Tells All." *AOL Travel*, 2007. Found at http://information.travel.aol.com/article/air/pilot-confession.

Wehrman, Jessica. "'Air Rage' Is Back." *Scripps Howard News Service*, January 14, 2002. Found at http://www.knoxstudio.com/shns/story.cfm?pk=AIRRAGE-01-14-02&cat=AN.

Weiss, Joanna. Associated Press (unnamed) article of August 17, 1999, cited in Elliott Neal Hester, "Flying in the Age of Air Rage." *Salon.com*, September 7, 1999. Found at http://www.salon.com/travel/diary/hest/1999/09/07/rage/index1.html.

"Where Do Aerotoxic Fumes Come From?" *www.aerotoxic.org*, found at www.aerotoxic.org or http://www.aerotoxic.org/categories/20070829_2.

"Why Airline Service Suffers." *ABC News* online, April 4, 2006. Found at *http://abcnews.go.com/print?id=1800726*.

"Woman on Frontier Flight Charged with Assault." *Rocky Mountain News*, July 26, 2007. Found at http://www.rockymountainnews.com/drmn/local/article/0,1299,DRMN_15_5644588,00.html

"Woman Says She Was Bullied by Southwest Employee." *USA Today*, February 8, 2006. Found at http://www.usatoday.com/travel/flights/2006-02-08-swa-lawsuit_x.htm.

"Woman Squashed by Plane Passenger." *BBC News*, October 22, 2002. Found at http://news.bbc.co.uk/1/hi/uk_news/wales/2346319.stm.

Yamanouchi, Kelly. "United's New Committee Targets 'Air Rage.'" *Denver Post*, September 17, 2007. Found at http://www.denverpost.com/business/ci_6913089.

Zeitz, Joshua. "Where Did All the Stewardesses Go?" *AmericanHeritage.com*, March 22, 2007, review of Femininity in Flight: A History of Flight Attendants. Found at http://www.americanheritage.com/articles/web/20070322-airlines-stewardness-flight-attendant-pullman-porters-unions-austin-powers_print.shtml.

Zellner, W. "Southwest: After Kelleher, More Blue Skies." *Business Week* Online, News: Analysis and Commentary, April 2, 2001. Found at http://www.businessweek.com:/print/magazine/content/01_14/b3726061.html.

"Zeroing in on Air Rage." *International Transport Workers' Federation* (ITF), 2000 (quoted by Agent Premium News [APN], 2001). Found at http://www.itfglobal.org/transport-international/airrage.cfm.

Zimbardo, Philip. *The Lucifer Effect: How Good People Turn Evil* (New York, NY: Random House, 2007).

Zimbardo, Philip. National Public Radio Discussion in May 2007 of Experiments Described in *The Lucifer Effect: How Good People Turn Evil* (New York, NY: Random House, 2007).

Index